W9-AAS-968

IN PLEASANT PLACES

Sidney A. Rand

1996

i

To family members, friends, loved ones and colleagues, named and unnamed in the pages that follow. Each of them helped me write this book.

© 1996 St. Olaf College, Northfield, Minnesota

Published by St. Olaf College; printed by Northfield Printing, Inc.

All rights reserved. Except for brief excerpts for review purposes, no part of this book may be reproduced or used without permission of the publisher.

Cover photos by Lois Rand. Back Cover portrait by Robert Paulson.

First Printing, 1996. Printed in the United States of America.

ISBN 0-9622931-7-2

CONTENTS

"The lines are fallen unto me in pleasant places;
yea, I have a goodly heritage."

Psalm 16:6, KJV

INTRODUCTION

Attempts at autobiography are quite varied. Some are simple accounts of life's events and activities. Some are platforms for the advancement of the author's ideas and convictions. What follows may be a combination of these. I have tried to recount as many of the events of my life as I believe the reader may find of interest, but I have not avoided flavoring the story with samples of the convictions which have undergirded my life and commanded my loyalty. I have found the experience exciting and completely enjoyable.

When I began to write this story several years ago, I thought of it as a purely family affair. My purpose was to provide members of the family and a few friends with a record of my life as I view it. As time went on, and with the urging of Lois and others, things began to take on a somewhat different aspect. I was encouraged to think of colleagues and others outside the family circle who might be interested in reading what I have to say. This was further encouraged when President Mark Edwards of St. Olaf College assured me that the college would be interested in seeing that what I have written be made available to a larger circle of friends. I am grateful for the partnership which has resulted, and indebted to the college for its assistance. Surely the St. Olaf portion of my life has provided the focus of a major part of my career. St. Olaf was, and continues to be, a "pleasant place" for the Rands.

My chief sources of information have been my own memory and certain personal records such as appointment books, talks and correspondence. Lois has put it all in the computer, something I am incapable of doing. She has corrected mistaken memories, straightened out my grammar and urged me to include certain experiences which had otherwise eluded my memory. She also edited the entire manuscript, which means that it reads better than could ever have been true otherwise. My son Peter has supplemented my memory at several points and has offered helpful suggestions regarding the structure and layout of the book. The errors and omissions that remain are mine.

Dan Jorgensen, Director of Public Relations at St. Olaf, provided helpful editorial suggestions and shepherded the volume through publication.

I am reminded of the way in which people's memories are being questioned in the courts these days. The issue is whether or not we remember correctly. I hope I have. No–one has tried to force my memory or hypnotize me as I have written. Most likely, what follows really happened.

Sidney A. Rand

Minneapolis
May 1996

BOYHOOD PLACES

1916–1934

Chapter 1

THE HOME IN ROTHSAY

Whack!

There went my croquet ball off into the woods. It wasn't the first time. My brother Lyman often did that to me as we engaged in our favorite summertime activity in Rothsay.

Of course, I wasn't surprised. After all, I hit his ball as far as I could whenever I had a chance. That's the way we played the game.

Our large croquet lawn was part of the garden place I called home. The lawns (yes, there were several) and the house were set in a large grove of trees covering several acres on the edge of town. It was a beautiful spot developed by my grandfather A.B. Pedersen after he moved from St. Paul to Rothsay, Minnesota, in 1879.

During my childhood I was made aware of the sterling qualities of my grandfather. He had arrived in Rothsay as the town was beginning, and built both his business and his reputation from scratch. Several years before his death in 1919 he sold his store to T.K. Brye. The farm at the edge of town was rented out. But until a stroke laid him low he continued to care for his large yard and carry on the several business interests he maintained both in Rothsay and in Breckenridge, the county seat.

One of grandfather's accomplishments of which we couldn't help but be aware was the yard and garden where we lived. On the corner of the farm immediately adjoining the village, he had laid out an elaborate home site. There were trees of many kinds — boxelder, cottonwood, poplar, fir, pine and several kinds of fruit trees. One of the joys of my childhood was the privilege of having fresh crabapples, plums, gooseberries, currants, strawberries and chokecherries as they ripened, and to enjoy them all year in the form of jam, jelly, sauce and pickles with which Mother stocked the cellar shelves. We were never without a supply of such homemade goodies.

Our house consisted of a kitchen, pantry, dining room, sitting room, piano room and parlor (we called it "the front room") on first floor, and six rooms on the second floor. The upstairs was divided into two unconnected parts, four rooms being the area we used for bedrooms, and a two–room area we called "the other upstairs." The other upstairs had served as sleeping quarters for farm helpers at the time our grandfather operated the farm, and also as an office and study. During the time we lived there it was the attic, a general–purpose storage area. We children enjoyed going there to investigate and play with old books and magazines together with miscellaneous cast–off items. There was an old gun in a closet, and that was declared off limits by Mother. That portion of the house, together with the kitchen, pantry and dining room, belonged to the part built in the 1890's. The sitting room, piano room and parlor, together with the four bedrooms on second floor, had been built in the 1880's.

The house was not modern. There was no electricity, no indoor plumbing, and no central heat. Among my most unforgettable memories is that of running to an outdoor toilet in below–zero weather. We called it "going down there" because it was about fifty yards from the house down a small slope toward the barn. There we kept our outdated Sears Roebuck and Montgomery Ward catalogs, which became reading matter for moments of contemplation and also served another practical purpose. We carried water for drinking and cooking from a well near the barn. There was a cistern under the dining room where rain water was stored as it drained off the roof. This was soft water and was favored for baths and washing clothes.

We did have a telephone. It was installed on a wall in the sitting room. To make a call it was necessary to turn a crank on the side and then pick up the receiver to hear the operator (whom we called "Central") ask for the number being called. We could even ask for the other party by name ("Will you call Serklands, please?"). If we were to be away from home, we would tell Central where we would be, and she would see that any calls for us would be properly directed. The operator I remember best was a Mrs. Johnson, known to everyone in the community as Lala. She was a wonderful woman, eager to help and serve. Our telephone number was 19 and we had a private line!

The cellar, a very important part of the house, was under the older part of the building and served as our refrigerator as well as general food storage area. There was also a large bin where the renter on the farm stored potatoes during the winter. The cellar steps were steep and represented degrees of coolness. We would usually store things on the steps according to their temperature requirements. Mother was expert at that.

I have special memories of the cellar. One has to do with lizards. As a little boy I was frightened by them, but as I grew older I assisted Lyman as exterminator of lizards and other unwelcome cellar guests. One day Mother discovered on a shelf in the cellar several bottles of dandelion wine. She disposed of it unceremoniously, explaining that "we don't need that around." Evidently my grandparents had prepared their own dandelion wine and, while I have no knowledge of their being great imbibers, they probably enjoyed a treat on occasion. My mother and father were teetotalers and never had alcoholic beverages in the house.

This reminds me of something quite unrelated to the house. Dr. J.C. Serkland, the local doctor and our uncle, together with O.H. Ekeren, the local druggist, had invented a cough medicine which mother believed to be the best. It was strong stuff, as I once discovered by stealth. She claimed it really cured a cold, or at least greatly alleviated it. I'm sure it was mostly alcohol, but being a medicine it was quite a different thing from alcohol in other forms. I remember well when I became old enough to enjoy its proper use.

We lived mostly in two rooms of the house — the dining room and the sitting room. In the summer the kitchen was used, but in the winter a wood– and coal–burning stove in the dining room provided both heat and the means for cooking. The dining room was large and had in it, besides the stove, a table with several chairs, a china closet, a large desk, Mother's sewing machine and a large safe which had been our grandfather's security storage place. The pantry and a closet were connected to the dining room. We ate our meals in this room, and the table was used for family games and occasional schoolwork. I say occasional because none of us brought home schoolwork with any frequency.

The sitting room contained a stove — first a hard–coal heater with ising–glass on the front and sides, then an oil–burning space heater in later years, also a sofa, a large bookcase, a smaller bookcase, a table and several chairs. The large bookcase contained books which had belonged to our grandparents, including the ninth edition of Encyclopedia Brittanica, which proved to be a helpful reference for school work as well as for general information. Throughout the house there were many articles of furniture and personal possessions which had belonged to the Pedersens, and most of them remained until 1953 when Mother died.

From 1920 to 1926, our grandmother's bed was located in the sitting room. This restricted our use of the room because she was paralyzed and confined to her bed. She employed a nurse full time during those years. The nurse slept on a cot near grandmother's bed. It was folded up each day and brought out again in the evening. I've often thought how the nurse lived with no privacy. It must have been a strain on her as well as Mother, to say nothing of the difficult situation in which Grandmother found herself.

I remember the nurses well. There was a procession of them and we called them all "Miss..." — no first name business in those days. They had names like Wold, Larson, Aaberg, Heggen, Rostvold, Lysne. Each one stayed a few months or a year and then moved on. I can understand why. The inconveniences under which they worked were not made easier by having two boys like Lyman and me around.

I learned my first Norwegian in connection with Grandmother's illness. When Mother was busy, she would tell me to go to the bedside and ask, "Er det noen du vil?", which is Norwegian for "Is there anything you would like?" If Grandmother said "Ja," I went to get Mother. If the answer was "Nei," I could report that all was well. I regret the fact that I did not learn to speak Norwegian at that time. Grandmother spoke only Norwegian by choice, and I could certainly have made use of the opportunity. But I don't suppose a three- to ten–year–old boy had much interest in a second language. And, as I remember it, we lived almost in fear of our grandmother. At least we lived in fear of disturbing her. So with her death in 1926, an opportunity to learn Norwegian in childhood was gone.

I must have picked up something from her and Mother, however, as they spoke to each other, because as I tried using my limited Norwegian when we lived in Norway I was reminded by several people there that my accent resembled that of the language as spoken a hundred years ago. One person even guessed correctly that my ancestors must have come from Sigdal because that was the accent I spoke.

The piano room and parlor were little used during my childhood. The piano room, with two south–facing windows, was the greenhouse. There Grandmother kept a display of several plants, which Mother tried to keep alive and growing. The piano in the room was not used. I'm not sure why my grandparents had it. My mother didn't play, and to my knowledge neither did other members of the family. Next to the piano was a special corner. That was where Christmas gifts were kept during the days before Christmas Eve. On that great day, and not before, they were brought to the sitting room where the Christmas tree was placed. Attached to the piano room was a closet where Mother kept her good clothes as well as boxes of family pictures and keepsakes.

The parlor, or front room, was a thing by itself. It was furnished, as was the piano room, with plush–upholstered chairs and sofas in late nineteenth–century style. This room was definitely off limits to us except when very special company came. The large folding doors which separated it from the piano room were often closed and in the winter sealed off with carpets along the base of the doors to keep out the cold.   One advantage of no indoor plumbing was the fact that parts of the house could be closed without fear of freezing pipes.

One special occasion for the use of the parlor was the marriage of my sister Mary to Harold Miller in 1936. Pastor Salveson officiated, and Alice Serkland and Lyman were the attendants. It was a beautiful summer day and the parlor was a cool and comfortable setting for the brief service.

In the late 1940's the house was wired, so Mother did enjoy the convenience of a refrigerator and a plug–in radio (instead of battery–operated) the last years of her life.We used kerosene lamps for lighting during the time I lived in Rothsay. They were collected on the top of the safe during the day, and in the evening would be distributed according to need. Sometimes we would use two or three together to give us adequate light for reading. Lyman and I were responsible for bringing kerosene from a fifty–gallon barrel in the woodshed near the barn. We used a gallon can with a spout, and from that would fill the lamps. Regularly we would trim the wick of each lamp so it would burn brightly and evenly, and we would wash the glass top of the lamp. Some time in the thirties we got a lamp that used kerosene under pressure, much like a gas lantern. That provided a great improvement in our lighting.

Lyman and I shared a bedroom and a three–quarter size bed with a lumpy, straw–filled mattress. Each spring we took it out of doors for a beating and a dose of sun, after which we would need to shape the mattress to our bodies again. I don't recall that such a condition interfered with my sleep then, but it would today. Charlotte and Mother had beds in a large room at the head of the stairs, which was also a hall leading to the other three rooms. Privacy was not a primary requirement in the Rand household. There was little heat in the bedrooms in winter — only what would find its way up the stairway. But in the summer it was very warm. The house had a gabled roof which cut down on the ceiling height of rooms, and the sun had a good chance to heat the upstairs. In the cold winter, we would dress and undress around the stove in the sitting room, and dash into or out of bed as quickly as possible. We used cotton flannel sheets in the winter plus lots of blankets and quilts. Sometimes we would heat a flat iron, wrap it in a piece of woolen cloth and place it near our feet in the bed. My, that felt good!

The two less–used bedrooms were rather special. One was used by Mary when she came to be with us in the summer, and the other was the guest room. In that room, two trunks contained dishes, linens and other items which had belonged to Mother's sister Seline, Mrs. J.C. Serkland, who had died in 1912.

The contents of the trunks were the property of Alice Serkland, and she chose to leave them in the house until after Mother died in 1953.

Mother was skillful at adapting a less than modern house to our comfort. The sitting room, for example, was on the north side of the house. On warm summer days, she would close the doors to this room, and in the evening open them. The room was always several degrees cooler than the rest of the house. In the winter, Mother practiced another tactic. She was a fresh air enthusiast, I think, for periodically she would open all the doors and windows for a few minutes or up to half an hour to "change the air," as she said. It seemed to work. The new air did seem fresher, and even seemed to warm more quickly than the other. So much for air–conditioning in the 1920's.

I don't want to give the impression that we lived a deprived life or that there was something heroic about the lack of plumbing and electricity. By modern standards it may seem so, but not by those of the 20's. In fact, we lived in a manner similar to most other folks in Rothsay. They lacked modern conveniences, too. To be sure, some had modernized their homes, and we were probably a bit envious of them. I made it a point to use the bathroom at the Serkland home several times during each of our visits there. That was certainly an experience to be prized in contrast to our outdoor facilities. I'm sure that Mother, not we kids, was the one who really knew what it meant not to have modern ways of doing her housework. I was happy when she finally got electricity.

When I am asked whether I like camping, I answer truthfully that I do not. I say I camped the first sixteen years of my life, and now I prefer electric lights, indoor plumbing, and hot and cold running water immediately available.

Our home was more than the house, of course. There was a great yard surrounding it, at least ten acres in size. Grandfather Pedersen had not only planted lots of trees, but had laid out gravel walks and planted lawns in a rather formal pattern around the house. We enjoyed it all. The woods, as we called the plantings around the house, provided fuel for the dining room stove, places for walks and hide–outs, and the possibility for childhood road construction. Lyman and I built several dugouts in the woods. Each was a hole in the ground, about four feet by six feet, and two feet deep. We would build a makeshift frame over the hole, and cover it with one of Mother's worn–out oilcloth tablecloths. The dugout was seen as a private preserve, meaning that we tried to keep Charlotte out. I remember once building a fire in a dugout and cooking slices of crabapple on the lid of a pail. The smoke was unpleasant and the apples tasted terrible, but it remains in my memory as at least a minor boyhood achievement.

Another time a friend of ours, Kenneth Jensen, brought three cans of Prince Albert tobacco and three pipes (I believe he had stolen them from the store of his uncle Ed Skugrud), and the three of us boys proceeded to have a smoke in the dugout. I believe I lasted three or four puffs and then fled to the house, where Mother was curious as to how I could become ill so unexpectedly. Of course I had no idea how it could have happened. I was nine or ten years old at the time, and didn't smoke a pipe again until I was in my thirties.

The grass of the several lawns needed regular mowing, and that was always the occasion for some sparring between Lyman and me. Our lawn mower was of ancient vintage and was not always in the best condition. And it needed to be pushed. Every once in a while we would take it to Arndt Johnson, the local blacksmith, who would sharpen the blades, make minor adjustments and oil it. It would then do the job for another year or two.

Mother would try to see that the mowing duties were equally shared by Lyman and me, but neither of us ever thought parity was reached. We had four lawns. One was about a hundred feet by forty feet, another about fifty feet square, and there were two smaller ones, so it was no easy task. Somehow, though, it got done, especially if the length of grass threatened the efficiency of our croquet game. That game was a major summer activity at our home. All of us played and we had many friends, young and old, who joined us, so at least the largest lawn always had to be in proper condition.

The lawns also required raking in the autumn after the leaves had fallen. When we were too young to rake, the job was done by Ole Sigmundstad, a handyman in town whom Mother could call in to do odd jobs. He was the one who culled the trees for firewood, prepared the wood in stove lengths, changed screens and storm windows, and covered the foundation of the house each fall with tarpaper and straw. Lyman and I took over some of those jobs as we grew older.

Gardening was not our long suit, even though we had plenty of space for it. Mother was not a gardener, but she encouraged us children to be. One year I joined the 4–H Club and undertook a garden project. It was a total failure, and I became an ex–4–H Club member.

Fruit trees presented another story, of course. They were there, and their marvelous produce was ours for the taking. I must have picked bushels of apples and plums and chokecherries, and at least many pounds of gooseberries, currants and strawberries. We had our grandfather to thank for that abundance.

Our yard had several gravel paths. One, to the north, led toward town. To the west, two paths led toward the barnyard and the outdoor toilet. Keeping these walks free of weeds was another task Mother assigned Lyman and me. We were reluctant and not very efficient weeders. However, we enjoyed these paths for bike riding, tire rolling and races with homemade cars, of which we built a few. We spent many pleasant hours in such pastimes, often joined by our friends.

Just beyond the woods to the south was a house occupied by the family that rented the farm. I remember the Otto Olson family, who lived there in the 1920's. The children in that family were of ages similar to ours, so they were friends and playmates. When the Olsons moved away, a family named Tosh moved in. They had two grown daughters. Later the farm was rented to the Torvald Martinson family, who lived in their own home across the road northwest of us. For some years the renter's house was vacant, but in more recent years it has been occupied off and on.

During my childhood we got milk and cream from the farmer as part of the rent arrangement. One of my favorite indulgences was to pour thick cream, beginning to sour, on a slice of bread and then, with or without brown sugar added, eating to my heart's and stomach's content. Ah, those were the days. I don't believe they had yet invented calories, butterfat or cholesterol.

I have often been asked if I grew up on a farm. I did and I didn't. During my childhood, the farm which adjoined our home was owned by my mother and by my three Serkland cousins. This was their inheritance from the Pedersens. After Mother's death in 1953, Lyman, Charlotte and I sold our inherited interests to Alice Serkland who had earlier bought out her brothers Alvin and Chester. She continued to own the farm, including the house where I grew up, until her death in March, 1996.

I was exposed to farming as a boy and learned something about it. I had experience in picking potatoes, shocking grain, picking mustard plants out of fields and trying to milk a cow. I never did learn how to do that. Most of my interest, however, was taken up by my attachment to the Moen Lumber Yard, so I never spent much time with farm work.

A favorite memory has to do with the home in Rothsay. On a nice summer day I would often lie on the grass and watch the clouds go by. I imagined the clouds to be animals or buildings or people I knew. I saw ships on the sea and characters from fairy tales. Those were my first travels. Imagination took me far from home as I dreamed of what might be. It was a refreshing experience and lingers as one of childhood's bright moments.

Chapter 2

ROOTS

When our family moved to Rothsay in 1920, it was a town of about 450 people. It still is about the same size. I call it my home town because, even though I was not born there, it was the place of my childhood, and the memories of my early years center there.

I was born a short distance north of Rothsay, at Eldred, Minnesota, in Polk County. I weighed in at nine pounds and was born at home, as was the custom in those days. The date was May 9, 1916. During the summer of that year, our family moved a few miles east to Beltrami, where I spent the next three years of my life. Every once in a while I've been asked by someone who is acquainted in Eldred or Beltrami if I know someone they know. I have to confess my only knowledge of either place is what was supplied to me by my mother later in life.

Soon after my birth, my family spent the summer in Rothsay with my mother's parents, Mr. and Mrs. A.B. Pedersen. Because my father was a school superintendent (they called it principal in those days), my parents were often free in the summer and would spend time in Rothsay. Some summers my father attended summer school. Once before I was born he had attended the University of Minnesota, and another year Syracuse University in New York. He never earned his baccalaureate degree, having gone into teaching after completing the two–year "normal training" course at the State Teachers College in River Falls, Wisconsin.

I was baptized on August 6, 1916, in Hamar Lutheran Church in Rothsay by Reverend Magne Langeland, who had earlier baptized and confirmed my mother and officiated at the wedding of my parents. He had also baptized my brother Lyman who was born in 1914, and later baptized my sister Charlotte in 1920.

My father, Charles William Rand, was born December 28, 1879, in Onalaska, Wisconsin, a small town near La Crosse. His father was Artemus

Reed Rand and his mother was Clara Evangeline Shove. My grandfather Art, as he was known to all his friends, was born in Dane County, Wisconsin, on January 25, 1852, the son of James B. Rand and Elizabeth Latimer. James was born in West Virginia on October 2, 1822, and died in Onalaska in 1896. Elizabeth was born in Pennsylvania in 1825. I do not know the date of her death. James owned a butcher shop and dray line, and was deputy sheriff. He lost his right arm in a farming accident while still a young man.

My father had one sister, Nell Elizabeth, born in 1881, with whom he shared both parents. Their mother Clara died in 1883, and Nellie, as she was known to the family, was taken into the home of an uncle and aunt named Merrill. She remained with them until she was grown, and, while she was never legally adopted, she took the name Merrill and was known as Nell Merrill during her entire adult life.

In 1886, Art Rand married Cora Shaul, and in the 1890's moved to Mississippi. He had been in the timber cutting business in Onalaska, and in the late nineteenth century that business was tapering off in Wisconsin. In Mississippi it was in a period of growth.

Four children were born to Art and Cora Rand. They were Wesley Edgar, born in 1888; Clayton Thomas, born in 1891; Joyce Viola (married Hugh Cassibry), born in 1893; and Benjamin Donald, born in 1905. The only one of that family that I ever met was Clayton, who became the editor and publisher of a newspaper in Gulfport, Mississippi, and, in addition, was widely known as a syndicated columnist and lecturer. He came to the middle west occasionally during the 40's and 50's on his lecture tours, and I visited with him on some of those occasions.

My father's mother, Clara Shove, was the daughter of Thomas Burtis Shove and Henriette Boardman. Thomas was born in 1837 in New York. I do not have the record of Henriette's birth. Clara was born on January 31, 1857, in Onalaska, Wisconsin, and died there on December 3, 1883.

The Shove line goes back to colonial times in New York, and, prior to that, to County Surrey in England. The family is of English and Scottish stock. One of the Shoves, who had done well in the lumber and mining business in Colorado, had a family history prepared which traces the Shove family back to Rev. Edward Shove, born in County Surrey about 1578. His grandson Rev. George Shove came to America and settled in Taunton, Massachusetts.

Like the Shoves, the Rands are also of English and Scottish descent. They can be traced back to the states of West Virginia and Vermont, and before that also to County Surrey in England.

On August 25, 1901, my father married Edith Ione Youells, who became the mother of Mary Ione Rand, born on July 14, 1902, and Elizabeth Lois Rand, born on July 22, 1906. Ione Youells Rand died shortly after the birth of Elizabeth, who was adopted as an infant by an uncle and aunt of my father. Their name was Dugan and they lived in New Haven, Connecticut. Elizabeth Rand Dugan, as she was then known, died in 1936 as the result of an accident. Although she was my sister, I never met her, a fact that seems strange to me now but was probably not strange at the time, given the fact that in the 20's and 30's travel was not as common or convenient as it is today.

I grew up knowing Mary as my sister. She spent much of her childhood with her grandmother in Wisconsin, but also spent time in our home, especially after she was grown and during the years she taught school in Wisconsin following her graduation from the State College in River Falls. In 1943, Mary and her husband Harold Miller moved from Minnesota to San Diego, California, where they spent the rest of their lives. For many years she worked for the Navy as a mathematician.

My mother and father were married on December 31, 1909. After a brief honeymoon in Kansas City and St. Louis, they returned to Grantsburg, Wisconsin, where my father was the principal and my mother a teacher.

My mother, Ida Alice Pedersen, was the youngest child of Anders Braatelien Pedersen and Jorgine Vatnaas. Somewhere along the way Mother dropped the first name and was known as Alice Pedersen. She was born in Rothsay, Minnesota, on March 9, 1884. Her brothers and sisters were Peder Georg (born December 7, 1873; died September 4, 1874); Berthe Seline (born December 1, 1875; died December 24, 1912); Oscar Edward (born September 11, 1877; died October 12, 1877); and Petra Olava (born November 17, 1879; died August 13, 1882). All of the children except my mother were born in St. Paul, and the three who died in infancy are buried there in Oakland Cemetery, as are their parents.

Both of my mother's parents were born in Norway. My grandfather, whom I was taught to call "bestefar" (Norwegian for grandfather), was born on the Braatelien farm in Sigdal, a wooded valley in the county of Buskerud, about seventy–five miles west of Christiania (now Oslo), the capital city. My grandmother, "bestemor," was born on the Vatnaas farm near the Braatelien farm. In Norway, farms carried names through many generations, and the families were known by the names of the farms. My grandfather, evidently preferring not to use a name as difficult for Americans to say as Braatelien, made a change when he came to this country. He made the farm name his middle name and took as his surname the first name of his father, Peder Erickson Solumsmoen, and added "sen," the Danish–Norwegian designation for "son of." Thus he became Anders Braatelien Pedersen. In the Rothsay area he was always known as A.B. Pedersen.

A.B. Pedersen was born October 8, 1838, and died December 27, 1919, in the hospital in Fergus Falls following an extended illness. Grandmother Pedersen was born June 10, 1843, and died June 12, 1926, at her home in Rothsay. She had been bedridden for seven years following a stroke.

Grandfather Pedersen emigrated from Norway in 1870 and settled in St. Paul following a brief time spent with relatives in Wisconsin and trying out several jobs in various towns. He had learned the tailor trade in Norway, having determined early in life that he couldn't continue to live on the Braatelien farm. He had several siblings and was among the youngest. Primogeniture determined that an older brother would acquire the farm. It consisted of approximately eighty acres, most of it in timber. Five of his brothers and sisters joined him in America, including the oldest brother who sold the farm in Norway to another family. America was economically attractive to Norwegian young people in the late nineteenth century, and my grandfather was among those who did well in the new land.

Jorgine Vatnaas immigrated to America in 1872, a decision having been made before my grandfather's departure that they would meet and be married here. In 1873, they were married at the home of my grandfather's sister, Mrs. Sarah Austerud, in Martell, Wisconsin.

Following a few years of tailoring in St. Paul, my grandfather decided to look for other opportunities. In 1879, he moved to Rothsay, Minnesota, two hundred miles northwest of St. Paul, and erected the first business building in that new community. The railroad was moving west, and, as it did, new towns sprang up. Rothsay was a station on what was to become part of James J. Hill's Great Northern Railroad.

Grandfather Pedersen opened a store in his building, and in addition to storekeeping, became postmaster and something of a banker. He soon built a small house next door, and it was in that house that my mother was born in 1884. He later bought 240 acres of land on the edge of town and built a house there — a house that was to become my home in 1920.

Grandfather's business pursuits were not always successful. For several years, he was in partnership with a man in Duluth, Minnesota, who had invented a new kind of razor. The business never succeeded, and Grandfather lost several thousands of dollars trying to promote the venture. The fact that he absorbed these losses and continued in business and farming indicates his over-all business success.

In his later years, he wrote two books. The first, *Mor Hansen*, is a novel of rural Norwegian life, underscoring the tensions of class distinction between land owners and those who worked for them. It was probably based on what he had observed in his home area. He published this in hard cover, and distributed it to relatives and friends. Lyman has contributed a copy to the folk museum in Prestfoss, Sigdal. Clara Serkland, wife of my cousin Alvin, translated it into English, and provided the translation to various relatives. The second book is autobiographical, and provides both facts about his life and observations he made concerning situations and people. He illustrated it with charming drawings tinted with colored pencil. It was never published, but was translated into English by my cousin, Alice Serkland, and provided to close relatives. A copy of *Mor Hansen* and the original of the autobiography have been placed in the archives of the Norwegian American Historical Association.

My parents lived in Grantsburg and West Salem, Wisconsin, and in Ulen and Reading, Minnesota, prior to my birth. My brother Lyman was born in Rothsay on July 25, 1914, and my sister Charlotte also was born there on July 25, 1920. I always thought it was peculiar that Lyman and Charlotte shared the same birthday, six years apart.

During the time my parents lived in West Salem, they rented the house owned by Hamlin Garland, a famous writer of American frontier stories. He had moved to New York earlier, but continued to own the West Salem residence. My mother prized a letter they received from Mr. Garland after he had found a poem in the house which my father had written and left there. It described the house and my parents' pleasure at having lived there. I am happy to have Mr. Garland's letter.

When Lyman was born, he was given the second name Burtis, no doubt from his great–grandfather Shove. Charlotte Juneva was named for our father, who had died six months before her birth (Charlotte for Charles) and for our grandmother Pedersen (Juneva for Jorgine). My second name, Anders, is for my grandfather Pedersen. No–one in the family seemed to be able to account for the names Lyman and Sidney. Mother used to say, "I guess we just liked them." I never told her that I have not cared particularly for the name Sidney. I have secretly wished they had called me by my second name. Anders is the Scandinavian form of Andrew, and I think of it as a good strong name as well as one having family significance. When I was the ambassador to Norway, the Foreign Minister, Knut Frydenlund, decided I should be known by my Norwegian name, so he called me Anders. Another friend in Norway, Petter Koren, did the same. He is a retired justice of the Supreme Court, and at the time we lived in Norway was governor of Akershus, an area adjoining Oslo, and an office similar to that of a chief county officer in America. His mother's people had come from Sigdal, and that gave him a special interest in us and in our presence in Norway.

My mother was a graduate of the University of Minnesota in the class of 1907. She had completed high school in Fergus Falls in 1903 when she was nineteen years old. She had started school in Rothsay a year later than most students because as a child she had suffered from a bone marrow disease in one leg which kept her out of school for some time. She had undergone surgery at St. Mary's Hospital in Minneapolis at the age of seven. She was always proud of the fact that she never returned to be a hospital patient throughout her entire life, but by strange coincidence she spent the last several days of her life in St. Mary's Hospital, and died there on February 18, 1953.

My father died on February 24, 1920, in Roseau, Minnesota. At that time he was principal of the school at Williams, a small village near the Canadian border, where we had moved in the summer of 1919. He had attended a meeting in Bemidji and was returning home by train when he became ill and entered Budd Hospital in Roseau. He had the flu, or, as it was often called in 1920, "flumonia." After several days of hospitalization he had recovered quite well and had been told he could go home the next day, but he died of heart failure before he could leave the hospital. He was buried in Williams after a service in the Congregational Church there. It was not permissible to transport bodies in other than private vehicles because of the flu epidemic; otherwise I imagine he would have been buried in Rothsay or Onalaska.

Regarding his funeral in the Congregational Church, it should be noted that my father was a lifelong member of that communion. In several of the towns where my parents lived, they attended Lutheran churches, but my father remained a Congregationalist. In Williams there was no Lutheran church in 1920, so the choice of a place of worship had been simplified.

I have vague memories of my father and of his death. I believe I recall some simple games he played with Lyman and me, and I definitely remember that the two of us were left with friends in Williams when Mother went to Roseau after receiving word of my father's death.

A family friend, Reverend Amon O. Johnson, who was a high school student in Ulen, Minnesota, when my parents taught there (probably the school year 1912–13) wrote later regarding my father, "I can still see him singing solos at church. He rounded out the notes vigorously and with a slight emphasis bordering on the theatrical at times. He was a fine principal of our school."

I have wondered about the fact that my father moved frequently in his work. I have no knowledge of his performance being unsatisfactory or of his being asked to move on. He seems to have been well liked wherever he worked. Mother used to say that she believed it was because he was drawn to the challenge of working out the consolidation of rural school districts. During the time he was a principal, small schools in rural areas were being brought together in order to provide a base large enough to support an elementary school offering grades one through eight, and a four–year high school. High schools were not common in small towns in the first two decades of this century. For whatever reason, my father seemed to enjoy the work, and went from town to town investing his considerable energy in the enterprise at hand.

It can't have been easy for Mother. Living conditions were often less than ideal, and moving was an inconvenience, to say the least. I never heard her offer a word of criticism or complaint, however. I believe my parents were a happy couple, content with what life offered them.

My father's death was the first unusual event of my life. I've often wondered what effect it had on me. Lyman, Charlotte and I grew up without a father, but I imagine none of us realized just what it meant to be members of a single parent family. I remember times when I observed friends who had close relationships with their fathers, and I would wonder what that was like, but I have no memory of being morbid about it or dwelling on it. Evidently Mother succeeded in bringing us up without our having a sense of being deprived. I also have pleasant memories of association with men like Edwin Skugrud and Ed Moen who, now that I look back on it, I believe took special interest in me at least in part because I had no father.

My wife Dorothy used to say to me during our days in Nashwauk that I was at my poorest in preaching at funerals, and she ascribed that to the fact that I had no personal experience with death. She reasoned that at three–and–a–half years of age I had been too young to be affected by my father's death.

The loss of our father did change the lives of all of us in the family, of course. Mother packed our things — in wooden crates in those days — and shipped them by rail to Rothsay. We moved in with my grandmother Pedersen, who was then an invalid as the result of a stroke she had suffered earlier. Grandfather Pedersen had died two months before my father. Bestemor required both nursing and housekeeping care, and Mother became the housekeeper.

Mother did her best to keep our father's memory alive. Because we did not own an automobile, we never got to Williams to visit the grave during my childhood. (I have done that several times as an adult). But Mother would tell us children about our father's sense of humor, his readiness to be the master of ceremonies at almost any function, his pleasure with "made–up" games he played with Lyman and me, and his strong singing voice. He also played the cornet, an instrument I inherited from him and tried to play for a short time as a member of the Rothsay band. That was a pick–up group which had an on–and–off existence. We had no organized music activity in the Rothsay school.

I have in my possession a copy of a poem my father wrote extolling the virtues of the house in Rothsay. He wrote a number of poems. One, in seeming anticipation of later developments, he called "Sir Coffin Nail." It is an attack on cigarettes and their deadly consequences. My father never smoked, and he did not drink.

He must have been a wise man, too. Mother told of a time when he learned a Norwegian song which he sang for our grandparents, much to their pleasure. He had not a drop of Norwegian blood in him, but he knew how to please his in–laws!

Chapter 3

MOTHER — AND THE REST OF US

Mother was the center of our home. Most people of my generation have grown up in what can be called a patriarchal family. Father earned the living, Mother was usually busy with the home and children. Because of my father's death when I was three–and–a–half years old (Lyman was five and Charlotte was born six months after our father's death), our family was different. Mother was the breadwinner, leader, single parent — everything.

From March, 1920, when we moved to Rothsay from Williams, Minnesota, until my grandmother's death in June, 1926, Mother stayed at home, took care of the house and assisted with the care of her mother. In the fall of 1926, she returned to teaching at the request of the local school board, and, with a few years off, taught in Rothsay High School until she retired in 1950.

I think we were a poor family, judged by some standards. We had a place to live without direct cost to us, and while Grandmother lived many of the household costs were borne by her with income from the farm and the inheritance from her husband. When Mother went back to teaching, our family income consisted of her salary and whatever return there might be from the farming operations. The latter was usually a few hundred dollars a year. Mother remarked more than once that we were blessed by the fact that during the dry years in the 30's when so many farmers lost their land, our farm was never mortgaged. Mother's salary as a teacher varied, but the highest it ever got was ninety dollars per month for nine months of the year. During that time, I spent four years at Concordia College and Charlotte attended Moorhead State College for two years. I regularly received money from Mother while I attended college.

Mother frequently told us we couldn't afford certain things, but I was never aware of her feeling deprived or wanting us to feel we were. She succeeded in providing for her children all that was needed to live a healthy and happy life. Living in a small town was of help, I am sure. There were lots of folks in about the same financial situation as we. And Mother's credit was good. We had perpetual charge accounts at Skugrud's store and Martinson's meat market. Mother would pay as she could, but I don't believe she ever caught up. The merchants were understanding, which Mother ascribed to the fact that her father had been generous to many people with regard to their credit. She thought there was some repayment of that going on with us.

Another benefit we enjoyed was freedom from doctor's charges, because we had our own physician, Dr. J.C. Serkland, in the family. He had been married to Mother's sister Seline, and after her early death had married Anna Langeland, daughter of the longtime pastor of Hamar Church. He was the father of my only first cousins, Alice, Alvin and Chester Serkland. Dr. Serkland never charged us for his services, and I remember Mother expressing her appreciation for that on many occasions. Our family had the rather normal need for a doctor's help. All three of us children had measles and chicken pox, and Lyman had scarlet fever as a boy. Once I opened a gash over one eye as I ran into a piece of playground equipment at school. That required a few stitches. In 1928, Mother was bedridden for some time with pericarditis. At such times we were especially happy to have Dr. Serkland as a member of the family and the sponsor of our own private HMO. Fortunately, none of us was hospitalized during my childhood.

Once our HMO failed us. In the summer of 1932, Dr. and Mrs. Serkland took a trip to Norway. During their absence, a young physician came from the University of Minnesota Medical School to serve the Rothsay community. While he was there, I broke an ankle playing baseball. Dr. Bunker, the replacement physician, set the bone, applied a cast — and charged a fee!

Dr. Serkland and O.H.Ekeren were the ones who concocted our favorite cough medicine, as I mentioned earlier. Their other great creation was Bronchiol, a liniment–like, oily substance which Mother administered at the first sign of a cold. It was rubbed on the chest and covered with a piece of wool flannel, one of our uses for worn–out winter underwear. It worked. I cannot forget the aroma, dominated by camphor.

On the subject of medications, I must report that Mother was "anti." She didn't believe in ingesting a medication or palliative except on doctor's orders. We never had aspirin in the house. The only exception to Mother's policy was the practice of having on hand a regular supply of Smith Brothers or Ludens cough drops.

Our home was a generally happy, busy place. We had the normal spats and fights as kids are wont to do, and of course I felt Lyman dominated me, even as Charlotte felt her brothers were mean to her. A few times I remember we brought Mother to tears with our behavior. But for the most part I think we were four fairly independent people who, especially as we grew older, went on our individually chosen paths. I think of my childhood as a time of great freedom to do and be what I chose within the outer limits set by Mother, such as no swearing, no drinking, no card playing. We were expected to be regular in church and Sunday School. There were assigned home tasks, some of which I've already mentioned. Lyman was more inclined to step outside the boundaries than either Charlotte or I. This is not to say the two of us were any better. Speaking for myself, I would say that I behaved as I did because I feared doing anything that would displease Mother. This was probably due both to my love for her and a general conviction that she knew what was best.

This attitude of mine is illustrated by an experience I had in 1934. I hitchhiked to the World's Fair in Chicago and made the rounds of the various exhibits, shows and entertainments. One day I stood before the Sally Rand tent. There she was pictured in her fine feathers! I thought to myself that as a Rand I should really see that show. But I didn't go in. It may have been the high price of twenty–five cents which discouraged me, but I really think it was the fact that I was convinced Mother would not approve.

Some of our indiscretions were both funny and naughty. One sunny summer day Mother was entertaining several of her friends at a coffee or tea party. She had set a nice table in a shaded corner of our croquet lawn. Lyman, probably nine years old at the time, induced me to go with him to the woodshed where the fifty–gallon barrel of kerosene was kept. He undressed me, set me under the pump at the top of the barrel and covered me with kerosene. Then he chased me around the yard in full view of Mother's guests. Of course Mother had to interrupt her party and take me into the house where she gave me a quick bath, and both of us the reprimand which was quite in order. As I recall, she got back to her party, but I'm sure the afternoon was one she remembered for all the wrong reasons.

We had good times as a family, and were great game players. Summer activities included tennis, baseball, long walks, biking and many made–up activities. Croquet was a leading summer pastime and included friends such as the Paulsons, Skugruds and Salvesons, who would often join us in tournaments on Sunday afternoons. Our croquet set was made up of the leftovers of at least two sets. Some mallet heads and balls were chipped, but we did our best. Mother was always ready to play croquet.

The croquet we played was special, as I have discovered in the years since

Rothsay. Many people see it as a polite, rather slow–moving game. Some with whom I have played even stroke the ball gently as they stand over it between their legs. Never would the Rand Rothsay brand be played with such gentility. We would send the opponent's ball flying into the woods, and we would try to make an arch (and sometimes do it) from half–way across the lawn. It was a no–holds–barred kind of competition, and we loved it. I am pleased to say that some of that highly competitive spirit lives on in the next generation. My son Peter plays in the Rothsay style, and so does my stepson Mark. I have reminded Mark that his dad Walt Ekeren was one of the great competitors on the Rand lawn in Rothsay.

In the winter, we enjoyed such outdoor activities as skating, skiing and snowball fights, and there was an abundance of parlor games. I must have played hundreds, if not thousands, of games of Rook, Pit, Old Maid, checkers and caroms. In all of these, Mother was a great participant. She didn't seem to mind losing; it was the love of the game that kept her at it. I think games were a form of relaxation, relief from some of the demands of what must have been for her a very difficult life. Her normal stoicism and reserve frequently melted into laughter and even shouts, rather mild shouts, to be sure, as she trumped a play in Rook or made a difficult shot in croquet. She was always ready for a game even though work enough for several days piled up around her.

Mother was not a great housekeeper and made no claim to be. As summer ended and she returned to her teaching duties, she would often say, "Now my vacation begins." Teaching was her great love. Housework was necessary, of course, and she got some minimal assistance from her children, but as a rule our house was neatly kept only when required by the expected arrival of guests or at special times such as Christmas. Otherwise, closets were normally a jumble, dusting was delayed and the normal muss and mess created by three youngsters was left unattended for days at a time.

Laundry was done on a regular basis, however. Mother insisted that we be clean. Even my clothes, dirtied by my involvement with lumber yard work, got the regular laundry treatment. And that wasn't easy. In the summer, Mother would wash clothes outdoors in large tubs, with a scrub board and hand–operated wringer. In the winter, she adapted the process to indoors. In either case, she used a copper boiler to boil white clothes. In the summer, she hung everything outdoors to dry, and in the winter most of the wash was hung on a folding rack placed on the screen porch. Then everything would freeze stiff as a board, but when it was brought back into the house it smelled so good. That's an aroma that occupies a special place in my memory.

Even as Mother was not in love with housework generally, she also had no special love for cooking. We ate good–tasting simple food, nothing fancy. Breakfast was toast and cereal or, for Lyman, always one hard–boiled egg crushed over a piece of toast deliberately burned and scraped of its blackness. I drank coffee from early childhood and enjoyed it not only for breakfast but in company with the others at Moen's Lumber Yard, usually morning and afternoon. Our noon meal at home was dinner with meat and potatoes. For supper we often had leftovers from the noon meal. Mother cooked by color. She used vegetables as available, but we never heard much about calories or vitamins. It seemed good to Mother to have some green, some orange or yellow and often some red along with the bread and butter and meat and potatoes. She was an excellent baker. Her pies, cinnamon rolls and bread bring wondrous memories to mind.

An exception to what I said above about minimum help provided by us children occurred in 1928, when for three months Mother was bedridden with pericarditis, an inflammation of the lining around the heart. During that time, Alice Serkland, who had recently graduated from the University of Minnesota, took Mother's place teaching and we kids pitched in to help at home. I did most of the cooking and Lyman kept house. Charlotte, who was eight years old, helped when we could get her to. I remember baking a cake — something I thought was a major accomplishment. I think it really was, because in those days we baked cake from scratch — no boxes of mixes to make things easier. We were very happy when Mother was well again.

Mother loved teaching. I had her as a teacher for English I, II and III and for algebra and geometry. She was thorough and demanding but always fair. Through the years, many persons who were in her classes have told me that she was the best teacher they ever had. She was old–fashioned, in that she believed in memorization and rote learning. She believed you either knew an algebraic function or you didn't. She believed you either knew a theorem in geometry so you could make use of it or you didn't. She believed committing some Shakespeare or Tennyson or Longfellow or Scott to memory was a good thing, because such literature had both linguistic merit and the ability to feed your mind. I shall not recite here any of the pieces I learned under Mother's tutelage, but I could do so if it were demanded.

One of Mother's students in Ulen, Minnesota, was Amon Johnson who later became a pastor. I have referred earlier to what he had to say about my father. His parents Henry and Julia Johnson were good friends of my parents. Amon Johnson's daughter Corinne Ehlke shared with me in 1989 some of her father's jottings in which he comments about Mother as his teacher: "Mrs. Rand was my teacher for a year in Ulen and her impression will always be with me. She even understood my fights and other tendencies, and through it all she taught me to think intelligently in my immature way. She was close to Mom, and kept in touch with me as long as she lived. Mrs. Rand was one in a million...she was remarkable. My enthusiasm for algebra skyrocketed, as well as my interest in Latin."

Mother was active in church, too. She often gave talks in women's groups and taught classes in Sunday School. She was regular in church attendance and at the communion table. Her Christian faith was not on evident public display, however. She spoke about her faith at times, she taught us evening prayers, and she insisted that we attend Sunday School, confirmation class and worship services. We did not regularly use a prayer before meals during my childhood.

I never doubted my mother's faith. Something about her indicated that whether things were going well or otherwise, she was relying on One greater than herself. Her life exhibited that trust in a quiet, consistent way. The fact she was of Norwegian descent may partially account for her stoic and unruffled manner. Also, the fact that our congregation had been affiliated with the Norwegian Synod may have had something to do with it. That church body represented orthodox, no–nonsense Lutheranism, and that's precisely what Mother typified.

Our family enjoyed certain special times and activities. There were walks to Hamar cemetery one mile south of town (each church had its own cemetery). Not infrequently we would walk there in the summer with flowers from the yard for the grave of Mother's sister Seline. We had lilacs, peonies and fruit blossoms in abundance, especially in early summer. Mother would tell us something about the family or about friends whose graves we saw. One grave always attracted us. It was marked by a memorial stone in which had been mounted the picture of the child buried there. We were impressed by that.

Two church cemeteries near Rothsay were the scenes of special Memorial Day observances. World War I veterans would march to the cemeteries with the children of town trailing behind. There would be shots fired in salute and the kids would scramble to recover empty shells.

Speaking of walks, I remember several longer walks taken with friends. More than once several of us boys walked to Lawndale, seven miles north, bought an ice cream cone at a little store there and then returned home. Once, in company with my Bergan cousins from Fergus Falls, I walked from Rothsay to Fergus, a distance of sixteen miles. My feet ached like everything. I wore tennis shoes with no arch support, and I believe my arches were permanently damaged, but we completed the walk. That's what mattered.

Annual or semi–annual trips to Fergus Falls were also special. A train left

Rothsay about nine in the morning and returned in mid–afternoon. That gave us time to go to the dentist, do some shopping and have lunch — all major events. Our dentist was Dr. Lafitte, who had his office on the second floor of the J.C. Penney store building. We went to him for a checkup once a year shortly before the start of school. Our clothing purchases were concentrated at the same time and usually were made at Penney's. Lunch was either at the Candy Kitchen or at Elton's Cafe. My standard fare was a hot roast beef sandwich. If hamburgers had been invented, we had not heard of them. Sometimes a dish of ice cream or even a malted milk was added to my lunch, and that would crown the whole trip with success.

I remember my first long pants. I had worn knickers as a youngster; all the boys did. I believe it was my confirmation suit that brought the change. That was the usual time for boys to graduate to men's clothing. I purchased the suit, dark gray with stripes, at Penney's with my own money. I suppose it cost ten or twelve dollars, a big investment at the time. After I started frequenting Moen's Lumber Yard at the age of eight years, I purchased most of my own clothing. Of course I received clothes as gifts from time to time, but otherwise I paid for what I wore and was proud of that.

Perhaps the most impressive adventure we experienced with Mother was a trip to the Twin Cities and Wisconsin in the summer of 1928. We visited Aunt Nell and the P.L. Johnsrud family in St. Paul, and Tanbergs and Austeruds in Spring Valley and Woodville, Wisconsin. Mrs. Johnsrud, Flossie, was my father's cousin but like a sister to Aunt Nell because it was Flossie's parents who had taken Nell to live with them following her mother's death. The Austeruds and Tanbergs were cousins of my mother. The mothers of Netta Austerud and Hans Tanberg were sisters of A.B. Pedersen.

We had a great time on that trip. We went by train, of course. I remember not being able to sleep much the night before we left. We were met at the station in Minneapolis by P.L. Johnsrud (everyone called him P.L., not Peter). He took us to a drug store in St. Anthony Park near where they lived, and treated us to malted milks. While in the Twin Cities, we visited the State Capitol, the Como Park Zoo, the fairgrounds and several parks and lakes. In Wisconsin we met second cousins about our ages. We spent several pleasant days there.

One purpose of the trip, probably the reason it was planned in the first place, was to attend the graduation of Alice Serkland from the University. The ceremony was held in Memorial Stadium, a place I had read about in connection with football, and such names as Herb Joesting and Bronko Nagurski. As a small town boy, I was appropriately impressed by the size of the stadium and the size of the crowd. I had never seen anything like it. Mother and Alice were always close to one another, and I'm sure Mother was eager to attend the graduation program for that reason. But it also was the first time she had been at the University since her graduation in 1907, so I would assume that was an attraction, too.

One other major trip I took remains a vivid memory. After my high school graduation in 1933, I remained in Fergus Falls for a year working in O'Meara's store. By the spring of 1934 I had saved a little money (I believe it was about two-hundred dollars), and decided it was time to go to college. But the World's Fair was on in Chicago and I wanted to see it, so I left my job in mid-August and went to the fair.

I've referred already to my experience of standing before the Sally Rand show and wondering whether to go in. But there was more to the fair than that. I hitchhiked to the Twin Cities where I stayed with Aunt Nell for two nights. She was in charge of public relations and advertising for the Rap-in-Wax Paper Company, and arranged a ride for me in a company truck from St. Paul to Chicago.

I spent three days in Chicago, staying at the YMCA for seventy-five cents a night. I spent the days at the fair seeing most of the exhibits and eating ten-cent hamburgers and hot dogs. I had arranged to ride back to St. Paul on another Rap-in-Wax truck and we took a different, less direct route than the one we had followed going to Chicago. We went into Iowa and then north to St. Paul, so I saw more of the country that was new to me.

After another night of free lodging, courtesy of Aunt Nell, I took a streetcar to Robbinsdale at the northwest edge of Minneapolis and returned to my hitchhiking routine. A man picked me up and gave me a ride all the way to Rothsay. On the way we stopped to see the Reformatory in St. Cloud, which neither of us had visited before. I arrived at home in Rothsay as Mother was preparing supper. I had started the trip with fifteen dollars, and when I returned I had fifteen cents. The trip had taken ten days. Travel was a bit cheaper then than it is today.

Perhaps because we had no car, automobile trips of any kind were special treats for us as children. The Skugrud family was especially generous in taking us for rides, often on Sunday afternoons. Sometimes it was a trip to Lake Lida, where the Skugruds had a cottage. On other occasions it was a drive to Pelican Rapids or Barnesville or Detroit Lakes. It usually included a treat such as ice cream or pop. T.K. Brye, the merchant who had bought our grandfather's store, also took us for rides. He had an open touring car, a Dodge, I believe. It was exciting to ride with the wind blowing at us as we sped along at twenty-five or thirty miles per hour. A trip to Fargo was very special for us. I remember such trips with the Serklands, the highlight of which was a meal at the Bluebird Cafe.

As important as any trip I took during my childhood was the one to Underwood, a few miles east of Fergus Falls. That was the home of Clara Wold, who was our grandmother's nurse when I was eight years old. Miss Wold took me with her and we stayed for two or three days. It was my first overnight stay away from Mother and away from home. I was royally treated by the Wold family, who lived on a farm and did their best to entertain me. We had huge breakfasts, exciting times with horses and other animals, but the chief memory I have is that of homesickness. The first night I could have died! But I didn't. I survived and returned home with a new appreciation of Mother, Charlotte and even my brother Lyman, I think.

My sense of smell evokes many memories of childhood and home. I have mentioned Bronchiol. That aroma was distinctive and lingering when used, and memory can easily recall it, together with the stuffed nose and woolen rags that accompanied its use. Another smell which lingers is that of fresh lumber. While working at Moen's Lumber Yard, I learned to distinguish the odors of oak, cedar, pine and fir, all of which were pleasant and inviting. Then there was quite another aroma — from the manure pile next to the barn. In the winter it steamed, and in the spring when the spreader hauled it to the fields the reminder spread over the farm and wafted to our house. It was a very special smell. I remember both the smell and the sound of wood burning in the cook stove. There was something cozy and inviting about that. And of course there were the smells associated with food — freshly baked bread or pie, fruit juice dripping through a muslin sack, and cheeses of various kinds. Grandmother Pedersen kept a strong cheese called pultost in a covered jar in the pantry. As a child I considered it sporty to go to the jar, lift the lid, take a whiff and run. It was awful.

In addition to aromas, there were tastes that I remember well. We rarely had a chicken dinner in those days. Baked chicken was our regular Christmas dinner entree and its tastiness was always a treat. Fresh apples and plums and berries from the orchard gave special meaning to life. And such a mundane thing as peanut butter on bread always reminds me of the hundreds of times that rather ordinary food brought pleasure, the pleasure of taste, to a young boy so many years ago. It still does, to an older man. Rich cream, was another favorite childhood taste. We had whipped cream on puddings and Jello, and cream beginning to turn sour was something special on bread, as I've said.

One of my fondest taste memories has to do with threshing. When I worked at the lumber yard, we would often use the trucks to haul grain to town from the threshing rigs. It was always a treat to arrive at the grain separator as morning or afternoon coffee was being enjoyed by the crew. Usually there were clothes baskets filled with sandwiches and doughnuts and cookies, together with large pots of coffee. Warm day or not, there is no taste quite like that one, sitting in the stubble with chaff blowing in your cup and the men joshing each other. Feasting on thresher's lunch made all of life worthwhile.

Because Walter Ekeren was a special friend of mine, and because his father's drug store included a soda fountain, I developed a couple of special tastes. One was for the overly–rich malted milks which Walt mixed for his friends. Usually I had a chocolate–flavored one, rich and thick, and costing all of fifteen cents. Another popular taste treat was a Little Dick, which consisted of a scoop of ice cream covered with chocolate syrup and red–skinned peanuts, all in a Coca Cola glass. Those were the days.

I have always enjoyed eating, and I like most foods. I have never been compelled to modify my diet for health reasons and, perhaps as a result, I went from a normal weight youngster to an overweight adult. As a teenager I was five feet ten inches tall and weighed 137 pounds. In my mid–twenties I went from that weight to 165 pounds, and finally to 185 pounds, which I weighed for several years, probably because I enjoyed food too much. In 1993, my weight changed again, but more of that later.

Lyman and I have had different interests in adult life, but as boys we played together quite a bit and shared many friends. We had the marvelous big yard with its woods and lawns to be a playground, and we made full use of them, often with friends who came to play with us. Lyman once invented two friends for us. His was named Daters and mine was Biggerbaggers. Who knows where kids get ideas like that? Another of Lyman's ideas was the Skratt family. This was definitely a Scandinavian group and was capable of absorbing the blame or credit for all sorts of things. As the years have passed, not only Lyman, Charlotte and I have been involved with the Skratts. Alice Serkland has met some of them as she has traveled, especially in Norway, and they have been known to send postcards and letters to us from various places. When Lois and I were living in Norway, a cousin of hers, Ellen Corneliussen, was introduced to them and ever since she has regularly inquired about their welfare. In Norway we met Skratts in far north Honningsvåg and, of course, in Sigdal. They have given us much pleasure and don't seem to bother us too much, so we are glad to have them in the family.

Chapter 4

A BUSY BOYHOOD

In addition to our life as a family, my childhood experiences centered in school, church and Moen's Lumber Yard. Each played a key role in my growth as a person.

During the 20's and 30's, the Rothsay school consisted of grades one through eleven. There had never been a kindergarten, and the last year of high school had not yet been added. Those who chose to complete high school went to Fergus Falls, Pelican Rapids or Barnesville. Until the early 30's, Park Region Lutheran College in Fergus Falls offered a high school program as well as the first two years of college, so some Rothsay students completed high school there.

No transportation was provided to students by the school district, nor did the district make provision for anyone to complete high school in another community. Students from the country ordinarily attended rural one–room schools through eighth grade, and then would find their own way into town for the high school years.

I finished eighth grade in a class of nine boys, all of us proud of the fact there were no girls in the class. When we returned to school in the fall of 1929, we were joined by several girls from the country. We managed.

The Rothsay school was housed in a square brick building of two floors and a basement, surrounded by an ample playground area, testimony to the fact that recess was an important part of the school day. There was no organized physical education activity.

At the edge of the school yard were two outhouses, one for each sex; Rothsay had neither a water nor a sewer system at that time. As I look back on school days, I am a bit surprised to remember that there were no graffiti or other defacements in the boys' toilet. We must have been an unimaginative and subdued lot.

The school building included two classrooms on the first floor and three on the second. Grades were grouped in the rooms as follows: one and two, three through five, six through eight, and high school. The fifth room was a science lab, Latin classroom and general purpose area. It adjoined the larger high school room which served as an assembly as well as recitation room. Because the larger room doubled as a study hall, it seemed to me that I took algebra, geometry, English I, II, III and some other courses three years in a row as I listened in to what went on in other classes while I was supposedly in study hall. It was no doubt something like a one–room school.

In the basement of the school building were the boiler room, a large coal storage area and a room which served as a manual training classroom. All the boys were required to take a course in manual training, and I believe I progressed from making a bread board to making a bird house. My better training in anything like carpentry came with my experience at the lumber yard.

I started first grade in the fall of 1922 when I was six years old. My teacher was Helga Bjorgen, a sweet and attractive young lady recently graduated from the two–year normal training course at Moorhead State Teachers College. All of my grade school teachers were persons with only two years of college, a common thing in those days.

After the first two weeks of school in second grade, Walter Ekeren and I were promoted to third grade. As I remember it, I took skipping a grade in stride and didn't make much of it. I imagine Mother was consulted before it was done, but I have no memory of it being discussed at home. I wonder what I missed in second grade.

In third grade, my teacher was Esther Paulson, our family friend whose husband Lawrence was the town banker. In fourth and fifth grades, my teacher was Cecelia Kunkel, a fashion plate. We used to say she went home at recess and put on a different dress. Years later, when I was at St. Olaf, and when she was Mrs. Peterson living in Milaca, Minnesota, she sent greetings to me through a mutual friend. I regret that I did not take time to visit her and renew our acquaintance.

From sixth through eighth grades my teachers were Mabel Edwards, Pearl De Otte and Edmee Elseth.

All of these teachers linger in my memory as helpful and dedicated persons. The very fact I remember their names says they made an impression on me. Some were tougher disciplinarians than others, but all of them succeeded in helping me understand that school and studying are important, that we learn only as we apply ourselves, and that education can be an enjoyable experience. I believe I am fortunate to be able to remember my grade school days that way.

I graduated from eighth grade on May 31, 1929, in the class of nine boys. Yes, we had a graduation program for the completion of grade school. The exercises, as they were called, were held in the Odd Fellows Hall, a building next to the Ekeren Drug Store, and the only place in town, other than the churches, for a public gathering. I gave the class prophecy and Walter Ekeren sang a solo at our graduation program.

When I returned to school in the fall to enter ninth grade, I had a new and different experience. My mother was one of my teachers. Following her mother's death in June, 1926, Mother had accepted a position in the school. I remember the summer day when R.S. Cowie, the editor of the local paper, the *Rothsay Enterprise*, and chairman of the school board, came to ask Mother to teach. There were new state regulations seeking to upgrade the quality of the schools, and Rothsay had no teacher other than the principal with a baccalaureate degree. Mother had her B.A. from the University of Minnesota with majors in German and English and a minor in mathematics. In other words, she was well qualified to teach in a two–person faculty where it was necessary for each one to teach several subjects. So she returned to her favorite activity and taught English I, II and III, and algebra and geometry. The principal taught history, social studies, general science and Latin.

When I started school, the principal was Richard Stafne. Others during my Rothsay school days were Lyle Johnson, George Bowers and Lyman Heyerdahl.

There were no electives in Rothsay High School. Each of us took three years of English, two years of math, two years of science, one year of Latin, three years of history and one year of social studies (it was called civics). In addition, the boys took manual training. I received good grades through high school, either A or A– in each course, and had no difficulty in my transfer to Fergus Falls for my senior year.

Extra class activities were few. Once a week we gathered as a school and sang songs in the *Golden Book of Favorite Songs*. That was a relatively undisciplined activity, with the skill of the accompanying pianist varying from year to year. We did learn the words for a lot of songs. I still remember "Darling Nellie Gray," "A Spanish Cavalier," "Tenting Tonight," "My Old Kentucky Home," and "Battle Hymn of the Republic," as well as others. Not much was made of the Pledge of Allegiance, which we used occasionally. There was no prayer in school; I guess you were supposed to do that at home or in church. It surely was no issue.

Recess was big. That's when we got to know the country kids, and that's when we threw ourselves wholeheartedly into such games as softball, marbles, tag and pump–pump–pullaway. It was a thoroughly enjoyable time. There were the usual fights, often town versus country. I remember Mother telling Lyman and me not to play marbles for keeps; that was a form of gambling.

There was no school lunch program. Either you went home, which is what the town kids did, or you brought a brown–bag lunch which was eaten at your desk. Occasionally we who were from town would view with some envy those who could have those bag lunches packed, as we suspected, with all sorts of goodies.

During the years Mother taught, we lived in style at noon. Mrs. Elling Flaten operated a boarding house in her home a block from school. Mother arranged for the four of us to eat dinner there. It was always a meat–and–potatoes meal with all the fixings, and it therefore relieved Mother of the need to prepare a major evening meal at home. Mrs. Flaten's table was regularly patronized by teachers, by visiting auditors at the local elevators or creamery and by traveling salemen. Conversation was sometimes boring to a young boy, but sometimes it was fascinating, too. Lyman and I would excuse ourselves as soon as we had eaten so we could get back to the school playground. In addition to the substantial meals Mrs. Flaten served, I remember her home for the phonograph she would let us use while we waited for dinner. A record I remember well featured the voice of Enrico Caruso. There were also issues of H.L. Mencken's *American Mercury* in the Flaten home, and I would browse in them. That was not standard fare in Rothsay homes, I must say.

One activity offered in school was dramatics, and I was a regular actor. In 1929, I was Willie Sterling, "a dear little angel of an adolescent," in the play *And Mary Did*. In 1930, I was Howard Wayne, "in love with Dolly," in *The Country Doctor*. In 1931, the play was *The Path Across the Hill*, and I was Dr. Jimmie Reed, "an ambitious, surly fellow." Finally, in 1932, I played Stumpy Smith in *Clover Time*. Stumpy was a "Susquehanna Valley tough guy" who walked with a stiff leg. Learning to walk that way was as difficult as knowing my lines.

All of the plays were put on in the Odd Fellows Hall before admiring crowds of a hundred or so parents and friends each time. It all sounds so amateurish to me now, and of course it was, but to Rothsay kids in the 30's it was the stuff of which real life was made.

The Rothsay school had no athletic program. However, during the time I was in high school, a new creamery was built in town and the second floor was not immediately needed for butter making. So the school arranged to use the space as a gym. We played basketball on a concrete floor with a ten–inch–square timber pillar in the middle of the court. It was quite a challenge to say the least, and I know of no NBA recruits who have come out of the program.

School continued for me in Fergus Falls. Lyman had preceded me there by a year and had secured an after–school job at O'Meara's Department Store. He graduated in 1932 and I inherited the job. Involved in that work were such tasks as sweeping and vacuuming floors after the store closed, delivering packages to the homes of customers, running various errands and assisting with window trimming. It was a good job to have and I stayed on full–time for the year after I finished school.

In my last year of high school, I took English, chemistry, physics and higher algebra, not exactly a balanced course load. It must have been that the Fergus faculty decided I needed more science and math, or else they might have been suspicious that my Rothsay courses were not adequate. I enjoyed the year and did not find it difficult. I earned mostly A's and graduated with honors in a class of 128.

In spite of the fact that I had a job, I did participate in debate during my senior year. I've always enjoyed appearing before a group, so speech activities attracted me. In the spring I competed in a contest at Moorhead State and won first place in extemporaneous speaking.

Since high school graduation I have attended reunions of the class in 1958, 1983 and 1988. I was a member of the committee which planned the fiftieth and fifty–fifth anniversary reunions.

Hamar Lutheran Church was another center of life and activity during my childhood. I was baptized in that congregation on August 6, 1916, by Pastor Magne Langeland, confirmed on May 11, 1930, by Pastor Emil Salveson, and ordained into the ministry on June 6, 1943, by District President R.M. Fjelstad.

Prior to the merger of Norwegian Lutheran church bodies in 1917, Hamar Church had been affiliated with the Norwegian Synod, the right wing of Norwegian–American Lutheranism. Purity of doctrine and adherence to accepted churchly practices were two major emphases in the Synod. Hamar Church exemplified these; traditional liturgy was followed in worship, education was emphasized and subjectivism in expression of the faith was uncommon. Our pastors were devoted to their work, well educated and examples of sober piety. Across the street in Rothsay was Our Savior's Lutheran Church, also of Norwegian background but not affiliated with any larger church body, and stressing informal worship, outward expression of personal faith, and evangelistic services.

Mother was a faithful member of Hamar Church and represented its tradition. She wouldn't think of doing anything other than to go to church, support the pastor and try to reflect her faith in her life. But she didn't talk much about it or make a fuss over church or religion. It was there, a part of life, and that was that.

In her later years, Mother was quite active in the national church organization of women, the Women's Missionary Federation. She held district and national offices for a time and enjoyed that work very much. During her teaching years, her church activities had been limited by time and energy.

As children, Lyman, Charlotte and I attended Sunday School and five weeks of summer Bible School each year. We also "read for the minister" in preparation for confirmation, and attended church services and Luther League. We were required to memorize Luther's *Small Catechism* and the Pontoppidan–Sverdrup explanation of it, and we read the familiar Bible stories from Volrath–Vogt over and over. I can still recite from memory the *Small Catechism* and much of the explanation. I am grateful I was required to commit these truths to memory as a child. I am also grateful to Mother, who not only insisted that we learn what we were assigned, but helped us understand what we studied.

Luther League was a social as well as religious gathering and included whole families. It was held on Sunday evenings every other week or once a month. There was always a program followed by refreshments, visiting and games in the church basement. We didn't speak of church parlors; in Rothsay the basement was the basement. With the lack of opportunity for social gatherings, the church played a leading role in planning such activity for young people. I have many pleasant memories of sitting near Mr. Salveson at Luther League meetings so that I could kibbitz on the choosing of hymns. And the parlor games such as Wink–'em, Skip–to–my–Lou and Row, Row, Row Your Boat gave us a chance to choose the girls we liked the best and avoid the others. The menu usually included sandwiches made with homemade bread or rolls spread with minced meat, and sometimes cake. What a way to spend an evening!

During my childhood, worship services in Hamar Church were conducted every other Sunday because Mr. Salveson also served Hedemarken Church six miles south of town. The first organist I remember was Mrs. O.F. Grangaard, the mother of my friend Don. When the Grangaard family moved from Rothsay, Mrs. Salveson became the organist. Off and on there was a choir, directed by Mr. Salveson and featuring Mrs. Serkland, a soprano soloist. Mr. Salveson also sang; he had a beautiful tenor voice. I sang in the choir briefly and not very well.

34

A highlight of church activity was the Sunday School Christmas program. We did the kind where each class would do a reading or recitation and the whole school would sing several songs. I remember once being gently pushed by Mr. Salveson back into the group, as I'm sure he sensed that my loud but not always musically correct voice would be better not seen if it must be heard. As a rule, Walter Ekeren was brought to the fore and featured because he had a good voice and knew how to use it even as a youngster. I was one of the "three wise men" a couple of times, dressed in someone's plaid bathrobe — a non–singing, non–speaking part.

In checking family scrapbooks, I have discovered that in 1928 I sang a solo at a Luther League program. The fact that I have no memory of it may indicate the degree to which I tried to forget. I wonder if it was a misprint in the program.

It seems to me I thought of church as an enjoyable experience. I liked people and wanted to be where there were others. I enjoyed the formality of the liturgy and the solemnity of worship. Lyman didn't take to it as much. As soon as he was old enough to escape Mother's direct supervision, he avoided church and church activities. Charlotte was faithful, and after she had a family she was diligent in bringing up her children with church as an important part of life.

Mr. Salveson was the first person to speak to me about being a pastor. He didn't push it, but gently suggested that it was something I should think about. On the trip to Moorhead when he took me to college, he spoke to me about the ministry and reminded me that I should give it serious thought. He told me then that he had also talked to Walter Ekeren about the ministry, but that Walt's father had asked him not to continue because Mr. Ekeren wanted Walt to be a pharmacist. That is what Walt did, and went into partnership with his father and his two older brothers Hal and Olaf. It is interesting, however, that when he was thirty–seven years old he went to the seminary and became a pastor. He served in the ministry from 1956 until his death in 1972.

Mr. Salveson did me another favor when I was invited to be on the program of the Luther League Convention to be held in Los Angeles in 1939. A pastor in Circle, Montana, Odean Borsheim, who had been one of Mr. Salveson's confirmands in Barnesville several years earlier, had let Mr. Salveson know he was going to the Los Angeles convention. Mr. Salveson suggested that I might ride to California with Pastor Borsheim. I did that, getting low–cost transportation in good company. He also took with him a young man from his congregation, so the three of us made the trip together by car. I traveled to Circle by train and there the car was loaded with our baggage and lots of food. We planned to picnic along the way.

On the trip we visited Glacier Park, Salt Lake City, Grand Coulee Dam, the San Francisco World's Fair, Death Valley and many other interesting places. The convention was impressive, but I believe I profited as much from the trip. It was the first extended trip away from home for a Rothsay boy now twenty–three years old.

My early years also found a center of activity at Moen's Lumber Yard. I probably shouldn't call it work, at least not what I did when I started to frequent the place. It all began in a rather interesting way.

In the summer of 1924 when I was eight years old, Moen's Lumber Yard received a carload of cedar and pine fence posts with bark still on them. The call went out over the efficient Rothsay grapevine that there were jobs to be had. The bark needed to be removed from the fenceposts. I hurried to participate and, in spite of my age, was permitted to take part.

The posts were peeled by pulling a draw–knife over them. A draw–knife is a heavy blade about twelve inches wide with a handle at each end and mounted at right angles to the blade. To use it, you would straddle the post held in place by a saw–buck and pull the knife toward you. That must have been risky business especially for an eight–year–old, and I'll wager that the Moens had no liability or workmen's compensation insurance. We were paid a penny a post. I peeled posts for several days and one day earned a dollar. That was the first dollar I ever earned. I was on my way as a participant in the capitalist society.

After the log peeling was over, the Moens let me hang around the lumber yard. There were four Moen brothers active in the business. Ed, the oldest, was the boss. Marvin was a craftsman in charge of the shop where he produced window screens, doors, wagon boxes, truck boxes, hog feeders and other articles made of wood. Ray and Luke (Lawrence) were younger, and soon after finishing high school left for employment elsewhere. For several years in the 20's and early 30's, the lumber yard was a thriving family business. In the late thirties it was sold. Ed moved to Michigan and Marvin became the Rothsay Standard Oil distributor.

One of my first jobs at the yard was placing laths between rows of lumber as it was unloaded from box cars on the railroad. All the lumber came from the Pacific Northwest by rail, and much of it was not dried out when it arrived. Stacking it with laths between the rows provided for a drying process. As time went on I did various other jobs. I ran errands, helped deliver lumber and coal, and made myself useful in the woodworking shop. I'm surprised the Moens let me stay. I must have been more nuisance than help at the beginning. By the time I left to go to high school in Fergus Falls in 1932, I was sixteen years old and was doing a man's work at the yard.

A bonus of my work with the Moens was learning to drive. They taught me to drive a Model T Ford with its three–pedal shift and brake system. Later I learned to drive a truck with a gear shift. The yard had two Samson trucks, the only ones I ever saw. They had Chevrolet motors and were without cabs. They were the perfect vehicle for hauling a load of lumber, but a bit breezy in the winter.

When I started at the lumber yard, Ed Moen would usually give me a dollar or two on Saturday afternoon. Then it became five dollars and finally ten. That was good income for a volunteer such as I was, especially considering the fact that it was a time when a dollar bought quite a bit more than it has since. Out of what I earned I bought my clothes and had adequate spending money.

During the school year I would run home at about three o'clock, change clothes and hurry to the lumber yard where I stayed until six o'clock. On Saturdays and during the summer I worked from eight to six.

An enjoyable part of the lumber yard experience was coffee time. Usually one or two of the men would take me to one of the Moen homes or to Larson's Restaurant for coffee and a doughnut or roll. This was usually both mid–morning and mid–afternoon. I cannot remember when I started drinking coffee. It must have been before I was eight years old, because I was included in the coffee break from the start of my time at the yard.

Ed Moen was a considerate and understanding boss, and the others treated me in a way that made me feel welcome. I learned something about the man's world, including exposure to profanity, shady stories and memories of World War I in France. I never reported those experiences to Mother.

While the lumber yard was the chief work experience during Rothsay days, there were others. At least once I participated in "potato vacation." In the '20's, lots of potatoes were grown in the Rothsay area. When they were ready for harvest in September or October, school would close for a few days and many of the children became potato pickers. The potatoes were dug from the ground by a machine which dropped them behind. The pickers followed with a potato sack around the waist and a wire basket in hand. As the basket was filled it was emptied into the sack. It was back–straining work but yielded five cents per bushel as reward. My goal was to pick twenty bushels a day and earn one dollar. I did that several times.

I also shocked grain as a boy. The harvester of those days, called a binder, dropped bundles of grain bound with twine. These were stacked by hand with the heads up, five or six bundles to a shock, in such a way that rain would drain away. After a week or so in the shock, the grain was threshed. I didn't shock grain many times, but enough to remember the uncomfortable feeling of barley beards inside my clothes.

Probably because my work at the lumber yard brought me some regular income, I early developed the habit of keeping track of what I received and what I spent. I used a composition book with a page for each month. I recorded nickels and dimes as well as dollars. I kept the book, with other things, in a box I called "My Business." When Mother died I claimed that box, but since have lost it. It was an important part of my very personal possessions for several years.

When I went to Fergus Falls in the fall of 1932, and inherited the job Lyman had at O'Meara's Store, I was fortunate to find another helpful and supportive boss. Ed O'Meara had emigrated from Ireland as a young man, and after working for others for several years started his own department store in Fergus Falls. He made it a practice to hire a high school boy to do odd jobs and some custodial work. I worked at O'Meara's part time during my senior year and full time the year following. As I have related earlier, the work was varied and pleasant.

I can't remember what I was paid for part–time work, but the year I worked full time I was paid fourteen dollars per week. I paid four dollars of that for board and room at the Bergans and tried to save at least some of the rest. I saved about $200 that year, and together with a childhood piggy–bank accumulation of about $150 I was able to start college in the fall of 1934 feeling quite well off.

It has been my good fortune to work for persons who have been congenial and understanding. Ed Moen and Ed O'Meara typify for me the best in what a young man should experience as he enters the world of work. They believed that a person should do the work he is assigned, should accept responsibility for his actions, and should do his part to work constructively with others. They treated me as a person, not just as a subordinate. Each had a sense of humor and a balanced view of life. The experience of working for them has shaped my view of work and its place in life.

Chapter 5

HOME TOWN FOLKS

During my childhood I was surrounded by few relatives but many close friends. The Serkland family in Rothsay and the Bergan family in Fergus Falls were the only relatives we saw with frequency. Compared with many Rothsay families, ours was evidently quite limited with regard to the number of uncles, aunts and cousins who played a part in our lives.

But there were many friends.

We were close to the Salveson family. For some reason or other, I always called Pastor Emil Salveson "Mr. Salveson." He came to Hamar Church in 1923 and was the only pastor during my childhood. Prior to his arrival in Rothsay, there was an interim following the death of Pastor Langeland in 1921. I remember going to church with Mother when Pastor Bjornson was in charge. He was the regular pastor of two country congregations near Rothsay, but came to Hamar Church on occasion. He used only the Norwegian language. My chief recollection of being in church while he served was to sit next to Mother and periodically poke her and ask, "When is it over?"

The Salvesons had several children, and they were among our best friends. Obert, the older of two boys in the family, was about my age and was part of a group of fellows who were my regular playmates. We were in the Salveson home from time to time, and we entertained them at our home. Because of the inconveniences in our house and the fact that Mother's teaching duties were demanding of her time and energy during the winter months, we would entertain mostly in the summer. Sunday dinner, with games and conversation following, was the normal schedule when Mother entertained.

Mr. Salveson was a kind, caring and faithful pastor. He was not particularly demonstrative, and his sermons, read from a carefully prepared manuscript, were not exciting to listen to. But his patient and persistent caring for the people made quite an impression on me even as a youngster. I'm sure his pastoral care was one of the chief reasons I remained interested in the church, grew in faith and made the decision to study for the ministry.

One indication of Mr. Salveson's pastoral concern was the fact that from the time I left Rothsay to finish high school in Fergus Falls in September, 1932, until I had completed the seminary in 1943, I received a letter from him almost every week. He showed interest in what I was doing, encouraged me and reported to me the important Rothsay news. I'm not sure how often I wrote to him, but I would guess it was not more than one–fourth as often. He was also the one who gave me a ride to Concordia when I started college. As a faithful Luther College alumnus, he had tried to persuade me to enroll there, but Mother and I agreed that Concordia was a more reasonable choice, being closer to home and well known to us.

Mr. Salveson's interest in me and my career and his pastoral concern shown in so many ways remain with me as treasured memories. There was no reason for him to show me special attention unless it was that I fostered serious questions of concern in his mind. Or perhaps it was because I had no father; he may have seen himself in some sense as a surrogate.

The Serkland family was special for us as we grew up. Alice, Alvin and Chester Serkland were all several years older than I, but they were my only first cousins. I remember the special times we had with them at Christmas or in the summer when they would come to enjoy our big yard with us. Alice was the most regular visitor in our home through the years. She was devoted to our grandmother and was also very close to Mother. She often remembered Lyman, Charlotte and me with special gifts, and through the years she has remembered birthdays and special occasions. I still have, and frequently use, a letter opener I received from Alice when she returned from a trip to Europe when I was twelve years old. It is from Heidelberg, Germany.

Dr. Serkland was really more than a relative and the town doctor. I remember several occasions, especially after I had left home to go to school, when I would stop at his office for a chat while home on vacation. He would invariably take time to visit, to quiz me on how my life was going and to offer me friendly advice. Once while I was in college, he asked me if I had started to smoke. I replied that I had not. "Well, then," he said, "if you haven't started by now, you probably won't."

The other family of relatives whom we saw regularly during my childhood was the Bergans in Fergus Falls. O.W. Bergan, "cousin Walter," was Mother's cousin. His mother was a sister of A.B. Pedersen. The Bergan children, Homer, Florence and Robert, were about the ages of the three of us. We would often see the Bergans during our trips to Fergus and in the summer would visit each other.

Cousin Walter left his family some time in the early thirties, and after that the father of Mrs. Bergan (Cousin Harriet to us) came to live with them. He was Grandpa Hale, a large, hearty man who had been a Case implement representative. He taught me to play cribbage during the two years I lived with the Bergans in Fergus Falls from 1932 to 1934.

There was a large Gronseth contingent in and around Britton, South Dakota, who were cousins on my grandmother Pedersen's side. We didn't see them often, but sometimes in the summer they would drive to Rothsay to visit us. The family we knew best of several in the Britton area were Ole Gronseth, Mother's cousin, his wife, Elsie, and their children Ambrose, Sylvia and Eunice.

There were also Braatelien relatives whom we saw occasionally. One of my grandfather's brothers, Tollef, had also settled near Rothsay. He had kept the farm name, and as a child I thought it strange that my grandfather had had a brother with a different surname than his. We saw several of Tollef's children with some frequency. Gilbert Braatelien lived on a farm near Rothsay. His sister Mathilda lived in Fergus Falls and was a frequent visitor in our home. A brother Olaf was an attorney in Crosby, North Dakota, and together with his family would often stop to see us on summer visits they made to the Rothsay area. Olaf had no children of his own, but was raising Newell Braatelien, the son of his brother Harold who was not well. Newell was a little younger than I, but I enjoyed his visits to our home. Our paths converged many years later in an interesting way.

I have fond memories of times spent with the Skugrud and Paulson families. We were regularly entertained by the Paulsons during the Thanksgiving season and the Skugruds at Christmas. These two families together with the Salvesons and our family were usually included. Good food, games and music filled the time. I can remember how impressed I was by the fact that Mrs. Paulson usually served two kinds of meat. What an event!

Ed Skugrud was a jack of all trades, not least in music. He sang, played the violin, the trumpet and the saxophone — even a little piano. In the summer the entertainment, often at our home, was croquet, softball or touch football.

The Skugruds and Paulsons were also generous in inviting us to enjoy their shared cottage at Lake Lida. Many a summer Sunday afternoon they would take us with them on the twenty-mile drive to the lake. There was a Rothsay Camp on Lake Lida with several cottages owned by Rothsay people. One of the challenges of the lake trip in the twenties was the fact that near Rothsay Camp the lake road went through a section known as the clay banks. The road, not yet hard-surfaced, was difficult to negotiate when it rained, so the time to leave for home was often dictated by the appearance of the sky in the west.

At the lake we swam (I never learned to swim much, but I liked getting wet), sometimes fished, and went for walks in the woods and along the shore. Ed Skugrud tried to make fishermen out of Lyman and me. He would sometimes take us together with his sons Erling and Russell on fishing adventures either at Lake Lida or another lake nearby. I never caught the fishing bug.

Other summer lake exploits I remember from childhood are trips to Melby Lake and Hovland Lake, just east of Rothsay. When there were boys who could get us there by car (often it was Alvin or Chester Serkland), we would cool off on a hot summer evening in the not–so–clear waters of those two lakes. There was also a small creek that ran through a farm at the north edge of town, where we would sometimes skinny dip.

Speaking of families who were close to me during childhood, I must mention two others. One was the H.A. Johnson family. Mr. and Mrs. Johnson, whom we called Uncle Henry and Aunt Ju, had been friends of my parents since both couples lived in Ulen, Minnesota, in 1912–13. Mr. Johnson was a banker who in the thirties and forties became an examiner for failed banks. The Johnsons and their son Amon to whom I referred earlier, would stop to see our family often. We enjoyed them and their visits. Contact with the Johnsons continued when I went to Concordia College, because Aunt Ju was a sister of President J.N. Brown, and during my college years she lived at the Brown home. Mrs. Brown had been in failing health and was in the hospital. Uncle Henry had died some years earlier.

The other special people in my life were the Ed Moen family. Ed was my employer at the lumber yard, but he was more. He and his wife Berniece often took me with them to the movies in Barnesville or Fergus Falls. That was a special treat, because we didn't have movies in Rothsay and I saw few of them as a boy. I remember once when we went to Barnesville in their new Essex. I sat in the back seat, became car sick and vomited. I was humiliated, but Ed was nice and didn't scold me. He simply cleaned up after me.

I've reflected on why people such as those I've mentioned were so kind to our family. I think it was, at least in part, the fact that Mother was a widow with her hands full trying to raise three children. I believe it was also because most of those folks had known the A.B. Pedersens and respected them. Whatever the reason, I was fortunate to grow up in a community where friend befriended friend, and where love and concern for others showed itself in many ways.

There were other Rothsay people I would call special, not because they were friends of ours but because they were different from many others, and added flavor to the community. Kids notice people like that.

Haldor Hanson had worked on the section crew, the maintenance men who kept the railroad track in shape. He had evidently retired fairly early from that job, because I remember him as a man in his fifties in two other roles. He was for several years the driver for Pastor U.D. Johnson of Our Savior's Lutheran Church. Pastor Johnson would ride in state in the back seat of a Model T Ford sedan, and was quite a presence in town. Later Haldor Hanson was the town constable who took his job quite seriously, not least the nine o'clock curfew for children. He spoke with a thick Norwegian accent and was the butt of many a joke or prank. The story was told that he once lectured a driver for not coming to a full stop at a stop sign. "Can't you read English?" he is reported to have said. "It says true stop and that means really stop." The sign read "thru stop," and in Hanson's Norwegian accent it came out "true stop." On nice summer evenings, we boys spent some of the time after nine o'clock eluding Haldor Hanson and his curfew enforcement.

Jorgen Dihle, another notable in Rothsay, fixed our shoes. He occupied a store building one lot wide and about fifty feet deep. In the front he had a harness shop that had beautiful horse equipment on display. That room was never heated in the winter. He stayed in a small room at the back of the store where he fixed shoes. He was a gruff, efficient cobbler who brooked no foolishness from young boys.

Then there was Bill Hawley. He had farmed west of town and later moved into a trailer house which was located on the corner of the Torvald Martinson farm northwest across the road from our home. He was not a veterinarian, but he made his living taking care of farm animals when they were ailing. He was a gregarious, tobacco–chewing man whose place displayed magnificent disorder. He lived alone surrounded by old cars and other pieces of equipment. We kids lived with a fear/attraction ambivalence toward him.

Tom Juvrud was the school janitor, and we were supposed to address him as Mr. Juvrud. One of my distinct memories is seeing Mr. Juvrud's head peek into the classroom door to read a thermometer on the wall of the room. Then he would disappear. He was a tall, gangling man with a large moustache. As janitor, he was regularly involved in the task of keeping order in the halls. There was no neat division of labor in the school, and if the janitor could be enlisted to help the school operate in an orderly fashion it was all to the good.

In a small town, those in an age group tend to know each other. During much of my childhood I played with eight or ten boys of my age, and, in true boy fashion, tended to avoid about the same number of girls. There were some exceptions to the latter statement, as I shall mention.

My closest friend was Walter Ekeren, the son of Mr. and Mr. O.H. Ekeren. He was three weeks older than I. We started school together in the fall of 1922, and were promoted together out of second grade after two weeks in the fall of 1923. We remained classmates through our sophomore year in high school, after which he went to Fergus Falls. I rejoined him for the senior year, and we graduated together from high school in Fergus Falls in 1933.

For several years the Ekerens lived on the second floor of their drug store building. Walt and I played in our yard or in a vacant lot next to the drug store. A part of playing with Walt was playing with Shep, his dog. Shep had wandered into Rothsay, supposedly from the flats west of town, and had attached himself to Walt when he and I were about ten years old. For the next several years, Shep was a constant companion, a willing playmate and a friend to many of us boys. We hitched him to wagons in the summer and sleds in the winter, and he took it all without protest. I can't remember what finally happened to Shep, but I think he just disappeared. He was golden in color, medium size, and resembled a collie in appearance. Whatever he was, he was a good dog.

One summer Walt invited me to stay with him at Lake Lida for a week while he and his mother were there. My chief memory of that time has to do with a trip Walt and I took across the lake about a mile and a half to the Crystal–Lida Store to get some groceries. On the return trip, a wind came up and there were waves large enough to cause some concern. Walt manned the three–quarter–horse Evinrude motor, and I bailed water with a tin can. A tin can was always in the boat, sometimes used for bait and other times for purposes which would keep the lake from being polluted. We got back safely to the Ekeren dock where Walt's mother was anxiously waving and calling to us.

After high school, Walt went to North Dakota Agricultural College to study pharmacy. We didn't stay in close touch during the next several years, but we did exchange Christmas and birthday greetings. Our lives became intertwined later in an unusual way which I shall relate when I get to that place in my story.

Other close friends were Obert Salveson, Donald Grangaard, Foster Song, Orris Melby, Kenneth Jensen and Walter Johnson. Donald Grangaard moved from Rothsay after sixth grade, but my friendship with him has been renewed because he completed his career as the president and chairman of First Bank System in Minneapolis, and our paths have frequently crossed in more recent years.

There were some girls in my circle of friends, in spite of what I have

44

written above. Eunice Paulson (of a different Paulson family) was my age, and I liked her. In Rothsay during my adolescent years we really didn't date, but I did walk Eunice home a few times from Luther League and from school affairs. That and evening visits on the lawn in front of her house were the extent of our relationship. Walt and I used to think we were vying for her attention. Eunice moved with her family to Fergus Falls during her high school days, and she married a Fergus Falls man. By interesting coincidence, they lived in Forest City, Iowa, when we moved there in 1951.

Other girls among my friends were Alvina Larson, Charlotte Salveson, Florence Moen and Lucille Bergerud. Contacts with them usually involved school activities, parties and Luther League.

I acquired a nickname among my Rothsay friends. Two fellows several years older than I, Marvin Teterud and Floyd Fisher, decided one day, for no particular reason, to call me Butch. I don't know any way in which I fit that name. I was not big or fat, nor was I aggressive or tough. But the name stuck for several years, I believe as long as I lived in Rothsay. I disliked it from the start.

I participated in giving another fellow a nickname once. Vernon Paulson, a younger brother of Eunice, was a popular fellow among us. One day, again with no special reason, some of us decided to call Vernon Soapy. Several years later, I was in his company with some of his close friends, and they still called him Soapy. I imagine he shed that name somewhere along the way. Don't ask me why kids do such things.

Some special places, activities and occasions in our small town made my life rich and satisfying.

A short distance north of town was a small hill. It was our mountain. In the winter we would slide or ski there. It had a name, Stygge, which is Norwegian for plain or ugly. Its ugliness was quite mild, but I guess the name was used to indicate it was the most dangerous natural place in our otherwise gently rolling terrain. The Rothsay community of my childhood enjoyed winter sports, and frequently on a Sunday afternoon Stygge was crowded with people. We had rather primitive skis with a single strap over the instep. Mine were a gift from Alice Serkland. We had Red Flyer sleds, and a few people had toboggans.

Skating was done on frozen sloughs. There was one at the Torvald Martinson farm, and another west of the barn at our place. A culvert under the road provided a connection between the two, and sometimes, if the water had been just the right depth when it froze, we could negotiate the way between the two sloughs. I started skating with double runner skates strapped to my shoes.

Then I went on to single blades clamped to the soles of my shoes. Finally, when I was about fifteen years old I got a pair of shoe skates. They were hockey blades, and that was the greatest one could hope for.

We played hockey by our own rules on ice that was rough and where the stubble of rushes protruded here and there. We built warming fires at the edge of the rink and fed them with anything that would burn. We played crack the whip, and the kid at the end of the line usually ended up in the rushes.

An activity which was truly a community affair in Rothsay was baseball. The men in town had a team each year and played teams from the surrounding area. Ed Skugrud was a leader in that, and Hal Ekeren, Walt's brother, was the star pitcher for several years in the 20's. I played on a boys team sponsored by the American Legion post, my position being outfield or first base. I was never a great baseball player, or athlete of any kind. I still play a little golf, and until recently also a little tennis, but those who know me are aware of my athletic limitations.

During the 20's, Rothsay regularly had a Fourth of July celebration sponsored by the American Legion. That was a big day for little boys. We would gather up town early in the day to watch the stands being readied, and then spend the day parting with what money we could for pop, ice cream, hot dogs and many a ring toss. I never won a prize. There was usually a speaker at a morning program that emphasized patriotism. We were not far removed from World War I, and the consciousness of sacrifices made by young men was very real. That spirit prevailed also on Memorial Day, which always included a program in our church, a parade to the two cemeteries near town, and the firing of a salute in honor of those who had died in the war.

In at least some of the years when I was a boy there was a fair in Rothsay. The fairgrounds were south of our farm, across the road from Hamar cemetery. The fair included exhibits of agricultural and home products, but also boasted a merry–go–round, ferris wheel and other entertainment. Besides enjoying the fair activity, I remember we would go to the grounds the day after the fair closed and scour the place for coins. We usually found a few and came home a bit richer. It probably didn't replace what we had spent at the fair.

Each summer for several years, the Rothsay businesses would sponsor a week–long series of traveling programs called the Chautauqua. A tent was set up in the center of town, and each day a different program was presented. There were lecturers, musicians and always a play. There was no admission charge because the merchants had reasoned that the Chautauqua brought people to town who would do business while there. It was a grand institution. Easy auto travel, together with radio and television, later rendered such activities obsolete, but it was a treat for a small town to have such a cultural and entertainment experience.

The chief celebration year after year was Christmas. That included our activites at home, but also the Sunday School Christmas program at church and usually an invitation to the Serklands and the Skugruds. At home, Christmas was observed on December 24. The tree would be put up that day, never earlier, and in the late afternoon the gifts that had accumulated next to the piano were placed under the tree. At about five o'clock we would light the candles — carefully. Alice Skerkland would usually join us and we would open our gifts. I always had my special place to sit — under the telephone mounted on the west wall of the sitting room next to the big bookcase. One by one the gifts were opened, and then we would go to the dining room where the standard meal was baked chicken with all the trimmings.

As long as my grandmother lived, Mother would fix lutefisk for her. That's an old Norwegian dish, codfish dried and treated with lye. I disliked the smell of it cooking, and have never learned to like it, but I eat it on occasion when it is served.

Our home was a busy and active place, and our town offered enough for a boy to do so that time would never hang heavy. Besides, I had my work at Moen's Lumber Yard to occupy a good share of my time. In one way, that was my chief activity away from home while I was a boy.

THE CHANGING SCENE

1934–1945

Chapter 6

ANOTHER WORLD

Although life tends to flow in a steady stream rather than in fits and starts, there are nevertheless times when there occur certain breaks or new developments.

My life through high school seems to me to have been of a piece. Even the two years in Fergus Falls continued to center in Rothsay. I went home via the hitchhike method most weekends, and I never developed any sizeable cohort of close friends in Fergus. My work at O'Meara's, my life with the Bergan family and, for the first year at least, school activity, were the sum of my experiences away from Rothsay.

In 1934 it was different. The move to Moorhead was truly a change in life's locale. In the thirties, "going away to college" meant just that. Even though I was only forty miles from home, I was caught up in college life that included weekends. While at Concordia I got home once or twice between September first and Christmas, and another time or two between Christmas and the end of the school year. Even Thanksgiving Day was usually spent in Moorhead. At the college, it was a special time because few students were able to go home. There was a festive meal at noon, and that was followed by a "mud league" basketball game between Minnesota and North Dakota students. The term "mud league" was appropriate. The game was rough and tumble. Minimum attention was paid to the rules. There was a pep band and a gym full of fans.

I should say a word about our staying at the college with few breaks. During the 30's there weren't many cars available to students. Most had traveled to college by train or bus. Also, those were the days we called the depression. No–one had much money. Most students worked part–time. The attitude was that we were lucky to be at college and we'd better enjoy it. We did, making up much of our own recreational activity and taking full advantage of whatever the college offered.

Earlier I referred to the fact that Mr. Salveson gave me a ride to Moorhead when I started college. As I recall, I had a footlocker, which could be stored under the bed in the dorm, and a suitcase to bring my clothes and other needed articles with me. I had, among other things, a collapsible, cardboard, canvas–covered laundry case which I was to use regularly to ship my soiled clothes home to Mother. I marvel at this fact now, but it was common practice for college students, the males at least, to send their laundry home. There was no provision for doing laundry in the dormitories. Through four years of college, Mother faithfully did my laundry in addition to all her other duties at home.

Mr. Salveson delivered me to the Men's Dorm. There was no fancy name for that building in 1934. Since that time it has been renovated and named Academy Hall, a reminder of the early days of the college when Concordia was a secondary school (1891–1917). I went to a room which had been assigned to me and met my roommate, who had also been asigned to me. He was Walton Myhrum of Thief River Falls. He became a math major, played saxophone in the band that toured Norway in the summer of 1935, and had a raccoon coat. He and I got along well. We didn't have lots in common, and each of us went his own way. I decided that was a good kind of relationship to have with a roommate. We lived on second floor of the dorm, with a washroom across the hall and the building's only shower in the basement.

Our room was about ten by fourteen feet in size. There were two single beds, one straight chair and a table in the room. In one corner, near the door to the hall, was a shelf mounted about seven feet off the floor. Under it were several hooks for clothes, and the top provided a storage place about twelve by thirty inches in size. That was our closet. Walt and I got along fine, usually by only one of us being in the room at a time, except when we were in bed. If one of us studied at the table, the other one would go to the library or lie on the bed.

In 1934, Concordia had been a degree–granting institution for seventeen years. The merger of Norwegian–related Lutheran churches in 1917 had resulted in Concordia becoming a four–year college, and Park Region Lutheran College in Fergus Falls a high school and junior college. The enrollment at Concordia in 1934 was about 450 and there were 35 persons on the faculty. All of that seemed adequate and quite respectable to me. I don't believe I was much aware of size when deciding which college to attend.

The campus was on the south edge of Moorhead, a city of about ten thousand. It was surrounded on the south and east by a cemetery and fields.

The nickname for Concordia students, Cobbers, is supposed to have come from the fact that the college was in a cornfield. The campus facilities consisted of a well–constructed, all–purpose stone and brick building known as Old Main, an older frame structure with brick veneer which was the original building purchased from Bishop Whipple School when the college was begun, a frame and stucco dormitory and a small gymnasium. The college also made use of two or three former residences. The former Bishop Whipple building housed a women's dormitory, and an annex to it provided space for the library. It was about seven blocks to the business district, and there was trolley–car service to downtown Moorhead and Fargo.

While considering college, I had received a scholarship offer from Carleton College in Northfield. It was worth $75 a semester for the two semesters' tuition of the freshman year. During the summer of 1934, I had occasion to tell Dean Paul Rasmussen, Concordia's Dean of Men and admissions counselor, about the Carleton offer. He countered with a scholarship in the same amount from Concordia. I'm not sure that is why I went to Concordia, but it helped, of course. Mother wanted me to attend a college of the church, and I had agreed with that. The scholarship, together with my savings and some help from Mother, got me through the first year. The total cost was between $450 and $500.

During my freshman year I took history, English, German, Norse, mathematics and religion. I received an A in all of them, except for a B–plus in the first semester of Norse. As I continued through college, I completed a major in economics, minors in history and German, and courses in education which qualified me to teach secondary school in Minnesota. During my senior year I did my three weeks of required practice teaching in Kindred, North Dakota. Many of us prepared ourselves to be teachers on the less–than–commendable assumption that if we couldn't get any other job we could probably teach school. Job security was non–existent in the 1930's, so one needed to be prepared. I did not plan to be a teacher, but when I became one later I discovered I liked it very much.

I worked part–time all four years of college, and did not find that it interfered with my studies. In fact, I thought the combination of work and study was stimulating and satisfying. I earned A's and B's in all my courses, graduated with honors and was valedictorian in a class of ninety. I was not the highest ranking student, but Concordia had the custom of permitting the senior class to elect a valedictorian and a salutatorian from among the five highest ranking men and the five highest ranking women in the class. It may say something about the sense of relationship between the sexes in those days that the valedictorian was invariably a male and the salutatorian a female. I remember that on the evening I was elected valedictorian, Dorothy and I drove to Rothsay to tell Mother. It was handy to have the use of the Holm car on such occasions.

I believe I am one who learns quickly, and, I am afraid, also forgets quickly. I always found it easy to retain the knowledge required to do well in class and on examinations, but I am convinced that some other students who worked harder than I did retained more of what they learned. In college I also did the unacademic thing of choosing classes because of the time of day they were scheduled. I liked early classes, so I usually picked first hour offerings which came at 7:45 a.m. I avoided classes that met later than 2:00 p.m., thus omitting all science courses, which had afternoon lab periods. That was because I knew I needed to have a job, so I wanted most of the afternoon clear for that. All in all, it worked well. I was not especially drawn to science, and other courses seemed to fall at convenient times.

There were some exceptions to this schedule. After I started working at Woodward's store in the fall of 1935, Mr. Hanson let me take time for debate practice, which usually occurred in the late afternoon. And I did get to go on debate trips. I did most of my studying in the evening and during open periods in the morning.

Students who had jobs were excused from physical education activity courses. My work at the store certainly did not include much physical activity, but not being in love with physical exertion of any kind, I was not one to argue with the policy.

In spite of the fact that I worked regularly, I was chosen for some student offices. I was elected a cheerleader as a freshman, class president my sophomore and junior years, and student body president my senior year. I was a member of the Mondamin literary society, one of four men's societies designed to maintain the tradition of debate/discussion and to cultivate personal friendships. There were no fraternities or sororities at Concordia. Dorothy belonged to Mondamin's sister society, Alpha Kappa Chi, which was a nice arrangement because we sometimes had meetings or parties together.

I was active in debate all four years, and in my senior year my partner and roommate, Allwin Monson, and I won the Red River Valley tournament, an annual affair sponsored by Concordia and participated in by thirty or forty other colleges. I took part in tournaments at the College of St. Thomas three times, and the national Pi Kappa Delta tournament in Topeka, Kansas, as a junior. I was in two or three plays while in college. I remember being the banished Duke in Shakespeare's *As You Like It*, but my memory fails me regarding other plays or other roles. As a senior, I was chosen to be included in *Who's Who in American Colleges*, and I remember being quite impressed upon receiving that recognition.

College activity of another kind involved a group of us as we journeyed one day to Fargo, the home of North Dakota Agricultural College. The Governor of the state, William Langer, had imposed some arbitrary controls on the college, and as a result the regional accrediting agency had withdrawn accreditation. Students and faculty were up in arms and mounted a protest parade in downtown Fargo. Several of us from Concordia joyfully joined. It was my only protest march.

Dr. J.N. Brown, president of Concordia, was of great help to me. Each semester at registration time, I would have a conference with him regarding my finances. He would listen to my story and let me sign another note. After my freshman year I was dependent on my own earnings, help from Mother and signing notes. That's the way I got through college. There was no formally organized financial aid program available; students were on their own to figure out how to make ends meet. President Brown was kind enough to let me sign a note each semester, and then I would work at paying it off before the semester ended. I did not keep up to date, and that is one reason I stayed out of school the year after college. I had a debt of about $300 which I needed to pay off. As I remember it, I paid off the debt and saved about $300 with which to start the seminary in the fall of 1939. These amounts do not seem large now, but they did then. My debt of $300 represented two months' salary during my first year after college.

I've never been certain as to how to account for my college finances. Mother sent me money regularly, usually $20 per month, out of a salary which never exceeded $90 per month while I was in college. I'm sure it meant a real sacrifice for her. I have often counseled students to start college even if they can't see their way financially. I have faith that with careful planning and hard work it can usually be done.

Certain Concordia teachers made a lasting impression on me. One was Carl B. Ylvisaker, chairman of the Religion Department and a man of deep and exemplary faith. He knew most students by name and was loved by almost everyone, even many with no strong Christian commitment. He was my teacher in a course in Bible when I was a freshman and a course in Christian Doctrine when I was a junior. He was later responsible for my being called to teach at Concordia, but he died of cancer in 1945 at the age of 49, a few months before I joined the faculty. I had looked forward to having him as a mentor as I began my teaching, but that was not to be.

W.F. Schmidt was our debate coach, and also taught religion, sociology and speech. He was a big man physically, with a booming, gravelly voice. He was a big man in other ways, too, shouldering a heavy teaching load and being a spokesman for the college on many occasions. He was from the old American Lutheran Church and had been president of St. Paul Luther College, a junior college in St. Paul, prior to its closing in 1932. He was my first contact with a person from a church body which would later merge with the one in which I had grown up. I liked Professor Schmidt. He became a close friend and remained so in my post–college years.

Other teachers whom I admired and from whom I gained much were Agnes Ellingsen, a brilliant and demanding historian; J.H. Hjelmstad, a quiet and methodical professor of economics and the advisor in my major field; G.L. Schoberg, a teacher of German; and Mae Anderson, a mathematician and a stickler for detail.

Among my best friends in college was Junior Melberg, a Moorhead boy. He had been named Julian after his father, but had been Junior all his life. Some years later he decided to become Jay. He was two years ahead of me in college. The Melberg family lived across the street from the college and regularly housed students in their home. I lived with them my sophomore and junior years, and again during the year after graduation. During my senior year I roomed with Allwin Monson at the home of Mr. and Mrs. Otis Wentzel, also near the college.

The Melbergs were kind and thoughtful people. Mr. Melberg was advertising director for the *Moorhead Daily News* when I came to live with them. By 1938, when I returned to live with them, he had started his own printing business. Mrs. Melberg was a gracious and kind woman who wore her faith on her sleeve and was eager to share it with others. She suffered from arthritis which caused her considerable pain and interfered with her activity. She was a "late in the morning, late at night" person, but she was a marvelous bread baker. One of my favorite memories has to do with sitting in the Melberg kitchen late in the evening eating sandwiches made of her fresh dark bread spread with peanut butter and jelly. We told her we were saving a slice of bread by putting both spreads on each slice. I can't remember what I paid the Melbergs for rooming there, but I'm sure they lost money on my patronage.

Harold Brown, the son of President Brown, was another good friend. During our junior year, Harold was editor of the *Cobber*, the college yearbook published once every three years! I was the business manager. Later Harold and I were roommates during my first year at Luther

Theological Seminary.

Harold Brown figured in one of the highlight experiences of my college career. As a freshman class, we had built a pile of wood and trash near the athletic field in preparation for a homecoming bonfire. So had the freshmen at Moorhead State nearby. One Friday morning in October, Harold and I, together with Paul Thorson, another freshman, skipped a class and went to Moorhead State, where we lit the bonfire which had been prepared there. We were caught in the act by Moorhead State students, whipped with their belts and had our heads painted green. Then we were led through some of the buildings where we were greeted with derision. The Dean of Men at Concordia was notified, and he came to rescue us after we had promised to rebuild the bonfire. We enlisted other Concordia students to assist us in gathering material and did a pretty good job of it. That evening, before Moorhead State students could enjoy it, some Concordia upperclassmen set it on fire — and they were not caught. It always has seemed interesting to me that the Concordia Dean of Men, Mr. Rasmussen, never chided us for burning the Moorhead State bonfire, only for being dumb enough to get caught.

Others who were good friends in college and with whom I have stayed in touch through the years are Richard Burges, Curtis Strand, Sidney Lee and Freeman Holmer. I distinctly remember how impressed I was with the fact that Dick Burges carried his own checkbook and could write a check for whatever he needed. He was the only student I knew who could do that. His father was the banker in Edgeley, North Dakota.

Of course the greatest thing that happened to me in college was meeting a young woman named Dorothy Holm. She was Dotty then; it was only after we graduated that we decided together that she would be Dorothy. We were classmates and met at the freshman mixer, a traditional event where every freshman met and shook hands with every other freshman. I noticed her for several reasons. She was physically attractive to me, a blond with a ready smile. She was bright and met people easily. My attraction was later strengthened by the fact that she drove a car to school from Dilworth where she lived. That was a rare thing at Concordia in 1934. Dilworth was about four miles from the campus, and was a division point for the Northern Pacific Railroad, for which her father was a locomotive engineer. By the way, Dorothy not only had a car, she had a fur coat. Ah, me, what attractions!

During our freshman year, Dorothy dated several fellows including a friend of her family, Gabriel Hauge of nearby Hawley, the son of a pastor who had confirmed Dorothy's mother and officiated at her parents' wedding. Gabe Hauge was a big man on campus — debater, top student, and student body president. He later went on to earn a Harvard Ph.D. and to become advisor and speech writer for President Eisenhower. Following that, he became chairman of a large New York bank. During that freshman year, I dated Mae Reiersgord from Ulen, Minnesota. After our freshman year, she chose not to return to Concordia, so that relationship was over. As sophomores, Dorothy and I started going together on a fairly regular basis. Debate was one common interest we had, but of course our relationship extended to things much more important than debate.

Those who knew Dorothy need no convincing from me regarding her personal appeal and attractiveness. She was liked and respected by fellow students. Her keen mind, her quick wit and ready tongue were all features I admired and enjoyed. I was eleven days older than she; her birthday was May 20. I used to tell people that I prevailed in family affairs for eleven days each year.

Our relationship became quite secure as the result of a debate trip during our sophomore year. We traveled by car to St. Paul together with Margaret Haugseth, Dorothy's debate partner, and Ralph Fjelstad, who was mine. Margaret and Ralph were going together, so there was nothing for Dorothy and me to do except to pair up. We did and I guess we enjoyed it. The day we returned from St. Paul, the movie, *Paris in the Spring*, was showing at the theater downtown. We went, and the song by the same name as the movie became our theme song for a while.

After we had been going together for some time, Dorothy began to invite me to her home, where I was treated to delicious meals prepared by her mother. They were just the kind a young man liked, hearty home cooking. Because Mr. Holm usually came home from his run on the railroad quite hungry, the custom prevailed in the Holm household that whenever Mr. Holm arrived it was time for a good meal. I shared in several of those at various times of the day and evening.

Dorothy's family included her brother, Elmer. He was known to everyone as Junior, and that name stayed with him until well into adulthood. He spent a year at Moorhead State and then received an appointment to West Point. After one year there, he left and went into the army. Following a period of service, he became an insurance agent. He married Gertrude Anderson of Henning, Minnesota. After a few years in the Fargo–Moorhead area, they moved to Evanston, Illinois, where Elmer joined Gertrude's brother in a glass merchandising company. He later bought out his brother–in–law and ran the business very successfully.

Dorothy's mother, Floyd Alice, had grown up in Hawley, Minnesota, part of a large family named Torgerson. I was early introduced to numerous uncles, aunts and cousins. Among them, Dorothy was closest to her mother's brother Al and his wife Inez. They lived in Detroit Lakes, where he was a district highway engineer. In retirement they lived in Arizona for a time, and in 1973 moved to Northfield to be close to Dorothy. We enjoyed several months of good fellowship with them, a time cut short by Dorothy's death in January, 1974.

Dorothy's father had grown up on a farm near Clitherall, Minnesota. He had attended business school in Fargo, and worked in an office for a short time before going to work for the railroad. While they lived in Dilworth, he served several terms in the Minnesota State Legislature as a staunch member of the Farmer–Labor Party. Dorothy's family did not see much of the Holm relatives. I met a few of them as the years went by, but the close connection was always with the Torgersons.

During the summer of 1939, Dorothy's mother died. Her father continued to live in the family home until his death early in 1943.

Before our college days were over, Dorothy and I were quite convinced that our relationship was serious. We were not officially engaged until the year after college when I could finally afford to buy a ring, but we had an understanding earlier than that. My job at Woodward's enabled me to buy an engagement ring at Neubarth's Jewelry in Moorhead. I paid $50 for it, a fairly handsome sum by 1938 standards, and it pleased Dorothy.

She accepted a teaching position at Paynesville, Minnesota, in the fall of 1938. Her assignment included English and social studies. At Christmas time she succeeded in getting a job in the school at Staples, teaching only English, which was more to her liking and in a larger school. She taught there until the spring of 1941, and that fall moved to Hastings, Minnesota, where she taught until I finished the seminary in the spring of 1943.

While in college I had several different jobs. The first few months of my freshman year I worked at the Fairmont Creamery Company feeding chickens from three to six in the afternoon. The creamery bought chickens from farmers and prepared them for market by placing them in stacked cages called batteries. Along each row of cages was a small trough. My job was to pass along each row pouring a mash food mixture into the trough. The chickens were not very polite. In their eagerness to get at the food, they spit and pushed and generally made a mess. It was a dirty and unpleasant job, so when the season ended in November I was not at all unhappy to be laid off.

But I needed to work, so for the balance of my freshman year I had an NYA job at the college. The National Youth Administration had been created as part of President Franklin Roosevelt's program to alleviate the effects of the depression. The college received government funds which were used to pay students twenty–five cents per hour for doing various kinds of jobs. I swept floors and cleaned blackboards for two or three hours a day.

In the spring of 1935, I was fortunate to get a job for the summer working for the Bergland Oil Company at a service station near the east edge of Moorhead, a mile and a half walk from the college. I remember one incident from that summer very well. A man drove into the station one evening and ordered his gas tank filled. When I had done that, he despaired because he discovered he had no money. He offered me a watch as security and said he would return. He never did, of course. It was my first experience with a scam, minor as it was. I later found out the watch was worth about one–fifth of the cost of the gasoline involved. I paid for the gas and I think I got rid of the watch. So it went for an innocent from Rothsay.

In the fall of 1935, I was hired by Joe Hanson, proprietor of Woodward's department store, to be a little of everything. Woodward's was a working man's store which sold moderately priced clothing for the family and a few other things like notions and yard goods. Our most popular line of women's dresses sold for $3.99 each and our main line of men's suits was priced at $16.75. We sold lots of shoes for $1.69 a pair and men's work shirts for sixty–nine cents.

Woodward's became my place of employment for the next three years of college and for one additional year. During the school year I worked from three to six o'clock Monday through Friday, and 7:30 a.m. to 10:00 p.m. on Saturday. In the summer I worked full time. I was paid $30 per month during the school year, and that provided a major boost to my treasury. Besides, I enjoyed the work.

Woodward's was only a block from the Leo Johnson Furniture Store where Lyman worked. I would see him occasionally, but we were involved with different friends and activities so we did not get together often. Lyman left Moorhead to work in a store in Billings, Montana, managed by a friend with whom he had worked in Moorhead. In 1939, he was married to a Fargo girl, Helen Huseth. In 1942, their only child, Robert Ervin, was born. Lyman and Helen returned to Fargo, where Lyman sold furniture in the Gamble Store. He was drafted and served in the Army, following which he returned to his work as a furniture salesman, this time in Minneapolis and St. Paul. Later he became a furniture buyer for Gamble's, with an office in their Minneapolis headquarters, and remained there until his retirement. During our adult life, Lyman and I have seen each other occasionally, but each has gone his own way. We have remained good friends, even as our lives have taken differing directions.

In Joe Hanson I found another fine employer, an experience I have had time and again throughout life. He was an unmarried man about thirty–five years old when I went to work for him. He owned one–third interest in his store, the Woodward Company owned a third, and a former employer of Mr. Hanson's owned the other third. There was a chain of Woodward stores, about thirty in all, scattered throughout Minnesota, Iowa, the Dakotas, Wyoming and Montana. The Woodward Company provided joint purchasing services and supplied advice and help with special problems. It was a system not unlike Penney's, and was well adapted to depression needs. Several years after I worked in the Moorhead store, the chain was dissolved and the stores were sold.

The Moorhead store included a street level sales floor with a balcony over the rear one–fourth of the room, and a full basement. The balcony provided office space and the basement was for storage of merchandise. In addition to Mr. Hanson, there were three other full–time employees. We were a congenial group. Often, when we weren't busy, Mr. Hanson would engage me in conversation. He became a valued counselor and friend. He also let me use his big, impressive Studebaker on occasion.

During the year following my college graduation, I managed the store while Mr. Hanson spent the winter in Arizona. He was not in robust health, and the time away from the business seemed to be good for him. I was honored by the fact that he entrusted the management of the store to me. I was paid $150 per month during the year 1938–39, a munificent sum for a new college graduate at that time. Many of my classmates took teaching jobs for $85 or $90 a month.

While working at the store the year after college, I made the decision to enroll at Luther Theological Seminary in St. Paul. Mr. Hanson had made me a generous offer of employment. If I would stay in business with him, he would help me get set up in a store of my own. I was encouraged and flattered by his show of support, but decided against a business career. I had thought seriously of going into business. That was the chief reason I majored in economics, I believe. I had also been encouraged by some faculty members to consider going into law or doing graduate work. It was not until my senior year that I gave serious thought to the seminary and the ministry. As I have reported earlier, Mr. Salveson had suggested to me that I think seriously about going into the ministry, and at college Dr. Brown and Professor Schmidt had talked to me about it. Dr. Ylvisaker did not. He belonged to the school of thought that held that one should not go into the ministry unless it became the sole and overwhelming drive in one's life to do so. I believe his own experience in choosing the ministry had followed that pattern.

I had no overwhelming urge to go into the ministry, nor had I experienced any deeply emotional spiritual event in my life which led me in that direction. My Christian life had been a matter of nurture and gradual development. I had not passed through a period either of strong doubt or of radical confrontation with the Lord. Many around me at the college could testify to a deeply emotional spiritual experience as the ground of their faith and the reason for going into the ministry. I was not one of that group. I was told by a fellow student that I had no business planning on the seminary because, as he put it, "You are not one of us." An organization at Concordia composed of pre–seminary students was called "Presteforrening," which is Norwegian for "pastor's organization." I was never a member.

Thus when I decided to leave Woodward's in the summer of 1939 and enter the seminary, I was to join some of my college friends who must have wondered why I was there, and, more to the point, how the seminary could accept a student with my background and experience.

I had tested the waters a bit prior to leaving Moorhead. During the year following college graduation, I had done some interim preaching. The pastor of the Augustana Synod congregations in Comstock and Wolverton south of Moorhead had asked me to fill in for him for a period of six weeks. He was to be on a leave of absence. I'm not certain how I came to be asked, but I suspect that the pastor, Marvin Raymond, had sought help at Concordia. I enjoyed the experience of preaching. It was helpful to me as I thought about the ministry. I've often wondered just how the people in the congregation felt about it.

One summer I filled in briefly for the Presbyterian minister in Dilworth. That was my first venture into ecumenical affairs. The church in Dilworth was the one where Dorothy's family had been active, there being no Lutheran church in that community.

I look back on my college experience and all that went with it with gratitude and satisfaction. Concordia College was a good place for me. We students were mostly from the farms and small towns of Minnesota and North Dakota. Our acquaintance with the wider world was meager, but the college helped broaden and deepen our vision. In later years, I have frequently reminded students who travel widely in the world as part of their college experience that I had a great off–campus experience while in college, too; I went to Topeka, Kansas. In the thirties, that was for me what going abroad is for a student of today. I had friends who did better than I, even in the '30's. The Concordia Band toured Norway in the summer of 1935. How well I remember the awe and the envy with which we non–musicians viewed that opportunity.

College was a serendipitous experience. I went not knowing exactly what to expect and left college not knowing exactly what I had received. But as the years have passed, I have come to recognize that at Concordia I not only gained knowledge but also an increased appreciation of other people and a better understanding of myself. It all seemed to happen by the way. I wonder if that isn't what the liberal arts are about.

In my valedictory at Commencement in June of 1938, I spoke of doubt and faith. I thanked Concordia for teaching us to doubt many things, and for helping us see that much of life is open–ended and not pre–determined for us. I expressed appreciation for the fact that we had been encouraged to ask questions and to wonder. But, I added, we were grateful that the college had shown us where "doubt ceases and true faith begins." I emphasized that the college had been true to its mission as an institution of the church, and had unequivocally urged us to faith in our God and what he had done for us in Jesus Christ.

I haven't changed my mind in that basic assessment. In the more than fifty years since my graduation, those sentiments have been confirmed rather than lost or altered in any fundamental way. Concordia prepared me for the next step in my life.

Chapter 7

NEW DIRECTIONS

When I arrived at the seminary in September, 1939, I was immediately reminded of some of my shortcomings. Perhaps my college friends who had doubted my qualifications for seminary admission had been correct. In college I had failed to take certain courses which were considered proper preparation for theological study. I took no Greek or Hebrew and only a few courses in philosophy. But the seminary had accepted me and I was determined to make a success of it. I never did take Hebrew, and I took Greek by way of a tutored short course taught by my college classmate Carlyle Holte. I didn't stay with it long enough to become proficient in the use of Greek in connection with the study of the New Testament.

The result was that when I finished the seminary I received the diploma called Candidate in Theology, which is not an academic degree but a certificate of completion. At that time the seminary awarded the Bachelor of Theology degree to those who fulfilled the Greek language and exegetical requirements as well as other courses taken by all students.

Except for the fact that I am not equipped as I should be in the area of biblical languages, I have not noticed that I have been under a handicap in my career. In view of this academic record, I was surprised when I was invited to teach at Concordia in 1945, and also when I was asked to fill in as a teacher of homiletics at the seminary in 1984.

When I entered the seminary, I realized that another of my shortcomings, non–theological, to be sure, was the fact that I had never learned to type. I had received an Underwood portable typewriter as a college graduation gift from members of my family, and even before that had done some typing with the "hunt and peck" system. I went through seminary and graduate school using my faithful typewriter and my sometimes faithful typing method.

Luther Theological Seminary was a merger in 1917 of three seminaries, each belonging to one of the three Norwegian–background church bodies which merged in that year to form the Norwegian Lutheran Church of America. It was located in St. Anthony Park, an attractive residential area of St. Paul. The school consisted of one building which housed students on two upper floors, classrooms, offices and boarding club on the first floor, and a boiler room, laundry and small gym in the basement. It is now known as Bockman Hall, named for a former president, and is one of several buildings housing the present Luther Seminary.

When I arrived, there were approximately 135 students enrolled in three classes called junior, middler and senior. A class of thirty–five interns was scattered on assignment serving congregations around the country. There were forty in our junior class.

The students came from all parts of the United States, but most of them were midwesterners. The majority were graduates of the colleges of the church. All full–time students were white males. Occasionally there would be a student of color from one of the mission fields of the church. There were no women enrolled inasmuch as the church did not approve women for ordination at that time.

Dr. T.F. Gullixson, a stern, orthodox and determined president, "ruled." In 1939, there were still some echoes of pre–1917 days. Dr. Mons Wee and Dr. G.M. Bruce made it quite clear that as former members of the Hauge Synod they represented a certain warmth of Christian piety not so much a characteristic of the other churches of the merger. It was interesting to me that each of these men was, in his own way, rather distant and forbidding and not at all what I would call warm in personal relationships.

Dr. Gullixson and Dr. Herman Preus had been members of the Norwegian Synod, and they represented it well. They stood for a no–nonsense kind of loyalty to the doctrinal position of the church, and gave ample evidence of wanting all students to share that loyalty. While Dr. Gullixson always kept his official distance from students, Dr. Preus was a warm and cordial man, a gracious host and conversationalist.

Out of the United Norwegian Lutheran Church, identified by many as the "broad" church influence in the post–1917 organization, had come Dr. Carl Weswig and Dr. Michael Stolee. Dr. Weswig taught church history and Dr. Stolee taught missions. Certainly they were orthodox Lutherans, but they seemed to make less of a point of doctrinal allegiance than did Gullixson and Preus. Dr. Weswig was a man of immense understanding of the church and its history, and had a blunt yet charming way of lecturing. Dr. Stolee was so wrapped up in his earlier missionary experience in Madagascar that one could hardly detect a distinct theological position in his lectures.

I have thought it interesting that even twenty–two years after 1917, an equal number of representatives of each of the merging churches remained on the faculty. That balance was altered the year I entered the seminary, for Dr. George Aus joined the faculty as a professor of dogmatics. He was a native of Brooklyn, had received his education at schools in the east, and had adopted a theological stance colored in its approach and structure by the method of the former White's Bible Seminary in New York. He taught theology on the basis of an inductive study of selected portions of Scripture rather than on the basis of the Confessions of the Church or the work of systematic theologians. He was essentially an evangelist — warm, outgoing, personable, dramatic. He was a short man and literally strode the boards as he lectured and tried to pry out of us observations we had made as we studied the Bible. His classes were different and popular with the students.

Dr. Aus was unconventional enough to permit Luthard Eid and me, in our senior dogmatics course, to do a paper together on the person and work of the Holy Spirit. We thought of that as somewhat revolutionary. The frequent comment on a paper which Dr. Aus had read was "Ta det med ro," which was Norwegian for "take it easy."

Dr. John Milton taught Old Testament on a part–time appointment. He was the pastor of First Lutheran Church in St. Paul, a congregation of the Augustana Synod. He had been a faculty member at the Augustana Synod Seminary in Rock Island but had left there in protest, as we heard it, against certain theological positions taken by members of its faculty. He later became a full–time member of the Luther Seminary faculty and transferred to the Evangelical Lutheran Church. He was a quiet, thorough teacher whose effectiveness became increasingly evident as one sat in his classes. His presence at Luther represented a first small step by the seminary toward merger with other Lutherans, or at least toward cooperation in theological education, even as Dr. Aus represented a conscious effort by Dr. Gullixson to expose the seminary and the church to a different and somewhat controversial style of studying church doctrine.

When I was a senior, Dr. Gullixson called me into his office and asked for my reaction to the classes I had had from Dr. Aus. I was surprised to say the least. I had not thought that Dr. Gullixson would ever ask a student for his opinion of a member of the faculty or his work. In this case, I had to wonder if Dr. Aus was under investigation. After all, his method was controversial and there were even those who questioned the orthodoxy of the outcomes of his teaching.

I remember trying to phrase my reply carefully. As I recall it, I said that I thought Dr. Aus had led students into an understanding of the Bible in ways which were new to most of us, but ways which were salutary to our appreciation of the faith. Further, I believed his way of approaching theology gave us a good start toward the fuller use of Scripture in our preaching. I also said that I believed his method left us without a solid framework or methodology for our personal theological position. I offered the judgment that in view of Dr. Aus's method it was well that we had also received a solid foundation in the formal structure of Christian doctrine through the apologetics course taught by Dr. Preus. I added that Dr. Weswig's church history lectures had provided a broader framework and setting for understanding the theology of the church.

Dr. Gullixson told me he had single–handedly decided to invite Dr. Aus to teach at the seminary, knowing that not everyone would favor it. He thanked me for my comments and I left wondering if I had said too much. I had said what I believed, and I hold the same position today regarding ways to teach dogmatic theology.

My interview with Dr. Gullixson brought to mind one of the things that disturbed our otherwise rather tranquil academic life at the seminary. There appeared to be a running debate between Dr. Aus and Dr. Preus, a debate that to many students seemed to be a matter of theological substance.

Dr. Preus represented the tradition in Lutheranism which is rooted in firm loyalty to the Scripture and the conviction that the Lutheran Confessions adequately, faithfully and clearly present biblical truth. Further, I believe he represented the position that the seminary was obliged to see to it that those who enter the ministry be advocates of the truth as thus presented, and that subscription to that truth should be used in evaluating those seeking calls to the ministry in the church. His position was clearly spelled out and forcefully presented.

On the other side, according to some, was Dr. Aus, who stressed the biblical basis for doctrine and the experiential approach to theology. One needed to know the grace of God in a personal and affective way in order to be a theologian. The official doctrinal statements of the church were important, but the emphasis was on the life of faith more than on formal subscription to the confessions.

As students took sides in this controversy — and many of them did — it became a favorite subject of discussion and debate. There were ardent supporters of each of the professors, and positions taken were frequently carried into parish life and work after graduation.

Many students failed to see the importance of the debate. I was one of those. To me, the differences between the two positions were more psychological and sociological than theological. I believed then, as I do now, that both Dr. Aus and Dr. Preus were faithful representatives of valid emphases within the Lutheran understanding of the faith. I do not believe it should be necessary to choose one over the other. I was not aware, as a seminary student, that either professor was trying to line up a following or eliminate from serious consideration a position other than his own. But I believe many students were ready to espouse one position and reject the other. Perhaps the discussion itself was the prime benefit of the experience. It certainly was true that our life needed intellectual stimulation. Not all of our classes encouraged or required it.

The curriculum at the seminary was prescribed. There were few electives. One could take a course in Norwegian homiletics (preaching) but it was not required. And, as I have mentioned, one could escape the study of Hebrew and Greek. But the rest was required. It was as though the faculty knew what constituted the ideal or necessary academic preparation for ministry, and that it was the same for all regardless of background or previous academic experience. There were courses in dogmatics, church history, Old Testament, New Testament, homiletics, apologetics, missions, Christian education, sociology, liturgics and speech. I received good grades, mostly A's and a few B's. In speech our instructor was Dr. L.M. Brings, a teacher of speech and a publisher of plays. I received a C the first year from him, a B the second, and an A the third. Either I truly made progress in that area or Dr. Brings was a very successful teacher, or both.

The first two years I lived at the seminary. Harold Brown, my college classmate, was my roommate the first year, and Karl Kildahl, a St. Olaf graduate, was my roommate the second year. We paid nothing for room rent. The general fee was $20 per year, and the cost of board and laundry averaged between three and four dollars per week. The boarding club was a cooperative student enterprise. The food was adequate and certainly not fancy. I had saved enough money to pay my first year's expenses. During the second year I earned a little money and Dorothy helped me financially, a practice common today but frowned on in 1940. During my intern year I earned enough to pay my expenses and saved a little. My salary that year was $75 per month. During my senior year, Dorothy and I were married and she paid the bills.

The seminary required each student to attach himself to a congregation during the first two years. There were four of us who worked and worshiped at Christ Lutheran Church in downtown St. Paul. The pastor was Joseph Simonson, an excellent preacher and a well–organized director of parish activities. I taught Sunday School, worked with the Luther League and performed other duties when called upon. There was a lively group of young people in Christ Church at that time, and the fellowship with them added variety and fun to seminary life.

My intern year was also a rewarding experience. I was assigned to First Lutheran Church in Sioux Falls, South Dakota, where Dr. H.J. Glenn was the pastor. He proved to be an excellent guide and teacher for me. That year I listened to some of the best–prepared and best–delivered sermons I have ever heard. My duties were varied. I did some preaching, taught confirmation class, advised a young people's group, and worked with a group of women who organized calling on shut–ins, new members and hospitalized persons.

One of my special duties was to conduct devotional services in various homes where older persons lived. There were few nursing homes in those days; instead, a couple would often buy a large home and care for four to six elderly, often bedridden, persons. In our ministry to those folks I had good help. Two Luther Leaguers, Kathryn Brende and Mavis Grevlos, became my regular assistants. On Sunday afternoons they would go with me to one or two homes where they would sing and I would give a brief talk. With my minimal musical talent, such assistance was much appreciated by me and by those we called on. By interesting coincidence, my path has crossed again with Kathryn's, because she is a cousin of Lois and lives in the Twin Cities with her husband John Kvinge.

Early in my intern year, Pastor Peter Troen, who served the congregations at Baltic and Renner, near Sioux Falls, stopped at the church to greet Dr. Glenn. I was introduced to him and, following a brief conversation, he suggested we have a cup of coffee. We went to a small restaurant near the church, and, as we entered, Pastor Troen greeted the proprietor in a way that told me they were acquainted. We seated ourselves in a booth and the proprietor came to wait on us. "Two regulars," Pastor Troen said. Soon we were each served a shot glass filled with an amber liquid looking for all the world like the beverage for which a shot glass is intended. "Here's to you! Welcome to Sioux Falls!" said Pastor Troen, lifting his glass. I wasn't sure what to do. After a slight pause, I decided, "When in Sioux Falls, do what Baltic does," and downed my drink. It was coffee. We both had a good laugh — and a real cup of coffee. I found out this was Pastor Troen's usual way of introducing himself. He was a delightful clown as well as a wonderful pastor.

I also became acquainted with Augustana College during the school year 1941–42. Dr. Clemens Granskou, whom I was to succeed at St. Olaf College many years later, was president of the college. I learned to know him and his wife, Ella, as well as many other members of the Augustana faculty and staff.

Little did I realize that forty–five years later I would return to Sioux Falls as president of Augustana.

An intern's tasks are varied. The chairman of the board of trustees at First Lutheran Church was Bert Ulberg, who, together with a brother, operated a machine shop and garage where one of their chief activities was the repair of wrecked cars. One day, Bert came to the church and asked me if I could go to Springfield, Missouri, to recover a stolen automobile which an insurance company had arranged to have them repair. With the approval of Dr. Glenn, I took a bus to Springfield, where, armed with the proper papers, I went to police headquarters to claim the car. I was taken to a garage and shown the vehicle, which I discovered had been riddled with bullets as the result of a police chase. The car operated all right, and I got back to Sioux Falls without incident. Along the way, I noticed some strange glances on the part of service station operators and others who saw the car when I parked. I am sure at least some of them wondered if I was some kind of gangster escaping the police.

I remember December 7, 1941, very well. I had spent a busy Sunday at church and returned in early evening to my rooming house. My landlady, Mrs. Eneboe, was listening to the radio. She asked me if I had heard the news; I had not. She told me about the attack on Pearl Harbor.

The war changed many things. Some of my classmates volunteered for the military chaplaincy. I'm not sure why, but I did not seriously consider doing that. All seminary students were classified IV–D, and were not subject to the draft.

In the Norwegian Lutheran Church of America, there was one seminary. Many of the church's leaders believed in one seminary for the training of the church's pastors as a matter of principle. It was a way to mold or form a homogeneous or cohesive clergy for the church. No doubt one reason for this was the memory of the merger of 1917, in which the combining of the seminaries of the three merging bodies was seen as an effective way to unify the church. The result had been that pastors knew each other, conventions of the church were meetings of friends, and the calling of pastors was influenced by personal acquaintanceships.

The spiritual formation of the individual pastor was not given much direct attention by the church or the seminary. We were expected to attend daily chapel, to be active in our assigned congregations and to live exemplary lives. But a discipline by which pastors are formed or prepared spiritually was not a practice at Luther Seminary, so the men who left the seminary to enter the ministry were a varied lot in many ways. A degree of heterogeneity prevailed, if not in doctrinal subscription, then certainly in the manner in which life was lived and the ministry conducted.

I thought the seminary experience was enjoyable and exhilarating; I did not find class work difficult. I met many new friends, with whom I shared moments of hilarity and fun. The boarding club was often the scene of humorous announcements and impromptu skits which displayed a broad range of natural talent among the students.

The gym in the seminary basement was the scene of many a rough and tumble basketball game. Some of the sem students were lettermen from college, and the rest of us filled in as we could. A park near the seminary was the scene of our touch football games. In one of them, I received a blow on my nose from another player's elbow. My nose was broken, and I carry a reminder of that event in my profile.

Dorothy and I decided to be married before I started my senior year at the seminary. Dr. Gullixson did not like to have seminarians get married. He reluctantly went along with it when all seemed to be on the up and up, and especially if it was for the senior year only. I remember going to his office one day to tell him of our plans to be married. He peered out from under his bushy black eyebrows and asked me about Dorothy. How long had I known her? Where was she from? He did not object to our plans, and even gave us his blessing at the end of our conversation.

We were married on September 1, 1942, in Trinity Lutheran Church, Moorhead, by Pastor S.G. Hauge of Hawley Lutheran Church. He had baptized and confirmed Dorothy. Dr. Carl Ylvisaker was the organist. Elaine Olson, Dorothy's cousin, sang and was a bridesmaid. The maid of honor was Dorothy's long–time friend and sister of her Aunt Inez, Margaret Buckland. Her other attendants were her cousin Barbara Shippey and my sister, Charlotte. My attendants were Lyman, who was best man, Harold Brown, Hans Thoreson, a seminary classmate, and Jay Melberg. We went to Bemidji on our wedding trip and stayed only a few days, as Dorothy was to start her teaching duties in Hastings a week after the wedding.

Our home in St. Paul was on Hillside Avenue a few blocks from the seminary. It was one large room with a small kitchen, about five feet square, adjoining it. We reached our bathroom by going through our landlady's kitchen. Our one room was supplied with a rollaway bed, a sofa, a couple of chairs, a table and a dresser. We got along fine.

Once during the fall, my friend Luthard Eid went hunting and brought us two ducks. We cleaned them and enjoyed eating them, and for some time thereafter found duck feathers floating around our little apartment.

Dorothy commuted to Hastings daily, leaving home about 6:45 in the morning and returning about 5:30 in the afternoon. I don't believe I fully appreciated her willingness to do that. She had lived in Hastings the previous year, and I had offered to live there and do the driving to St. Paul, but after some discussion we had decided to live near the seminary. We led a modestly busy social life that year. We entertained the faculty members of the seminary, one couple at a time. They seemed to enjoy it, and some of them told us it was the first time they had been in a student home.

Dorothy's father visited us in St. Paul shortly before he died early in 1943. Our extended family began to shrink as we began our life together.

During a few weeks of my senior year I reverted to type. I got a job clerking in the J.C. Penney store in Minneapolis from late fall through the Christmas season. A classmate, Glenn Husby, joined me and the two of us frequently returned home to enjoy supper at our house. His favorite meal was goulash, a dish Dorothy prepared very well and which seemed to fit nicely into our limited budget.

As the senior year reached midpoint, we began to live in anticipation of our future. Some of my classmates had decided to enter the military chaplaincy. The war had caused a large buildup of manpower in the armed forces, and the need for chaplains had grown in proportion. I decided to volunteer for a call in a regular parish and not enter the chaplaincy. Perhaps the reason was the combination of a basic fear of war and a sense that I would not be the chaplain type if I were to go into the service.

Seminary seniors faced two types of final testing, each of which provided me with special memories. One was a set of oral examinations by the seminary faculty. The exam in New Testament was conducted by Dr. G.M. Bruce, who met with three of us at a time for about an hour of questioning. I can't remember what I was asked, but Dr. Bruce posed to one of the others the question, "What is the name of the town where Jesus was born?" The student became rattled, squirmed in his seat, tried to think of the answer and could not. Dr. Bruce, obviously enjoying the situation, kept prodding, and finally started to hum "O Little Town of Bethlehem." The student jumped in his seat and shouted, "BETHLEHEM! BETHLEHEM!"

In the Old Testament oral, I was asked, "How many men accompanied Abraham when he met Melchizadek?" I did not know the answer, but of course since that time I have learned what it is. Anyone interested can find it in Genesis 14:14.

The other testing came in January, when each candidate for a call met with a committee of three district presidents of the church in colloquium. Through this system, the church sought to examine the theology and churchmanship of the candidate and to provide the district presidents with the opportunity to look over the prospects. After all, the district presidents were responsible to recommend candidates for specific calls, and wanted to have at least minimal knowledge of those involved.

I remember my colloquium very well. Dr. N. Astrup Larsen, president of the Iowa District, was the chief examiner. He asked me if I had read *Law and Gospel* by C.F.W. Walther, a founding father of the Missouri Synod and one of its respected theologians. I answered that I had; it had been assigned reading during the intern year. Dr. Larsen asked what I thought of it. I said I believed it was an over–statement of an important truth. Some eyebrows were raised. After all, the distinction between law and gospel is a cornerstone of Lutheran theology. I certainly didn't disagree with the thesis of the book, but I did think the author was pedantic and verbose.

The questioning continued. I was asked if I was acquainted with what Paul writes to Timothy in II Timothy 2:15 which, in the King James version reads, "Study to show thyself approved unto God, a workman that needeth not to be ashamed, rightly dividing the word of truth." It was especially the last phrase that was of interest. I explained that I understood Paul to be saying that Timothy must be faithful to what the Scripture says, but that he probably did not have in mind Luther's law–gospel dichotomy.

The questioning continued briefly on other matters which I have now forgotten. I wondered if I had said the wrong thing. I knew I had said what I believed.

Dr. R.M. Fjelstad, president of my home district in northern Minnesota, came out into the hall after I was dismissed. With a generous smile on his face, he shook my hand and congratulated me on what I had said. I was grateful for that. He added that he hoped I would go into the parish ministry for a few years, because that would be good experience. "Then," he said, "I think the church will have some special things for you to do." I didn't think much about those words of his until later, but it would seem that he was something of a prophet.

I went home and checked up on the Greek wording in II Timothy. I discovered that the words "rightly dividing" are the translation of a Greek phrase which could properly be rendered "cutting straight." One commentator said it called to mind a tailor cutting a piece of cloth and being certain that he follows the pattern exactly. The Revised Standard Version of the New Testament translates the phrase with the words "rightly handling the word of truth," and the New Revised Version has "rightly explaining the word of truth."

The colloquium experience was valuable for me. I learned something about being careful with the use of words and being diligent in the study and interpreting of the Scriptures.

In the distribution of candidates done by the district presidents in the spring of 1943, I must have been assigned to more than one district. At any rate, I received calls to churches in Absarokee, Montana; New England, North Dakota; and Nashwauk, Minnesota. In addition, and quite outside the normal process, I was approached by First Lutheran Church in Sioux Falls asking if I would consider a call to be assistant pastor there. There was also one other, rather strange, development. Before I had accepted a call, one of the middler students, Arthur Jothen, approached me to say that his father–in–law–to–be, Dr. Nils Kleven, who was president of the Southern Minnesota District, had asked him to request that I hold off on any decision regarding a call for about two weeks, because he was recommending me to a congregation in his district. I never found out what congregation that was and never received a call from that district. I've wondered what would have happened if I had turned down the other calls I had and waited for one from southern Minnesota.

In addition to talking over the calls with Dorothy and asking for the Lord's guidance, I sought counsel from my friend Dr. Weswig. In spite of a rather gruff manner, he had endeared himself to me on several visits to his office. I liked his straightforward, no–nonsense approach to things. "Well, don't go to Sioux Falls," was his first piece of advice. "You've had that experience. Get out on your own," he said. We talked of the other calls, but he gave me no specific direction. I guess he knew I must finally make my own decision.

I'm not certain just what led me to accept the call to Nashwauk. It might have been the fact that it was in my home district. I believe it was also, at least in part, due to the fact that I made a visit there and was impressed that it was an industrial area with iron mines going full blast to serve the war effort. Also, the congregation was receiving home mission aid, having been started eighteen years earlier. A small rural congregation, Trout Lake, about twenty miles from Nashwauk, was part of the parish. That seemed like a bit of a challenge, too. So I accepted the call.

My salary was to be $1,500 per year, with $300 of that coming from the home mission department of the church. We were to be provided with a five–room house, rent free, including utilities. We later learned that the mining companies provided free coal or fuel oil for the three churches and parsonages in town. The others were a Roman Catholic parish and a Community Church which was affiliated with the Methodist Church. I was to be paid nothing for automobile expense, but I would be supported in the pension program of the church.

I've thought many times how my salary has grown since 1943. The interesting thing is that during the two years we spent in Nashwauk we always had a few dollars available. Of course prices were much lower than they have been since, in fact many prices were controlled by the government because it was war time. But even so, we must have lived quite frugally. One's needs and wants obviously change during a lifetime. We must have lived the simple life in Nashwauk.

Chapter 8

A CALLING — A CAREER

I was ordained in Hamar Church in Rothsay on June 6, 1943. The ordinator was Dr. R.M. Fjelstad, the District President in what was then the Northern Minnesota District of the Norwegian Lutheran Church of America. My first service in Nashwauk was on June 20, and I was installed on July 11.

My ordination was a special event in Hamar Church. In its long history I was the first son of the congregation to enter the ministry. Mr. Salveson and I had planned the service. We had decided to invite the pastors of the Pelican Valley Circuit to participate. This led to an interesting situation. Across the street from Hamar Church is Our Savior's Church, a Norwegian Lutheran congregation which had remained independent of synodical affiliation. It maintained that status until 1986, when it joined The American Lutheran Church. It stressed informality in worship, evangelistic services, and the avoidance of clergy vestments as being too formal and ostentatious. The pastor in 1943 was B.J. Ostrem, a member of the clergy of the Norwegian Lutheran Church but a man quite in sympathy with the principles I have mentioned.

When I invited Pastor Ostrem to take part in my ordination, he hesitated. He explained that he would probably be out of place inasmuch as he did not use vestments and he assumed the other pastors would. I urged him to participate anyway, wearing whatever he normally did in his congregation. He accepted and came to the ordination service wearing striped morning trousers, a cutaway coat, a white shirt with wing collar and a white tie. He certainly had been right about not fitting in; he really stood out among the group of clergy, all the rest of whom wore black gowns and white surplices.

The vestments I wore, a black cassock and white surplice, were a gift from Arthur Johnson, owner of a shoe store in Sioux Falls, who had insisted that he wanted to give me my vestments in appreciation of my service as an intern in First Lutheran Church. During the time I was in Sioux Falls, he had given me a suit and three pairs of shoes.

My ordination service went well despite the varied clergy attire. Jay Melberg, my good friend and college roommate, sang a solo for which he had written the words and his mother the music. The text is as follows:

Lord, wilt thou bless thy servant
    Who kneels before thee now.
Give grace to e'er remember
    To keep his sacred vow.
Give knowledge, strength and wisdom
    To cope with worldly wrong,
Give victory over evil and
    Fill every heart with song.

Give love to little children
    Who look for guidance now;
Give tenderness and patient care
    To all with furrowed brow.
Give willingness to follow
    The path thyself hast trod,
And, overcoming Satan, bring
    Repentant souls to God.

Oh, bless him, God the Father,
    Oh, bless him, God the Son,
Oh, bless him, God the Spirit,
    United, three in one.
Make him to preach thy message,
    Salvation full and free
Brought to mankind by Jesus' blood
    Poured out on Calvary.

I've had that song, and the rest of an impressive service, to remind me of my ordination as I have moved through the years. The text assumes that my life would be spent in the parish ministry, but the spirit of it is appropriate wherever one's area of service may be.

When I left Sioux Falls in the summer of 1942, I was given a wall plaque which, like Jay's song, has given me encouragement through the years, and is a reminder of my calling. A sweet woman named Samilena Rasmussen operated a religious bookstore in Sioux Falls. She had the plaque lettered for me in proper calligraphy. It is a quote from II Chronicles 18:13, and is the word of the prophet Micaiah who was tempted to speak words which would be sure to please his king. His reply was, "As Jehovah liveth, what my God saith, that will I speak."

The ordination service took place on a Sunday afternoon. In appropriate Rothsay fashion, it was followed by a fellowship hour which included a bountiful lunch served by the Hamar church women. Mother was proud and happy. She didn't say much, as was her custom, but she let me know how pleased she was that I had entered the ministry.

We moved to Nashwauk piecemeal. Some of our things were in St. Paul, some in Rothsay and some in Dilworth. We did what many young couples do — we accepted contributions of furniture and household supplies from family and relatives. In Minneapolis we had purchased a dining room set and a sofa and chair for the living room. We engaged a truck to pick up those pieces, come to Rothsay for some more things, and stop in Dilworth on the way to Nashwauk. From Dilworth, we brought a bedroom set, a cedar chest, a desk and chair and several smaller items. Our house in Nashwauk was furnished in ministry eclectic style.

The house in Nashwauk was a five–room bungalow. We used the second bedroom as a study, and furnished it with my office furniture and a sofa that could double as an extra bed. Dorothy had given me as a graduation gift an office desk, chair and typewriter table. I used those pieces until we moved from the old house in Northfield in 1977. Then I sold the desk and Mark took the chair, refinished it and uses it to this day.

We got along quite well in the small house. When Peter was born, we added a crib to our bedroom, and when Mary was born, we moved to Moorhead.

The parsonage was located two blocks from the church and across the street from the school. Next door on one side was the home of the superintendent of the Cleveland Cliffs Mine (a Roman Catholic family named Whitney), and on the other side our neighbors were the Gust Weggum family. Mr. Weggum was superintendent of the Butler Brothers Mine, the largest operator in the Nashwauk area. He was also chairman of the Board of Trustees of the congregation. Mr. Weggum was always available for counsel and help regarding the affairs of the church. A grown daughter, Marie, who was confined to a wheelchair, was part of their household. We were frequently entertained by the Weggums for a meal. Once, after we had moved to Moorhead, we were back in Nashwauk and were their guests for dinner. Peter was then old enough to speak up and let us know what he thought of things.

Mrs. Weggum served her usual delicious meal with a pudding for dessert. As the dessert was served, Peter tasted it and announced, "This is poison!" At that moment we were glad the Weggums were understanding friends.

Nashwauk was a town of about 2,500 people. World War II had provided a spur to the single industry, the production of iron ore. There were three companies with plants and mines in the Nashwauk area, and most of the people were employed by one of the mining companies. The mines operated twenty–four hours a day, seven days a week. I did not see some members of the congregation for months because their jobs kept them busy on Sunday mornings. For a short time I tried having a Sunday evening service, but that did not prove successful.

The Nashwauk community was ethnically diverse. In the congregation we had people of various backgrounds. Besides the expected Norwegian, Swedish, German and Finnish folks, there were those whose ancestors were of Czech, Yugoslav and Polish stock. Among the names in our membership list were Tuomola, Ferraro, Gustafson, Carlson, Weggum, Hill, Beckman, Damyanovich, Raatama, Mattila, Erck, Potter, Vangen, Buescher, Niemi, Trythall. There were of course also some Johnsons, Olsons and Nelsons. It wasn't exactly a carbon copy of Hamar Lutheran Church.

I remember my first trip to Nashwauk, perhaps in March, 1943. I had received the call through the Home Mission Board, because that agency was still paying $300 a year of the salary. I traveled to Nashwauk on the bus, arriving after dark on a Saturday evening. My impressions were mostly negative. Piles of slag and red ore dust surrounded the town. Houses were crowded together on twenty–five foot lots. Everything looked dirty. I wondered if I really wanted to live in such a place. The following day I preached in church and met several people, and they seemed warm and welcoming. I returned to St. Paul, talked things over with Dorothy, and we decided together that I should accept the call. During our two years in Nashwauk, we were happy and found the work challenging and satisfying. Even the ore dust and the slag piles faded in prominence as we got to know the people and became busy with our work.

For many years the Nashwauk congregation had worshiped in the basement of what was to be the church. The congregation had been organized in 1925 by Pastor Harold Farseth of Hibbing. He had served it intermittently since the beginning, but there had been three full–time pastors before I came, J.C. Lysen, Constantine Nestande and Carl J. Hanson. The superstructure of the church had been completed during Pastor Hanson's time of service. It was a frame building with a stucco exterior. The sanctuary seated about two hundred people. It had a small balcony and a conventional chancel with a sacristy off to one side. There was no organ; a grand piano was used for worship. A small choir loft was built into one side of the nave near the chancel. The basement provided the usual multi–purpose room and a kitchen. I thought the facilities were quite adequate for our congregation of about three hundred members. Our average Sunday morning attendance was between seventy–five and a hundred. On festival days we filled the church.

I was called to serve not only Nashwauk Lutheran Church but Trout Lake Lutheran, as well. That congregation worshiped in a small frame church on the shore of a lake about twenty miles west of Nashwauk and not far from Grand Rapids. The congregation was composed of about seventy–five members, all of them farmers or at least people who lived in the woods. In the summer, the church was a delightful location for worship. In the winter it was inaccessible because of snow, and we worshiped in a school along the main road near the church. Ladies Aid always met in one of the homes, and always included the men and the children. There was no sex or age discrimination in Trout Lake in the 1940's.

Dorothy was active in the work of the churches. She was with me at most of the special meetings, regularly attended the services at Trout Lake as well as in Nashwauk, accompanied at the piano on many occasions and did quite a bit of parish calling with me. Peter was born on January 8, 1944, and Mary on April 16, 1945, so much of the time we were in Nashwauk Dorothy's activity was limited somewhat by her pregnancies.

Our usual Sunday schedule included Sunday School and worship sevices in Nashwauk, and, on alternate Sundays, an afternoon service in Trout Lake. I taught confirmation class on Wednesday afternoons or Saturday mornings in Nashwauk, and irregularly at Trout Lake. I also taught a class in the city hall in Keewatin, five miles east of Nashwauk, for a few months one year in order to accommodate some members who lived in that area.

Ladies Aids (yes, they were called that) were active in both congregations. A choir in Nashwauk was directed by Louis Erck, a mining engineer who faithfully kept a group of twelve to fifteen persons together to enhance our worship. Eleanor Anderson was the capable Sunday School superintendent and was also active in Ladies Aid and choir. There was a Luther League in Nashwauk, and that group had its ups and downs in terms of persons interested and active.

A feature of our experience in Nashwauk, which I have learned since is not typical of Lutheran congregations, was that the pastor had nothing to do with the money. The Trustees prepared a budget, conducted an every member visit and paid all the bills. I never saw a financial report except the annual one distributed to the members of the congregation. I preached on stewardship from time to time, but that seemed to be my sole responsibility with regard to the temporal affairs of the church. Church and parsonage repairs and maintenance were not my concern. It was wonderful.

Our membership was quite scattered, and hospital calls were made either in Hibbing, fifteen miles east, or in Grand Rapids, twenty miles west. Gasoline was rationed because of the war, but pastors were entitled to a "B" card, which meant they could purchase more gasoline than those who had an "A" card. Stamps or coupons were issued for gasoline, as well as for sugar and meat. Tires were also rationed, and a special permit from a County Ration Board was required for new tires. The speed limit was thirty–five miles per hour, a measure aimed at conserving gasoline and tires. I believe the speed limit was generally observed because of the emphasis on the need to support the war effort.

Soon after we arrived in Nashwauk, I decided we should communicate regularly with the members of the congregations. We secured a mimeograph, a Gestetner as I recall, from a company that provided one free of charge on the basis of ads sold in the community. The businesses that advertised had their names printed in the newsletter we sent to members. It was a tricky way to get a copying machine, but it worked, and I heard no complaints from the businesses that contributed. As a result, we put out "The Pastor's Aide" once a month. I typed it on the Underwood typewriter I had been given by members of the family when I graduated from college. I also did the Sunday bulletins by the trusty hunt–and–peck method. I never learned to type correctly.

We also set up a committee to stay in touch with the servicemen; there were no women from the congregation in the service. Between sixty and seventy persons, not all members of the church, were on the list of those with whom we corresponded. The chairman of the committee was Margaret Buescher, a tireless, able woman full of ideas and energy. To this day I have not met personally most of the men we corresponded with, but many of them wrote to us to say how much they appreciated being remembered. I felt I knew them quite well, even if I didn't meet them.

During the two years we were in Nashwauk, I officiated at 115 baptisms, thirteen weddings and eighteen funerals. One of the funerals was a memorial service for a serviceman, Toivo Tuomola, who was killed in action and buried overseas. One of the weddings at which I officiated was that of my sister, Charlotte. She was married to Francis Heiserman in June of 1944 in Hamar Church in Rothsay.

Not long after we arrived in Nashwauk, a woman and her daughter came to the parsonage to arrange the funeral of the woman's husband. They explained that they were not members, but would like to use the church for the service, and would like me to take part. They named a certain woman pastor whom they wanted to officiate at the service. She would preach in Finnish, the family's native language. I wasn't certain what to do, so I asked for time to consult with the church council. The council members I consulted professed ignorance of what to do, so I called Pastor Harold Farseth, neighbor and friend in Hibbing. When I mentioned the name of the Finnish woman preacher who had been suggested by the family, Farseth laughed his deep bass laugh and said, "She's a Unitarian." He went on to tell me she was a person who traveled through the communities on the Iron Range and preached to groups of Finnish people, especially those who had left the Lutheran Church. I contacted the family of the deceased man and informed them that I would not be able to join in their service, but that they were welcome to use our church. They declined.

The next week I read in the local paper that the funeral had been in the Community Church, conducted by the minister of that church. One day soon after that, I met him in the post office, and we engaged in conversation. I told him that I had been asked to have the funeral in our church, and tried to explain why I had refused to take part in such a service. I had concluded that I should not take part in joint services with a Unitarian minister. The minister replied that he looked upon any funeral as an opportunity to preach the gospel, and had no scruples about conducting the service with the Finnish minister. In fact, he said he didn't know any Finnish, so he had no idea of what she had said. As he turned to leave, he stopped and said to me, "Say, Rand, what's a Unitarian?"

Another funeral experience lingers in my memory. It was a warm summer day, and we were to have the funeral in Trout Lake Church for a pioneer of the community, Sven Rydberg. The little church was filled, and we opened the windows both to get some air circulation and to permit people to stand outside the church and participate in the service. The church had no basement, so it was built low to the ground, and open windows provided a good view for those standing outside. As I went into the pulpit following an opening prayer and hymn, there was a creaking noise; something was breaking. I looked up to see the casket start to move toward one side of the church. The floor had given way and had fallen about a foot. Several men rushed forward to steady the casket, the church was vacated, and an inspection was made all around. It was determined that nothing more would happen, so people re–entered and we continued the service. I looked out upon a congregation of pious Lutherans all carefully tilted to the left.

To conclude my memories of strange funeral experiences, I must tell about another time a woman came to arrange for a funeral for her husband. She didn't want the service in the church because, as she said, her husband was not a believer. I agreed to have the service, and it was conducted in the yard of the farm home where the family lived. In the course of planning that service, I learned that the man was what on the Range they called a Red Finn. Those were Finnish people who were sympathetic to the Communist cause, having been influenced by their coming from Finland during a period when the country was dominated by Russia following the Revolution there. The funeral went as planned; I don't remember what I said.

The Iron Range gave rise to many new experiences for me. The ethnic mix was something I had not encountered before. I had never lived in as thoroughly industrialized a community. The sense of community did not run deep. People tended to be attached to their jobs and their company. Each of the mining companies maintained "locations," which were groups of homes provided for workers. They were often cookie–cutter groupings of several homes of identical shape, size and construction. There were several such communities near Nashwauk. The mines paid most of the taxes, and as a result the schools were well financed. I never quite got used to the fact that anyone in town could walk into the school and help himself to pencils, paper and other supplies which were piled on tables in the halls of the school buildings. A Community Building was the center of much of the activity of the town. Service clubs and volunteer groups of all kinds met there. We usually had church suppers there, as did the other churches in town.

There is a story to be told about one of those suppers. The women of our church were going to serve chicken, which was not rationed and therefore in better supply than other meat. It was also popular as the entree for church meals. So the day before the dinner, chickens by the dozen were cooked in the kitchen of the church. The meat was taken from the bones and left to cool over night. The next morning, all the chicken was spoiled.

What to do? In a hurried conference, it was decided to serve ham. But that was rationed. A friendly butcher in town agreed to let the women buy all the ham they needed on the promise that they would deliver the ration stamps later. The supper went on as planned, with everyone being told at the door that the entree was ham and not chicken.

Incidentally, gathering the food stamps for the meat was not too difficult. We had several farm families in the congregation who seldom used their stamps, because they either produced their own animals for meat or hunted and fished to supply their needs. So even that part of our experience, which caused near panic at first, ended well.

I helped with suppers such as that one. I enjoyed transporting food from the church to the Community Building and being available for other errands. I got to know the women better that way. Besides, these were events of community value because everyone showed up for the suppers. It gave me a chance to become acquainted with people who were not members of our church.

During the first summer we were in Nashwauk, we decided to have an open house at the parsonage. The congregation had repaired and decorated the house before we moved in, and we thought the people would like to see it. It was August, and wild blueberries were ripe for the picking in the area around town. Dorothy decided we would serve blueberry tarts. Her friend Margaret Buckland, who had been her maid of honor at our wedding, was visiting us and she would help.

How many would come to the open house? We guessed 150, but decided to make 200 tarts to be on the safe side. So Dorothy borrowed muffin tins from neighbors, and baked 200 shells for tarts. In each she placed some of the cooked blueberries — we had picked a few gallons of them. In hindsight, the whole operation seems foolish. The tarts would be hard to eat, and they were quite a bit of work to prepare. And what if blueberries were spilled on the carpet? But we were young and enthusiastic and went right ahead.

We didn't have 200 guests. We didn't have 100 guests. We didn't have 50 guests. We had 37 guests! After it was all over, we headed for several of our Catholic neighbors with free blueberry tarts. So ended our first open house.

We had a second one. When we had decided to leave Nashwauk after I was called to teach at Concordia in 1945, we decided to have another open house, because many people had told us they were sorry they had missed the first one. Shortly after Christmas of 1944, when holiday cookies rather than blueberries were in vogue, we invited the members of the congregation to come on a Sunday afternoon. Thirty–seven people came. Most of them were the same ones who had been there for blueberry tarts.

That took care of our attempts at a certain kind of social life in Nashwauk. We decided an open house was not customary in that community.

On July 2, 1943, after a couple of weeks on the job, I officiated at my first wedding. Ernest Gustafson, who was in the Navy, had a few days off to marry Eunice Kent. I had not met either of them until a couple of days before the wedding, so counseling was minimal.

After the wedding, I came home and asked Dorothy, "What is the date today?" "It's July second," she said. I had put July first on the marriage certificate. The couple had left right after the wedding, he to board ship for the South Pacific.

Early in 1993, after having had no contact with the Gustafsons for fifty years, I received a letter from them. They were now retired and living in Nashwauk. They wondered if I would come to their Golden Wedding celebration in July and repeat the wedding vows with them. Lois and I were there, and we enjoyed the reunion as much as the Gustafsons did. In repeating the vows, I used the same Service Book as I had used fifty years earlier. I discovered that throughout those fifty years they had remembered the mistake I had made in dating the marriage certificate. I was the subject of lots of kidding from many guests when this was reported.

At another wedding I recall, I raised my hand at the conclusion of the ceremony to give the benediction. As I did, the groom, a serviceman in uniform, raised his hand in reply. It was a perfect Nazi salute! On another occasion, as I began the benediction the groom slowly sank to the floor in a faint. He spent his first married moments flat on his back before the altar.

While making arrangements one day for a baptism, I asked if the family would like to have the service in connection with a Sunday worship. "No," the mother said, "we would like to have it here in the pastorage."

Another experience I remember well has to do with the hand–fired, coal–burning parsonage furnace. It smoked, and some days the smoke was quite thick in the house. One evening while the church council was meeting at our home, the furnace acted up. The men headed for the basement, made an inspection and conferred informally. The next week we got a new furnace. The Lord works in mysterious ways his wonders to perform.

A boy in confirmation class quit coming to class one winter. I inquired of his mother why he had dropped out. She told me they had been advised by their pastor to withdraw their son from the class. They were affiliated with a group known as the Finnish Apostolic Church, served by a layman from Minneapolis who came to the Nashwauk community on occasion and gathered his followers. I asked the mother if she would let me speak to the pastor the next time he came to town. She said she would, and in a few weeks she did call and invited me to her home.

The pastor turned out to be a telegrapher who donated a certain amount of his time to his church work. When we met, I told him I was sorry he had advised the boy to leave my class, and asked him why. "You're ordained, aren't you?" he asked. I admitted I was. "You're a college graduate, aren't you?" he added, and I acknowledged I was. "You went to seminary, didn't you?" was his final question, and I of course had to admit that also. "You aren't a Christian," he said. I'm not certain how things turned out with the boy, but I did learn something about one lay preacher of the Finnish Apostolic Church.

As I have said, the Nashwauk community was an ethnic mix. Among those with whom we became acquainted, other than members of the congregation, was a Greek family who operated a restaurant in town. One day when I was in the restaurant, no doubt for a cup of coffee, the proprietor asked me if the family could use our church for the baptism of a new baby girl. We arranged for the ceremony, so there was a Greek Orthodox baptism in Nashwauk Lutheran Church.

Dorothy and I were invited to attend the service. The church was filled with family and friends from near and far. As the service began, the priest led the family down the aisle to the front of the church to the shouts and laughter of the congregation. A small tub had been placed on the piano near the chancel. It was the baptismal font. The baby was immersed three times, each time to more shouts of glee from the congregation. After the service, we all went to the church basement and enjoyed a bountiful Greek meal.

I have never, before or since, attended such a happy, noisy baptismal service.

There were many wonderful people in the congregations at Nashwauk and Trout Lake. The Weggums were stalwarts and always helpful. Louis Erck and his family were pillars in the church. He had a jaunty way of leading the choir, and even got some music out of them. By the way, I sang in the choir, something many friends and relatives may find it hard to believe. I think I sang bass. A Mrs. Rostvold, growing quite old in 1943, had been soloist in the choir for years, and continued to be while we were in Nashwauk. Eleanor Anderson was one of those dependable persons of boundless energy. She was Sunday School superintendent, sang in the choir, was active in Ladies Aid and directed anything that needed directing. Margaret Buescher, a refined and gracious lady, was the chairman of our Servicemen's Committee, and in that she was ably assisted by Mrs. Holger Larson, whose husband was one of the servicemen. Gust Carlson and his wife were custodians of the church. They were Swedes — practical, hardworking, trusting people. They added luster to their crowns, in my mind, when they volunteered to take care of fifteen–month–old Peter while Dorothy was at the hospital for Mary's birth. In the Trout Lake congregation, the standout family was that of Mr. and Mrs. John Rydberg. They were farmers, salt–of–the–earth people. They could be called on to lead a service, teach a class or provide music for worship.

I have mentioned that there were "locations" in the area, little settlements where families of mine employees lived. There was also a small village three miles away, Pengilly. Located on Swan Lake, Pengilly was the home of some who worked in the mines, but others also. There were farmers, workers in the woods and people employed in various businesses. One family in Pengilly, the Vangens, became especially well known to me. Their son, Orel, came home from the Marines in less than good health. His spirit was low, he was given to moodiness, was a sensitive person by nature and didn't know what to do with his life. I would visit with him, play golf with him and try to befriend him. It happened that he had completed two years of college before going into the service, and was trying to decide whether to continue with his education. In April of 1945, he went with me to Moorhead to attend the funeral of Dr. Carl Ylvisaker. The Concordia Choir sang, and I believe that visit convinced him that he should go to Concordia and study music. He did, and after graduation became a high school choir and band director.

I kept my typed copies of the sermons I preached in Nashwauk until we moved from Northfield to Minneapolis. I looked at them occasionally while they were in my files, but I made it a point not to repeat sermons. While in Nashwauk I regularly preached on one of the texts for the day, usually the gospel. My sermons were normally twenty minutes in length. I tried to preach the text, giving what I believed to be its context as well as explaining its meaning in contemporary terms. I didn't use many illustrations. The people were kind; they said they appreciated my messages. I remember working quite diligently on sermons, believing then, as I still do, that preaching is the pastor's chief business. I've always enjoyed preaching, but since leaving Nashwauk in 1945 I have preached only occasionally. In later years, most of my speaking in public has been other than preaching sermons.

In the Norwegian Lutheran Church of 1943–45, there were circuits composed of several congregations in a compact geographical area. There was an annual meeting of representatives of the churches, and usually an annual conference of the pastors. Nashwauk and Trout Lake were part of the Arrowhead Circuit, which included about thirty congregations in the northeastern corner of Minnesota and a few in northwestern Wisconsin. Most of our circuit meetings were held in Duluth or Superior because there was a concentration of congregations in that area. It was a 180–mile round trip for us to attend a meeting in Duluth, and with gasoline rationing in effect it became a major effort to gather a group for a circuit meeting. Often the pastors, for whom gasoline was more available than for others, would take a carload, and that would be the extent of the delegations to meetings.

During the time in Nashwauk we drove a 1937 Pontiac. It was a dependable car, one we had bought just before we left St. Paul. We drove it until we went to Chicago for the school year 1947–48. During the time we were at the seminary for my senior year, we had driven a Model A Ford which Dorothy had been given by her father when she began teaching.

A project sponsored by the congregation on the Range was Camp Hanson, a Bible Camp located on a lake north of Hibbing. The congregations in Hibbing, Virginia, Cook, Floodwood and Cromwell joined with Nashwauk in the support of that camp. Its accommodations were quite primitive, but that was the way with most Bible Camps at that time. The camp was a useful tool for serving the young people of the congregations.

The work with the young people in Nashwauk was enjoyable for me. There was a faithful group of about fifteen high school age people who met for Luther League once a month, and could be counted on for other church activities.

One sad event in this connection stays with me in memory. A girl from the congregation went to Minneapolis to work shortly after completing high school. One day, members of her family called to say she was in jail in Minneapolis. I went to see her and found she had been picked up for vagrancy. She was contrite and we had a good talk. She was later released and stayed in Minneapolis. I lost contact with her.

Another time I had a funeral for a young serviceman who had been killed in New York City. He had fallen into the subway tracks and been hit by a train. I never did learn the details of that accident.

Certainly the most important events to us personally while we lived in Nashwauk were the arrivals of Peter and Mary.

Dorothy and I had enjoyed one year of married life before we moved to Nashwauk. the apartment in St. Paul was small, not well arranged, and lacking in things of our own. So when we moved into the parsonage in Nashwauk, it seemed like our first real home. Now we had a house of our own with furniture of our own, interesting as the collection was, and a new life to share.

We were delighted when we learned shortly after our arrival in Nashwauk that Dorothy was pregnant. We found it necessary to go to Hibbing for medical care, even though there were two clinics in Nashwauk. We could not use the local doctors because they were entirely obligated to care for the needs of the employees of the mining companies. We were outsiders, medically speaking. That was our first contact with a system of socialized medicine. Medical care for the mining company employees was contracted and paid for by the companies.

In Hibbing, we found Dr. C.N. Harris at the Adams Clinic. He was not only a competent physician, in our view, but also a friendly, concerned human being. We were glad he was our doctor, not least because we knew that Dorothy's high blood pressure was likely to cause complications during the course of the pregnancy. As the time for her delivery approached, Dr. Harris recommended that Dorothy enter the hospital in Hibbing so he could watch her closely. Peter was born on January 8, 1944, six days after Dorothy entered the hospital. We thought for a while he might be an Epiphany event, but he missed that by two days.

January 8 was a Saturday, and I had confirmation class that morning. A few minutes after I arrived at home about noon, the telephone rang. A nurse at General Hospital in Hibbing said I should come right away if I wanted to be present at the birth of our baby. The doctor had induced labor and the time was short.

I remember the fifteen–mile drive to Hibbing very well. The thirty–five–miles–per hour speed limit was not helpful. I kept breathing a prayer that all would be well with both Dorothy and the baby. Peter arrived before I did. As I entered the delivery room area, a nurse came out with the baby in a blanket. "Would you like to see your son?" she asked. She opened the blanket and there he was. "Hi, Peter," I said. We had decided on the name Peter Anders for a boy before Dorothy went to the hospital. We liked the name Peter because it is a strong, traditional Bible name. We wanted a name of two or more syllables to go with our one–syllable family name. Anders was chosen because it is my second name and was the name of my grandfather Pedersen. It strikes me now as I write this that Peter also reflects the family name Pedersen, although that was not in our minds when we chose it.

At the worship service the next day, I included the announcement that an assistant to the pastor had arrived, and that his name was Peter. I told the congregation that he would soon be with us in Nashwauk. After the service, as I greeted people at the door, one member said to me in all seriousness, "I didn't know we were getting an assistant pastor. We must be growing." My attempts at humor do not always come off as I intend.

Dorothy recovered well, and in a few days she and Peter came home. We set up a crib in our bedroom, and watched with interest the new member of the family. It was not long before we learned that Peter had a thymus condition. That meant the possibility of a problem with the development of the thymus gland. Dr. Harris recommended that we consult a specialist at the University. We did that, and found out there was no serious problem. Peter developed into a normal, healthy child. My mother observed that a declevity in Peter's chest, which was a sign of the condition, reminded her that my father had had the same thing.

Peter was a favorite in the congregation. We would often leave him in his buggy or stroller in a little cloak room at the rear of the church during worship services. Dorothy was never very far away, but even closer was Gust Carlson, the friendly custodian. Gust was all Swede — tall, raw–boned, and with a big, gravelly voice. He was as soft–hearted as they come, and he enjoyed keeping an eye on Peter. Once while I was preaching, there was a thud in the room where Peter was supposed to be sleeping. Somehow he had awakened and fallen out of his buggy to the floor head first. Gust Carlson was there before Dorothy, and there were no serious after–effects. No doubt this was some kind of test of the state of a Rand cranium.

It was not long after Peter's birth that we learned Dorothy was pregnant again. When Peter was fifteen months old, Mary was born in Hibbing General Hospital, and again Dr. Harris was the attending physician. He seemed to me to be even more solicitous than before regarding Dorothy's condition. As the time for her delivery approached, it was evident that she would need to be hospitalizedfor several days. What to do with Peter? After all, I had a job and could hardly be a full–time baby sitter.

The Gust Carlsons came to the rescue. They offered to care for Peter, and he spent several days with them. He was very good about it. I went to see him a couple of times a day, because Carlsons lived only a block away. Their teenage son spent time entertaining Peter in appropriate fashion, and he was often content to lie on the floor in front of a radio that played mostly western music.

Once again, I missed being present at the birth. Because Dr. Harris induced labor, we knew approximately when Mary would arrive. I was at the hospital about 5:00 p.m. on April 16, and was told that nothing would happen for at least a couple of hours, so off I went to stroll the streets of Hibbing and eat a leisurely supper. When I returned to the hospital at 6:30, Mary was there. Things had gone well and Dorothy was fine. So even though I had missed the great event, we were overjoyed to have a little sister for Peter.

We named the baby Mary Alice. We liked the name Mary, and there were Marys in the family, including my older sister. Alice was even more common among us. It was Dorothy's second name. Both our mothers were Alice — Ida Alice and Floyd Alice. I also had a cousin named Alice, and we thought Mary Alice was a euphonius combination. Many years after Mary's birth, we discovered there had been another Mary Alice in the family line. Kinsey Rand, a brother of my great–grandfather, James B. Rand, had a daughter by that name.

Dorothy tried to use both names for the new baby, but as time went on, we more and more used only the first name. And as Mary grew to be able to decide for herself, she definitely chose to be Mary rather than Mary Alice.

Peter was baptized in the Nashwauk church on February 13, 1944. I officiated, of course, and my sister Charlotte and her husband Fran Heiserman were sponsors. Mary was baptized, also by me, on May 13, 1945, with Dorothy's cousin Elaine Olson Seal and her husband Orv (later called Joe) as sponsors.

Dorothy and I were grateful we had two children, and that one was a boy and the other a girl. They have been the delight and pride of my life, even as they were for their mother.

One advantage of living in Nashwauk was that it enabled us to establish our own home and family customs. The ministry required our presence there at times such as Thanksgiving and Christmas, so the center of our life came to be separated from the homes which were formerly our focus. We didn't regret that new development; we welcomed it.

During our time in Nashwauk, we enjoyed the special friendship of two neighbor pastors and their families. One was the Farseth family in Hibbing. Harold Farseth was the dean of the Range, having been pastor in Hibbing for more than twenty years. He had been widowed and was married for a second time. He and his wife Elfrieda regularly entertained us in their home and came to see us in Nashwauk. Pastor Farseth was also the one I would go to for counsel and advice whenever a parish problem suggested it.

Pastor Maynard Halvorson and his wife Henrietta lived in Floodwood, about forty miles southwest of Nashwauk. They, too, were kind to us younger folks, including us in festive dinners and casual visits. We appreciated and enjoyed that.

Some of our relatives visited us in Nashwauk. Mother came and stayed several days, as did Al and Inez Torgerson. Margaret Buckland was there to help with the blueberry fiasco. The Heisermans and the Seals came for the baptisms. Because of wartime limitations, we didn't expect to see people from away often. Traveling even a few hundred miles was difficult.

A special family event I remember well was the wedding of my sister Charlotte to Fran Heiserman. They were to be married in Hamar Church in Rothsay on June 15, 1944, and I was asked to officiate together with Pastor Salveson. Dorothy and Peter went to Rothsay a few days ahead of the wedding date, and I was to drive there on the fifteenth. A few days before that, I found it necessary to conduct a funeral on the day of the wedding. The family was kind enough to schedule it for the morning, so I could drive to Rothsay in time for the wedding. All went well at first. The funeral was in the Nashwauk church and the burial in a Hibbing cemetery. When I left the cemetery, I had barely enough time to reach Rothsay on schedule, and I'm afraid I exceeded the speed limit in my efforts. On the way, I had a blowout and had to stop to change tires.

I arrived at the church in Rothsay twenty minutes late. Charlotte and some of her attendants were at the church door watching for my arrival. I hurried to the sacristy, donned my vestments, and the service began. It was only toward the end of the ceremony, as I placed my hands on the heads of the kneeling bridal pair, that I became aware of my dirty hands and my blackened fingernails. But the wedding was official and legal, despite dirty hands. Charlotte said she didn't notice.

One morning in November, 1944, I walked to the post office to get the mail, as was my daily custom, since there was no home delivery in Nashwauk. I took from the mailbox a rather bulky letter with a Concordia College return on it. My heart sank a bit, because I thought it was a list of names of persons I would be expected to contact in connection with a fund appeal the college was carrying on at the time. I had already spent several days on a similar assignment, and I felt I had done my duty.

I opened the letter immediately. There, instead of a request to make some more fund–raising visits, was a letter of call signed by President Brown inviting me to join the Concordia faculty in the Department of Religion. It was a complete surprise. I did not know the college was looking for anyone for such a position, and I had no hint that I was under consideration. How different, I have thought since, was that way of doing things from what is done today. I did not apply for the job, I submitted no dossier, I was never interviewed, I was simply called to teach by persons who knew me from previous contacts and who had evidently followed my career development.

Of course I was impressed. I was puzzled, yes, but deeply moved. I had been in the ministry less than two years. I had not considered leaving the parish ministry; on the contrary, I assumed it was to be my life's work. I hurried home to share the news with Dorothy. She was as surprised and excited as I was. What should we do? Should we tell anyone? Should we go to Moorhead to talk to the folks at the college? Was it right even to think of leaving Nashwauk so soon?

As the days passed, we thought and prayed about the matter. I acknowledged the receipt of the call, and several persons at the college urged me to accept. I realized this might be a turning point in my career. I recalled the words of District President Fjelstad following my colloquium in 1943, when he had said he thought that after I had been in the ministry a few years the church would find other things for me to do.

There was another concern. I had done no graduate work beyond the seminary, and my seminary program had not been exactly loaded with solid academic subjects. Would I be able to succeed as a teacher? What would my colleagues on the faculty think? After all, many of them had been my teachers.

On the positive side was encouragement from Dr. Carl B. Ylvisaker, chairman of the Religion Department. He knew me well from my days as a student in his classes, and I had to believe that if he thought I could teach, I should take that judgment seriously.

Dr. Ylvisaker was ill in the winter and spring of 1944–45. He had cancer and was confined to his bed much of that time. I went to Moorhead in March and had a good heart–to–heart visit with him. He knew he was dying and spoke with regret about not being able to teach with me. At that time I believe I had either accepted the call or was about to. The conversation left a lasting impression on me. Here was a man loved by almost everyone at the college, only forty–nine years old and the father of three small children. (One of the children, John, has since distinguished himself as a composer of contemporary hymns, and a sort of gospel troubador.) It seemed tragic to realize that Dr. Ylvisaker did not have long to live.

I was particularly moved by Dr. Ylvisaker's words about his colleague on the faculty, Dr. J. Walter Johnshoy. It had been common knowledge among students and faculty members that the two of them did not see eye to eye in theological matters. Dr. Johnshoy represented the formal, objective, reasoned approach to the Christian faith. He was apparently wary of any show of emotion or outward display of religious feeling. He was critical of Dr. Ylvisaker's rather personal and pietistic emphasis in matters of faith. As I visited with Dr. Ylvisaker, he said his one great regret about his years at Concordia was the inability to get along with Dr. Johnshoy. There were tears in his eyes, and mine, as he recounted this experience.

That was the last conversation I had with Dr. Ylvisaker. He died in April on the day our Mary Alice was born. I attended his funeral at Trinity Church in Moorhead and grieved at the loss of a great teacher, pastor and friend.

I do not have a record of the exact date on which I accepted the call to teach at Concordia or exactly how I arrived at the decision. I believe the conviction gradually grew in me that it was the right thing to do. Dorothy was quite willing to move to Moorhead. Both of us had positive memories of our student days, so life at the college seemed inviting. The decision to go into teaching seemed to come quite naturally without struggle or anxiety.

I have often said that I have never wrestled with a call as I know many pastors have. My career decisions have seemed to me to have been made with anticipation and gratitude for the opportunities presented, but have not involved deep personal soul–searching or struggle. As I did not seek or apply for the position at Concordia, so I did not seek or apply for the positions I went into later in my career. I firmly believe that God has guided my life in this respect as in others. Why he has spared me struggle in the process I do not know. But I do know that I have never regretted a career change I made. That certainly was true of the Concordia position. I enjoyed teaching and, as with the pastoral ministry, I went into it believing I would spend the rest of my career as a college teacher.

When I decided to accept the Concordia call, I met with the Nashwauk church council to explain my decision. The members listened and gave me no argument. But one man said, "Do you mind telling us if you will get a higher salary?" I believe at that time I was getting either $1,800 or $2,000 a year as pastor. The salary at Concordia was to be $2,400, but we would need to provide our own housing. So I told the council that the salary was about the same. The council members said they couldn't understand why I wanted to leave if the Concordia salary was not larger than I was getting in Nashwauk. They even suggested that they might increase my salary if I would stay. I assured them that salary was not the determining factor.

Shortly after I had decided to accept the call to Concordia, I was in the Twin Cities and decided to stop at the seminary. While there, I knocked on the office door of Dr. Weswig, one of my favorite professors. "Come in," his gruff voice shouted. I went in, sat down and proceeded to tell him that I had accepted a call to teach at Concordia. "Too bad, Rand," he replied, "I had hoped you would stay in the ministry and make a success of it." With that blessing I changed my career.

So we prepared to leave Nashwauk. My last service was on June 3, 1945. On that occasion we celebrated the twentieth anniversary of the Nashwauk congregation, and we burned the mortgage on the church building.

As of that day the two congregations also went off home mission support. That was a significant step, because it meant they were no longer financially dependent on the church at large. All in all, it was a good way for us to leave. It moved the emphasis away from the Rands to the congregations and their accomplishments. I felt good about the way things had come together in two short years.

We had arrived in Nashwauk wondering if we could ever enjoy living with the red dust and slag heaps. When we left, we both wept. The first call often does that to a pastor, my friends have told me. For Dorothy and me, it had been a learning and growing experience. We could not have started out in the company of more congenial and cooperative people, and we could not have begun our ministry in a more varied and challenging environment.

I must confess that I have not kept up any regular contact with

Nashwauk–Trout Lake people. Dr. Gullixson used to say to us at the seminary, "When you move, move." He meant that a pastor shouldn't continue to cultivate relations with people in a parish once he leaves. It can prove difficult for the successor pastor and actually create problems in the congregation. I have returned to Nashwauk once for an anniversary at the invitation of the congregation, in addition to the occasion of the Gustafson's Golden Wedding. Otherwise I've heeded Dr. Gullixson's advice.

BROADER EXPERIENCES

1945–1963

Chapter 9

TEACHING — AND LEARNING, TOO

Prior to our moving in June of 1945, I went to Moorhead to find housing. The college offered to rent us a house a half block south of the administration building on Seventh Street. The rent would be $50 per month. We accepted the offer because the location was convenient and the house seemed to be adequate for our needs. Also, in 1945 housing was in short supply, because during the war few houses had been built. We felt fortunate to find the house we did.

It was a frame–stucco, story–and–a–half home with living room, dining room, kitchen and sun porch on first floor, and two bedrooms and bath on second floor. The basement was useful for storage, and of course included a furnace, water heater and coal bin. We hand–fired the furnace and controlled the hot water supply by lighting a gas burner under a tank in the basement. The house in Nashwauk had included a stove and refrigerator, but in Moorhead we needed to supply those ourselves. We bought a stove, and Al and Inez Torgerson gave us a refrigerator. I believe they bought a new one for themselves, not because they needed it but simply to help us out. They often did things like that for us; Dorothy was a favorite niece.

The sun porch on first floor became my study. In the winter it was too cold to use, so I would then transport books back and forth between the porch and the dining room table to do my studying. The bedroom where we put up two cribs for the children was quite small, and, because Peter and Mary shared a room, Peter would frequently entertain Mary with various antics, not least when Mary should be sleeping. It is interesting that even as our house in Nashwauk was proving to be too small when Mary was born, so when the bedroom in Moorhead became next to impossible for a seven–year–old and a six–year–old to share, we decided to move to Forest City. I wonder if the Lord keeps track of such mundane matters as he directs calls to people in the ministry of the church.

At the time we moved to Moorhead, we were driving a 1937 Pontiac which we had purchased during my senior year at the seminary. It served us well until 1947, when we sold it as one way to raise some money to underwrite the costs of going to Chicago for graduate study. One feature of the Pontiac which I liked, and which I have never found in another car, was a heat distributor under the front seat. It directed heat both forward and back, and provided the most even heat I've ever experienced in a car. I wonder why that didn't become a permanent feature of car design.

We had no sooner gotten settled in Moorhead than I was off to Bible camp and admissions work for the college. I had spent an earlier summer doing admissions work for Concordia following my first year at the seminary, but the Bible camp routine was new to me. I really should have spent the summer of 1945 getting ready to teach my classes in the fall, but the college wanted me to do the representational work, so I did it. Besides, I got paid a few dollars for it, and Dorothy and I agreed that that was welcome. Being away from the family was the real adjustment and not a small sacrifice.

Bible camps were in full bloom in the 40's. They had been started at various places in the Lutheran Church in the 30's, and had become quite popular. Congregations and groups of congregations rented or purchased facilities which became centers for programs especially for junior and senior high school youth. Teaching at them was a test of one's acting ability as well as command of the subject. In my case, I ordinarily stood before seventy–five to two hundred youngsters seated on hard benches for forty to fifty minutes at a time in a room that was often too warm to be comfortable. So I would try to be serious, funny, entertaining and informative, all at the same time or in some kind of sequence. I enjoyed it. During my years at Concordia, I taught at thirteen different camps in Minnesota, North Dakota, Iowa, Wisconsin, Montana and Idaho, several times at many of them. One summer I taught for nine successive weeks; most years it was five or six.

Sometimes it was possible to take the family with me to Bible camp. One summer we went to Park River Bible Camp in northeastern North Dakota. The facilities were better than at many camps; however, we were housed in a building that was a converted grain storage bin. The four of us managed quite well, going outside for sanitary facilities. Mary was a toddler and we took with us a stroller for her. The terrain was rough, and during the week the stroller's wheels were twisted beyond repair. Other than that, it was an enjoyable week with many fine people.

The extra work continued during the school year, and was considered normal for those of us who were clergy. In the five years I spent at Concordia, I preached or spoke in 28 communities in Minnesota, 35 in North Dakota and five in South Dakota. During the school year 1945–46, my first year of teaching, I had 69 speaking engagements off campus. In the school year 1946–47 I had 126. These were in addition to a full teaching load of eight or ten class hours a week, some counseling of students, speaking in chapel and serving on various college committees. Needless to say, I didn't get any scholarly work done.

My records also show that while I was at Concordia I officiated at 40 baptisms, 27 weddings and eight funerals. These pastoral acts were normally connected with my supplying vacant parishes or filling in for pastors who were ill. During two months of 1947, I assisted at Trinity Lutheran Church in Moorhead, the congregation to which we belonged, preaching on Sundays, teaching confirmation classes and doing some other pastoral work. This was after Pastor Roy Harrisville left for Bethlehem Lutheran Church in Minneapolis and before Pastor Erling Jacobson arrived.

The Trinity assignment taught me a lesson in humility. Glenn Midthun was the seminary intern that year, and he and I made big plans for Easter. We would have three services with special music and all the trimmings. I was to preach. Easter Sunday dawned with a fresh six–inch snowfall, even though it was April 6. We had a dozen people at our first service, about 35 at the second, and 55 at the chief service at 11:00 a.m., this in a congregation of more than 2,000 members, and a church seating 700 people. Glenn and I have joked about it since, but it was a real blow to our pride at the time.

In March, 1946, I was invited to preach in Glasgow, Montana, for a homecoming worship honoring returned veterans. My friend Tom Boe was the pastor there. I accepted the invitation several weeks in advance and made arrangements to travel to Glasgow on the fast mail train that made daily runs on the Great Northern line. On the Saturday I was to leave, I found out the train was to be two hours late; it normally left Fargo in mid–afternoon. As the rescheduled time approached, I called the station and was told the train had just left. I called Northwest Airlines and found I could fly to Miles City, about a hundred miles south of Glasgow, arriving there about 6:00 a.m. I called Pastor Boe to explain my predicament, and he said he would drive to Miles City to meet me. So off I went about one o'clock in the morning.

We had not been in the air long when an attendant came to me to ask if I was the one who wanted to get off at Miles City. She said the plane couldn't land there because of fog. We went on to Billings, 150 miles farther west, and landed on a bright, sunny Sunday morning. I called Glasgow and spoke to Mrs. Boe, who informed me that Tom was in Miles City. I told her I would try to get to Glasgow, and proceeded to inquire about a charter. A charter service was available, and the man in charge told me I could have a choice of a Piper Cub or an open cockpit plane which would get us there quicker. He said he had a sheepskin coat I could use, so I said we should go in the open cockpit, even though it was mid–March. He wanted $120 for the trip, an amount I didn't have with me. That was also pre–credit–card time. I sent a telegram to Dorothy asking her to wire money to Glasgow, knowing that she might wonder why I was in Billings and in need of $120.

The pilot went to check the weather and came back to report that we couldn't go because Glasgow was blanketed with fog. So I never got to keep my appointment. Instead, I got on a bus headed east, and in late afternoon it stopped in Glendive, the termination of that run. I got a hotel room and went home the next day. But that Sunday evening I noticed that at a theater next door to the hotel, the movie was Ray Milland in *The Lost Weekend*. I went, and found that Milland had lost his weekend in a different way than I lost mine.

The sequel to this story is that I got my money back from Glasgow, and the folks there paid my out–of–pocket expenses. They also reported that they had had a great homecoming service with last minute fill–in preachers!

On one of my off–campus trips I went to Leonard, North Dakota, to speak at a high school commencement with two boys and a girl in the class. We had the usual program including my talk. Then the time came for awards and diplomas. The superintendent proceeded to give an award to the highest ranking girl in the class. That was easy. Then he made an award to the highest ranking boy. That left the second boy without an award. Now, I thought, what will happen next? The superintendent was equal to the occasion. The second boy received an award for the largest number of successive free throws of anyone in school during the past school year.

High school commencements were fun. Everyone was in a good mood and one could sense the vitality of a community. The school was the center of community life, at least for most of the places where I spoke. It was a privilege to take part in those events. I felt almost like an intruder into a closely knit, family–like situation, but I was always welcomed warmly.

One spring, J.L. Rendahl, Director of Public Relations at Concordia, sent a memo to faculty members asking for the date and place of any commencement talks we were to give. He also suggested we tell him the title of the talk. I responded, and a short time later received a call from Mr. Rendahl telling me that the superintendent of one of the schools where I planned to speak had called, and, because I wasn't in, Rendahl had spoken to him. The superintendent had thought my title wouldn't fit with the motto the class had chosen, so he and Rendahl had agreed on another title for me. "You will of course give the same talk," Rendahl said. I did.

Another off–campus opportunity I appreciated was leading the Bible Study at the 1951 national Luther League convention in Seattle. I prepared a study on Jude, not the most widely studied book in the New Testament. My friend Cy Running, chairman of the Art Department, drew sketches to illustrate the study outline. A brief portion of Scripture such as Jude, which has numerous allusions to events recorded elsewhere in the Bible as well as a couple that are not, proved to be a handy, workable and interesting basis for a series of four lectures to a large group of people. Visuals such as movies, slides and overhead projection were still in their infancy, so I depended simply on my voice and the outline which each Luther Leaguer had in hand to communicate my ideas. Many people have told me years afterward that the studies were meaningful to them.

My chief responsibility at the college was the teaching of classes, however, and not all of the other work, interesting as it was. Because of Dr. Ylvisaker's death and the fact that by the fall of 1945 no–one had been appointed to replace him, I entered upon my duties as the only full–time teacher in the Department of Religion. Dr. Johnshoy taught courses in religion as well as in philosophy. Dr. W.F. Schmidt taught religion and also sociology and speech. My rank was Assistant Professor, and I was named chairman of the department for the year.

In the years that followed, I was joined by others — Otto Bratlie, Sigvald Fauske, Eugene Fevold, Arne Unhjem, Lowell Satre, Arne Sovik and Reidar Thomte. We were a congenial group, in fact we almost had to be, because for at least three years four of us shared one large room as office space, with a desk in the middle for a part–time student secretary. A small room across the hall was our counseling center for one–on–one conversations with students.

All freshmen were required to take a two–hour course in Bible each semester, the Old Testament in the fall and the New Testament in the spring. Sophomores took a two–hour course in church history each semester. Juniors took two courses in Christian doctrine. Seniors could choose one course among several electives in areas such as ethics, work of the church, and missions. My first year of teaching I taught two sections of freshmen, two of sophomores and one of juniors. It was of course impossible to do justice to such a schedule, especially for an inexperienced teacher. But somehow I lived through it, and the students did, also.

In the school year 1946–47, the college experienced a sharp increase in enrollment from about 900 students to more than 1,200, due chiefly to the large number of veterans returning to college under the G.I. Bill. They brought a breath of fresh air to the college. Most of them were older than the other students, and many of them had experienced the gruesome aspects of war. This background, together with the fact that they had been in various parts of the world, added flavor and color to classroom discussions, to say nothing about campus organizational life and political activity.

I tried not to lecture all the time. My aim was to involve the students in discussion of what I thought were important concepts or events that we studied. It met with a mixed reaction. Many of my classes were large. The smallest I had was 25 students, and I often had 125–130 at a time. In many of the larger classes only a few of the students participated in discussion, so it was often discouraging. But my basic procedure persisted; I would usually lecture for twenty to thirty minutes and then try to provoke discussion with a few probing questions. The system sorted out the aggressive and talkative students from the others.

I discovered I liked being a teacher. Perhaps it was in my genes. Both my mother and my father had been teachers. Maybe it was my apparently natural desire to stand up before a crowd and speak. I've always enjoyed that — trying to get a reaction from people as I express my ideas. Also, I like to see the subtle nuances and the humor in life, and found teaching provided a vehicle for expressing myself in that regard. I've always taught with a chalkboard at my side, the only visual aid with which I am well acquainted. I usually filled several chalkboard sections each class period.

It was my custom to write two things on the board at the beginning of each semester. One was the name of the course; I wanted to be sure the students were where they expected to be. The other was my name. I wrote "Mr. Rand." We were not in the first–name period of faculty–student relations at that time! I used "Mr." rather than "Reverend" or "Pastor," both because "Mr." is always proper and because I wanted the students to see me as a teacher rather than as a pastor. I didn't try to hide the fact that I was a clergyman, but have always felt that the teaching of religion should be as academically solid as possible, and not an occasion for preaching or evangelism. I even reminded the students that the grade they received from me was not to be taken as my estimate of the state of their religious life, but rather a reflection of the degree to which they had performed the work expected of them in the class.

It was difficult for some students to accept that distinction. One day a student came to see me after she had received a grade of D in an exam. She couldn't help feeling that I had made a negative judgment on her spiritual life. That problem arose off and on as long as I taught.

Because of the number of students I had in class each term, it was impossible to give essay examinations. I would usually prepare an exam which consisted of several types of objective questions (true–false, multiple choice, blanks, etc.). At the end of the exam I would add one or two questions to be answered with brief paragraph replies. Dorothy was a great help in this. She would type the test and check the answers to the objective questions for which I had prepared a key. One semester I had 385 students in my classes. To give a quiz or two during the term, require a term paper and then give the final exam meant that I gave myself an almost impossible assignment, but somehow it got done. Maybe that's one reason the presidency of Waldorf College looked great in 1951.

Because of the size of most of my classes, and because I wanted to get to know the students by name, I would always seat them alphabetically and require them to remain in those places for two or three weeks. During that time I tried to put names and faces together, and thereafter I let them sit where they chose. It was then that I found out who the couples were. I've always felt I promoted some campus romances by my seating policy.

One day I was teaching the doctrine of the resurrection of the body in a class on the Christian faith. I compared that idea with the concept of immortality. To emphasize my point, I wrote the two words on the chalkboard. Pointing to the word "immortality" I said, "Everyone believes in this." There were gales of laughter from the class. I had written "immorality."

Another day I was teaching a class in a room in the Science Building, a World War II converted barracks. Peter, then three or four years old, and a playmate busied themselves outside the window with rather loud shouting amid their play. Of course that diverted the attention of the class. I told them to remain while I went outside to banish Peter and his friend from the area around the classroom. Our home was a half–block from the Science Building, so Peter's play area frequently included parts of the campus.

Our house had a porch with a wide ledge at the front. One day Dorothy discovered a row of beer cans neatly lined up on the ledge. Peter and friends had done the job. When quizzed about where they had found the cans, Peter replied, "Over by Brown Hall," a men's dormitory nearby. Students passed our house regularly as they went from one college building to another. That day they had evidently been amused by the display at our house, and even wondered at the various brands of beer we must have been using. There was of course a strict prohibition against beer on the campus.

I had an office at the college, as I have mentioned. It was on the third floor of what was then called the Old Library Building, which actually was the only library building. I shared it with others. In fact, in the years I taught at

Concordia I never had a private office. Classes met in various buildings around campus. In all of the locations the ventilation was poor, the heating undependable and the lighting inadequate, but we got along, as did several generations before us who had lived and worked in similar conditions. Facilities at the colleges of the church, indeed at all colleges, are much improved since that time.

I liked morning classes, so I often started the day at 7:45 a.m. The two periods before chapel were my favorite times to teach. The period right after noon was my least favorite. Frequently both the students and I were drowsy at that hour.

Speaking at chapel was a part of the assignment for those of us in the Department of Religion. I gladly did my share of that. The chapel was located on the second floor of the administration building, and was used for plays and lectures in addition to chapel services. Chapel was held daily in mid–morning, and usually consisted of a hymn, Scripture, prayer and a short talk. President Brown presided whenever he was on campus.

During part of the time I was at Concordia I acted as advisor to the Lutheran Student Association, meeting regularly with the officers and assisted them in planning their programs.

Counseling with students took some of my time. I soon learned that there were students who seemed to thrive on counseling sessions with one of their teachers, and that they would take up more time than I could possibly give. On the whole, however, I found the one–on–one sessions profitable. I got to know students well, and thus kept a finger on the pulse of student concerns. Some students were troubled about their academic work, but more often their problems or questions had to do with personal spiritual difficulties, relations with their parents, or what I called "just growing up."

We enjoyed having students in our home. We would regularly entertain small groups such as the officers of the Lutheran Student Association, or my advisees, or the student body officers. We hit upon a game, called "hug the candle holder," that proved to be a good socializer and conversation piece. Everyone would sit in a circle, we would place a candle holder in the middle of the group, and then ask one or more students to go out. Someone remaining in the circle would hold a candle, often partially disguised. We brought in the victims one by one and told them all they had to do was hug the candle holder. Some would get down on the floor and do their best to hug the candle holder there. Finally they would discover the real live holder, and hugs of various degrees of passion would ensue. Usually the groups that played the game would keep the secret so we could repeat it with successive gatherings. So you see, we taught some things other than religion to Concordia students.

It was quite evident to me that I must get on with graduate work if I were to remain a college teacher, so early in my time at Concordia I began to consider possibilities. In the summer of 1946, I attended Union Theological Seminary in New York for a term of three weeks. That was my first exposure to New York, and I profited from experiencing some of life in the Big Apple. At the seminary I enrolled in a course in theology from Paul Tillich, and courses in Bible and speech. It is Tillich I remember. He was then a widely recognized and highly respected professor. He had emigrated from Germany, spoke with a heavy German accent, and used a vocabulary which included theological language to which he had attached quite special meaning. Once I caught on it was a treat to listen to him. I also heard lectures by Reinhold Niebuhr and Paul Scherer, but I did not take courses from them.

I roomed in a seminary dormitory with a Congregational minister from New Hampshire. He was as ignorant of the middle west as I was of the east, and admitted that he had never been west of Philadelphia. He asked me, in all seriousness, if there were railroads in Minnesota, if Indians roamed wild, and if we had any cities. I must admit that I was intrigued by his ignorance and that I possibly added to it by giving some fictional replies to his questions, along with some truthful information. I hope he traveled to the middle west some time later and got straightened out.

My brief stay at Union Seminary was worthwhile, but I decided it was not the place I should pursue my graduate work. My special interest was church history, and I concluded that the faculty of the Divinity School at the University of Chicago was stronger in that field. So I decided to go there, and was not disappointed. I studied there during the school year 1947–48 and the summers of 1948, 1949 and 1950.

During the summer of 1947, I continued with my Bible camping. Dorothy, Peter and Mary lived in an apartment in South Hall, a men's dormitory. We moved out of our house for the summer in order to accommodate the Otto Bratlie family. Otto was to join the faculty for the fall of 1947, when we would be in Chicago. Living in the dorm was a bit like camping. We sold our piano and lent some furniture to friends for the year we were to be gone. The children thought it was quite a lark to live in a dorm, but I'm afraid it was less than enjoyable for Dorothy. One weekend when I returned from a week at camp, she reported to me that on a recent evening while the children were saying their prayers, Mary had made a special request of the Lord. "Bring Daddy home soon," she prayed, "so we can have good meals again." Dorothy realized that she had been doing quite a bit of lunching with the children. The next day Mary's prayer was answered; Dorothy bought a chicken and prepared, as Mary had asked, a "good meal."

The time we spent in Chicago was a good experience for the entire family. We were able to rent a university–owned apartment on Maryland Avenue, half a block from Lying–In Hospital and about three blocks from Swift Hall, where I had most of my classes and where the library of the Divinity School was located. Our apartment was on the second floor of an older building, but quite adequate for us. It was the largest home we had had as a family, with two living rooms, a dining room, a kitchen and two bedrooms. There was a large porch across the back. The apartment below us was occupied by a black family which included two children about the ages of Peter and Mary. The four children played together daily in the small back yard. Not once did Peter or Mary mention the color of their playmates' skin, even though this was their first exposure to black friends.

In other nearby apartments were more students of the Divinity School. They were from various cultural and religious backgrounds. It proved to be an interesting and profitable living experience for us.

My advisor was Dr. Sidney Mead, Professor of Church History, whose specialty was American history. I met with him regularly. At the beginning of the year he counseled me with regard to courses I should take and the way to plan my studies. I decided to work for the Ph.D. degree, and the first step in that program was to pass seven comprehensive exams, one each in theology, church history, New Testament, Old Testament, history of theology, Christian education and ethics. The entire battery was given each fall and each spring term. I decided to be brave and took all seven of them in my first term at the Divinity School. Somehow I passed! Dr. Mead had told me that if I had studied church history with Dr. C.M. Weswig they couldn't teach me anything at Chicago, so I shouldn't have any trouble passing that exam, and I didn't.

I was enrolled in a regular load of courses each term. Among my teachers, in addition to Dr. Mead, were James Hastings Nichols, Wilhelm Pauck, Bernard Loomer (the Dean of the School), Joseph Haroutunian, Daniel Day Williams, Ed Chave and Amos Wilder. I benefited from all of them. Dr. Pauck, who had come to the United States from Germany as an adult, was a brilliant lecturer and was at his peak professionally at the time I had him. He lectured without notes and told us not to take any. Few of us obeyed. "Listen to the lecture," he would say, "and then go and read." His course on Luther was one of the finest I have ever had. Dr. Nichols was a young man with a brilliant mind and a sharp tongue. I had him for a seminar on church historians, and recall doing a paper on Philip Schaff. Dr. Chave was considered an authority on Christian education. He was the poorest teacher I had at Chicago — a weak lecturer and a wishy–washy personality.

Jaroslav Pelikan was completing his doctorate while I was at Chicago. I learned to know him, respect him and appreciate his scholarly contributions. He has remained a good friend since that time. Others with whom I became acquainted and who have remained as valued friends are Jerry Brauer, Emmet Eklund, Walter Wietzke and Paul Sonnack.

The year in Chicago was a family time. Peter became four years old and Mary three during that year. We took them with us on various trips and sightseeing expeditions. We had sold our old Pontiac before leaving Moorhead in order to raise some needed cash for our year in Chicago, so we made abundant use of street cars, buses and trains to visit zoos, museums, churches and beaches. We took in ballgames at Comiskey Park and Wrigley Field, viewed the Christmas decorations in the Loop, and for several months traveled to Nazareth Church every Sunday morning. Pastor Carl Hanson, who had been my predecessor in Nashwauk, had been pastor there and had left for a church in Minnesota. I helped out by conducting Sunday worship. That not only helped us get acquainted with some fine people, but it provided us with many a good Sunday dinner in the homes of Nazareth members.

One Sunday I preached in a congregation on the north side of the city where a seminary friend, Ray Farness, was pastor. He had a set of football shoulder pads and a helmet which he gave to Peter. All the way home on the train Peter wore the gear, proud as a peacock and noticed by everyone on the train.

Another Sunday we journeyed to Evanston, where I had been invited by Pastor L.O. Anderson to preach in Trinity Church. After the service, we were invited to the Anderson home for dinner. We were seated at a beautifully arranged table, and the food was passed. As Pastor Anderson handed me a bowl of peas, each of us thought the other was holding it. It fell between us on the table, with peas rolling all about. Mrs. Anderson was kind and acted as if all was well while she removed the mess. A few minutes later, I took up a knife to cut the piece of ham on my plate. The knife broke in two. Such embarrassments tend to cause a person to remember an event otherwise quite ordinary. Peter has remembered it well, and often has said, "Dad, tell about how you spilled the peas."

One evening Peter and I were wrestling on the bed. Somehow or other I threw him against the metal bedstead, and opened a gash over one eye. There was a burst of blood. We bundled him in a blanket and ran to the hospital a block away. What I remember most is how tough I had to be with the doctor who served us. He placed Peter on a table and prepared to suture the cut. Peter was screaming, as one might expect. The doctor scolded him, and the more Peter screamed the louder the doctor scolded. Finally I said to him, "I'll hold the child, you quit your scolding and do your work." He did, and all went well. Peter still has a scar above his eye.

My graduate work continued through that school year and the three succeeding summers. During the last two summers the family stayed in Moorhead while I lived at the dormitory of Chicago Theological Seminary, an affiliated institution at the edge of the university campus. In the summer of 1950, I took a hurry–up course in French and passed the exam I needed as part of my Ph.D. program. I never did pass the German exam, despite the fact I had a minor in German during my undergraduate years. When the decision was made to go to Waldorf in 1951, I also decided to discontinue my doctoral studies. The lack of financial resources for further full–time study, together with a fading enthusiasm on my part for pursuing the degree, led to that determination. I have never regretted my decision, although I must admit that, having been in educational work most of my career, it would have made sense for me to have completed the terminal degree. The deficiency has never seemed to be a handicap in my work, and I am quite certain I would never have been a great research scholar had I possessed the doctorate.

The year in Chicago had been a financial maneuver in a combination of ways. I have mentioned the fact that we sold our car before we left Moorhead. We set aside $500 of the $900 for which we sold it, knowing we would need to buy another when we returned. The college paid me half of my salary for the school year we were away. That amounted to $1,250. We had a few hundred dollars which Dorothy had inherited from her father, and the university had granted me some help.

One day, not long after we arrived in Chicago, the Dean of Students called me in and asked me if I needed money, and I acknowledged I did. He took a large looseleaf book out of a drawer in his desk and started paging through it. He had scholarship funds designated for Baptists born in Kentucky, for the sons of ministers, for Minnesota Congregationalists, and so forth. Finally he found one which could be used even for a Lutheran! As I recall, I was granted $800, which was a big boost to us. Since that time I have contributed regularly, in small amounts to be sure, to the University of Chicago out of gratitude for the help I received.

We returned to Moorhead in the fall of 1948 without any debt. When we arrived, we needed a car. They were difficult to come by because during the war cars had not been made. We were fortunate to be able to buy a 1941

Chrysler for $350. It provided us with adequate, if not always reliable, transportation for more than two years, at which time we traded for a Chevrolet which was one of the post–war products.

We also had to gather furniture which had been on loan to friends in Moorhead. We moved back into the house at 807 South Seventh Street, and lived there until we left for Forest City in 1951.

The routine at the college continued quite as before. Sig Fauske was chairman of the department, which had expanded since my arrival in 1945. There were five of us in the department, including Eugene Fevold, who was part–time while serving a congregation in West Fargo.

One of the most interesting aspects of my time on the faculty at Concordia was the opportunity to get to know and interact with other faculty members. Several of them had been my teachers, and I saw them in a new light as colleagues. Faculty meetings were an education. I learned that intelligent people could exhibit pettiness as well as generosity of spirit, and that convictions expressed in debate often had as much to do with personal agendas as with college goals. I also learned that a faculty can do noble things, rise to challenges and overcome difficulties. The lack of funds and equipment often dogged our work, but that was good training for the future, when, as a college president, I would face such matters with regularity.

Dr. J.N. Brown, who had been president of the college when I was a student, was still in that position while I was on the faculty. In fact, I believe he and Dr. Carl Ylvisaker selected me for the faculty without much consultation with anyone else, and without interviewing me, as I have indicated earlier. Dr. Brown retired in 1951 after 26 years in the presidency. He was a man of determination, with strong convictions about the identity of the college as an institution of the church. Regular worship, the study of religion and the encouragement of religious organizations for students were, for him, vital marks of a church college. He brooked no opposition if he felt anyone was trying to interfere with or alter any of the chosen goals or programs of the college.

I was of two minds about President Brown. I owed him much because he had permitted me to go through college signing promissory notes which he had no assurance would be paid on time. He had also been a willing and helpful counselor, speaking with me several times about my life and career plans. But when I became a faculty member, I grew convinced that he did not exercise enough latitude with students, and that it was probably impossible for him to change the habits of mind which had become a part of his quarter–century of work at the college. As World War II veterans returned to campus, it became increasingly difficult to enforce arbitrarily the old rules regarding drinking and dancing. Many of the veterans were adults who had developed habits of life while in the service which were not exactly what the college condoned or encouraged. I was elected a member of the college disciplinary committee, and together with others tried to shift college practice to an emphasis on counseling rather than punishment. We succeeded only in part, and in much of what we tried to do found ourselves to be in opposition to the president.

All of this grew into more than it should have. We transferred our differences with President Brown over student affairs to college affairs in general. I am not proud of the fact that in a faculty meeting devoted to planning the sixtieth anniversary of the college in 1951, when Dr. Brown suggested awarding six honorary degrees, I had the temerity to ask how many would be appropriate on the seventy–fifth anniversary! The faculty did an interesting thing with the honorary degree matter, however. It voted to award one degree — to President Brown, who retired with the conclusion of that academic year. It was an ironic way of rebuffing and honoring the man at the same time.

President Brown had served Concordia through difficult times of depression and growth. The college had become a degree–granting institution in 1917 at the time of the merger of Norwegian–background Lutheran church bodies, so it was a relatively young institution when he became president in 1925. He saw the college through the depression years of the thirties and the days of World War II. A solid foundation for the future was laid during his time, as is borne out by the great growth and increasing academic quality of the college which followed during the presidencies of Joseph Knutson and Paul Dovre.

Several Concordia faculty members were special friends of ours. Among these were Cyrus and Eldrid Running. Cy taught art, and was a naturally talented musician and clown. Paul and Eleanor Christiansen were also good friends. Paul directed the choir and continued on the faculty for 49 years. Sig Fauske was chairman of the Department of Religion the last three years of our time at Concordia. He was a generous and supportive colleague, and Dorothy and I were often with him and his wife Iylla socially. Reidar Thomte taught philosophy and religion. His wife Amanda became a special friend of Dorothy's. We continued the good relationship we had enjoyed in undergraduate days with Allwin Monson (speech), my former debate partner and roommate, and his wife Dorothy. Others with whom we spent personal time, and who enriched our lives professionally and otherwise, were Carl (physics) and Carol Bailey, Eugene (religion) and Dorothea Fevold, and Vic (Dean of Men) and Hilda Boe. We belonged to a reading group which included several of the couples named above, and which met irregularly to discuss books, visit and drink coffee.

I have been gratified to have had as students persons who have gone on to make fine records for themselves in various walks of life. Several of them attended the seminary and have served the Church in various capacities. I have had continued contact with many of them. Lloyd Svendsbye became a pastor and has served as an editor at Augsburg Publishing House, and, while I was president of St. Olaf, served as vice president and dean of the college. Later he became president of Luther Northwestern Theological Seminary and of Augustana College. Paul and Don Sponheim both became pastors; Paul has spent much of his career as a professor at Luther Seminary. Peder Waldum was one of many World War II veterans who enlivened class discussions with stories from their war experiences. Pete became a pastor and served his entire career in Montana. Arland Fiske became a pastor and newspaper columnist. We have had many theological discussions through the years, and I wrote an introduction to one of his books of collected columns about Scandinavian history and life. Albert B. Anderson attended the seminary but went on to earn his doctorate in philosophy. He has been a professor and college president, and now lives in Minneapolis, so we get together with some regularity for breakfast and interesting discussions. His wife, Anita, was also my student.

Ellwood Bohn was a big, strapping fellow from Bismarck, North Dakota, a star basketball player and a very able student. He majored in mathematics, went on to get a doctorate, and spent his career as a university professor. A good friend of his, and fellow basketball player, was Carl Zander, also an exceptional student. He became a psychologist, and was at the University of Minnesota for several years. Mary fell for Ellwood Bohn and Carl Zander. She was five years old when she announced to us that she was going to marry Ellwood or Carl. She was really planning ahead.

From time to time I see couples who were my students. Among them are Cal Larson, an insurance agent in Fergus Falls and a Minnesota state senator, and his wife Loretta Pederson. Our paths have crossed often, not least in connection with legislative matters affecting education. Clark Ringham and his wife, the former Ruth Satre, live in Minneapolis and we see them frequently. David and Eunice (Nordby) Simonson went as missionaries to Tanzania, where they began and continue the work of Operation Bootstrap, a program through which schools are built and teachers provided for the people of Tanzania. Funds for the schools are raised in America, and their construction is carried out by the parents of Tanzanian students. Our granddaughter Amy is now a teacher at one of these schools in Monduli, Tanzania.

When I arrived at St. Olaf as president, I was welcomed as a colleague by Miles (Mity) Johnson. He and his wife Myrna Hanson had been students at Concordia and were among those who carried on their courtship in my classes. Mity has had a distinguished career as director of the St. Olaf Band, and Myrna has made great contributions to the college and community, particularly as founding director of the Northfield Arts Guild. Two other former students, Rodney Grubb and Jack Schwandt, also joined the faculty at St. Olaf.

This is only a sampling of many students whom I have continued to see and enjoy through the years, many of whom have spoken warmly about my classes. That always makes me feel good. I have officiated at the marriages of several of my students, and even some of their children. I must say that my teaching experience left me with most pleasant and nostalgic memories.

Peter started school while we lived in Moorhead. He attended the model school operated by Moorhead State College as a teaching laboratory. It was about eight blocks from our home. One day, soon after he had started school, he arrived at home and announced to Dorothy, "I whistled all the way home." There were no school buses to ride, and he often walked to and from school with other children. But that day he had evidently walked home alone and whistled to keep up his courage. Another day he protested to his mother that he could just as well stay home from school. "All we do is play," he said.

I must record the fact that I built a house while we lived in Moorhead. In our back yard was a pile of used lumber, left over from the construction of World War II barracks buildings which the college had acquired for classroom and office use. I secured the approval of the college to appropriate some of the lumber to build a playhouse for Peter and Mary. It was a structure about four by six feet with a four–foot ceiling and a peaked roof. It had regular siding, a door in one end and windows on the sides. We named it Marpet, using parts of the children's names. When we left Moorhead we sold it to Allwin Monson for his children's enjoyment.

One day while I was building the house and had just laid the floor on joists that were propped up to adjust to the uneven ground, Vic Boe, the Dean of Men, came by. "Is it level?" he inquired. "I don't know," I said, "I don't have a level; I've only sighted it." "I'll go get my level," he said. Peter watched as Vic returned and placed his level on the floor, first one way and then another. "It's dead level," he exclaimed, surprised that it could be, I guess. Ever after that, when Peter showed the house to anyone, he would announce, "It's dead level."

When Peter and Mary were little children, I invented Johnny and Tinky Squirrel. In Moorhead (and later in Forest City, Minneapolis and Northfield) we had squirrels as regular visitors in the yard. I made up stories about Johnny and Tinky. They would chase each other, get into difficulty, have fun with children and generally live the lives of squirrels. Some human characteristics such as speaking were added to make the stories come alive. In more recent years, Luke, Leah, Amy and Dorothy were exposed to Johnny and Tinky, and seemed to enjoy them.

Another of my creations was the "long–billed beetle–hawk." When we were on automobile trips, I would spot such a creature in a tree and call on Peter and Mary to see it. At first they insisted they couldn't see any bird at all, but as time went on they developed that sixth (or seventh) sense which enabled them to discover and appreciate long–billed beetle–hawks as we traveled.

While we lived in Moorhead we traveled frequently to visit Mother only forty miles away in Rothsay. She had taught school for many years, but retired at about the time we left Moorhead for Forest City. Her life had been eased somewhat by virtue of the fact that the house had been wired for electricity. In her late years, she enjoyed a radio and a refrigerator as well as electric lights. The house never benefited from modern plumbing.

On our trips to Rothsay, frequently on Sunday afternoon or for holidays, our route took us through Barnesville on old Highway 52. There was no interstate highway yet. As we approached Barnesville from the north, we passed the Catholic church, in front of which was a statue of Christ. Mary would always exclaim, "I see JeeJee," her favorite name for Jesus when she was three or four years old. Also in Barnesville was a restaurant which served delicious ice cream cones. We could never avoid a treat as we passed through. As we neared Rothsay, the children would vie with one another as to who would first spot the grain elevator, the most conspicuous building on the horizon. Here Mary would shout, "I see Grandma's elebator." Yes, she said "elebator."

Mother was always a considerate hostess. She knew what we liked to eat and would usually have it. A favorite meal with all of us was meatballs, mashed potatoes and gravy. We didn't care what the vegetable was. If she had advance notice that we were coming, she would often bake a pie, knowing my weakness for that. One of my favorites was butterscotch. Lyman's favorite was chocolate, and in her later years Mother didn't always remember which was which. As a consequence we sometimes were served chocolate pie, certainly quite acceptable but far down the list of my favorites.

It must have been in January of 1951 that I received a telephone call from Arndt Halvorson, pastor at Immanuel Lutheran Church in Forest City, Iowa, and acting president of Waldorf College. Morton Nilssen, who had been Waldorf's president, had died in December, 1950, and Arndt, whom I had known since seminary days, was pressed into service on a temporary basis.

Would I be interested in meeting with a committee of the Waldorf board, a committee charged with finding a new president for the college? I told Arndt I might be interested, but the date later in the month when they suggested we meet in Minneapolis was during exam week at Concordia. I told him I could not come, and thought that would end the matter. A few weeks later Arndt called again suggesting a new meeting time, one that proved possible for me. So on a day in February I met with Waldorf representatives at the Curtis Hotel in Minneapolis. Those who came were Harlan Rye, chairman of the Waldorf board and a banker in Emmons, Minnesota; Irv Weiseth, another board member and a businessman in Mason City, Iowa; and Pastor Blaine Gunderson, also a board member and a pastor in Emmetsburg, Iowa. We talked for about three hours. As I remember the conversation, we discussed Waldorf College very little, and also said hardly anything about me or my expectations or plans. I went home thinking it had been a strange interview and probably no more helpful to them than it had been for me.

A few weeks later, with no contact since the interview, I received a call to be president of Waldorf. The salary was to be $5,000 per year "plus the normal travel allowance," whatever that meant. I accepted and the die was cast. I was to leave teaching and become an administrator.

While at Concordia I had had other inquiries about my future. I had been asked if I would consider a call to be pastor of Trinity Lutheran Church in Crookston, Minnesota, and I had received a call to be pastor of St. John's Lutheran Church in Hatton, North Dakota. I had been elected president of Clifton College, a small junior college in Clifton, Texas. In each of these situations, I chose to remain at Concordia.

But now I had decided to leave, and planning began. We moved on Saturday, June 30, 1951. It cost us $350 to move the contents of a five–room house, including a library of several hundred books. We didn't have a piano any more. The piano Dorothy had inherited from her parents, and which had accompanied us to Nashwauk and to Moorhead, had been sold to the Allen Hansons before we went to Chicago in 1947. Allen was a faculty colleague in the Department of Chemistry. I believe we sold the piano for $50, and that sum was fairly significant to us as we headed for graduate study in 1947.

In the spring of 1951 the Trinity Lutheran Church building had burned. That was the congregation to which we belonged, and I had participated in planning for its rebuilding. We had made a pledge toward the cost of that program, a pledge to be paid over a three–year period. We paid it during our Waldorf days in time to make a pledge to Immanuel Church in Forest City when an addition was built there. Before that pledge was paid, we moved to Minneapolis where we joined Bethlehem Lutheran Church and, sure enough, there was soon a building fund drive. Of course we pledged, and before we had completed our payments we moved to Northfield. Yes, St. John's Church in Northfield had a couple of building fund drives while we were there. Fortunately, we stayed in Northfield long enough to pay what we had pledged. It's rather nice to know that we've been able to help build so many church buildings.

An interesting postscript to this little story is the fact that when we moved to Minneapolis in retirement in 1981, we joined Central Lutheran Church and discovered the congregation had just completed a fund drive, the purpose of which was to build an addition to the church. But of course there have been other special appeals since!

Rand family crest with the motto, "Not for ourselves alone."

My father and mother, Charles W. and Alice Rand.

My childhood home in Rothsay.

Hamar Lutheran Church in Rothsay.

With my brother Lyman and sister Charlotte at home, the summer I chose to have my head shaved.

Walt Ekeren and I as Boy Scouts.

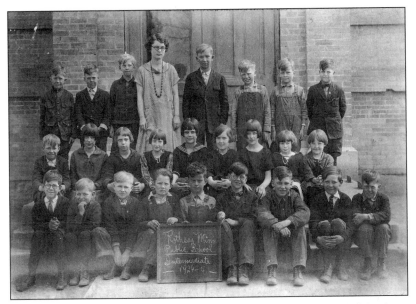

Grades three, four and five at Rothsay School. My brother Lyman is behind the sign in the center of the front row. My friend Walt Ekeren is at the right end of the last row, and I am next to him. The teacher is Cecelia Kunkel.

Mother with Lyman, Charlotte and me in the mid–30's.

Dorothy Holm and I at our graduation from Concordia College in 1938.

Naskwauk Lutheran Church with me in the pulpit.

At Bible Camp in Montana in the late 40's. Faculty (George Aus, Phil Hyland, Erling Wold, Orin Thompson, Reidar Daehlin, Sidney Rand and Glenn Husby) together with family members.

During my Waldorf days, a conference with Fred Thompson (left), Director of Public Relations, and David E. Johnson (right), our consultant from St. Olaf.

Teaching at Concordia.

With Dorothy, Peter and Mary in the early 50's.

My 1956 installation as Executive Secretary of the Board of Christian Education at Bethelehem Lutheran Church, Minneapolis. Also installed was C. Richard Evenson as Assistant Executive Secretary. Officiants were Dr. Fredrik Schiotz, President of the ELC, and Dr. Arthur Tolo, Secretary of the Board.

With my family on Inauguration Day at St. Olaf. Retiring President Clemens Granskou is in the background.

Five former presidents of Waldorf College later came to St. Olaf. Four of us were present on my Inauguration Day, and posed before the portrait of the fifth, Lars W. Boe. From my left, Clemens Granskou, Carl Helgen and Martin Hegland.

Leavy Oliver, president of the student body, and I visit with King Olav V during his 1968 visit to St. Olaf.

The Danforth Foundation awarded me a grant for a three–month leave of absence in 1972. Dorothy and I took a round–the–world trip, and here we are in Japan.

122

During the St. Olaf Centennial, President Elwin Farwell of Luther College joined me in examining the desk at which the St. Olaf Articles of Incorporation were signed in 1874.

Dr. Antonia Brico, pioneer among women orchestral conductors, and Lois's former teacher, directed the St. Olaf Orchestra in one of the concerts dedicating the new Christiansen Hall of Music in 1977. Here she visits with our daughter–in–law Nancy and granddaughters Dorothy and Amy.

Lois and I with Tanzanian Bishop Josiah Kibira, president of the Lutheran World Federation, and his wife Martha, when they visited St. Olaf in 1978.

Norway's Crown Princess Sonja (now Queen Sonja) visited St. Olaf in 1978. She drew laughs from ALC President Fredrik Schiotz, Norway's Ambassador to the United States Søren Chr. Sommerfelt and me when she reminded us that she should have been an American because she was born on the Fourth of July.

Johannes Cardinal Willebrands of the Papal Congregation for Christian Unity lectured at St. Olaf and received an honorary degree. On a later visit he presented to the college a Luther Bible from his personal library.

Lord Caradon, retired British diplomat, was a popular repeat visitor to the St. Olaf campus.

Luke and Leah Williams of California appreciated the St. Olaf campus as much as their grandfather did.

With my friend and successor as president of St. Olaf, Dr. Harlan Foss.

Chapter 10

COLLEGE TRANSFER

I am quite aware that this story of my life, as it relates to my adult years, is being seen from the standpoint of my work. There would be other ways to do it, but for me it seems to be right. Certainly family has been at the center of my life, and I don't mean to imply anything else. But I am like many others of my generation; my work tends to say who I am more than any other single factor. It has certainly determined where we have lived, and it has also given my life its cast of characters.

When we arrived in Forest City in June, 1951, the college had no president's residence to offer us as a home. Dr. Morton Nilssen had owned his own home, and his widow continued living there. The college had offered me an option regarding housing. I could receive a salary of $5,000 per year and provide my own place to live, or the college would pay me $4,000 and provide a home in addition. We chose the latter arrangement, both because we were quite certain that a home would cost us more than $1,000 per year and because, as when we went to Forest City, we found ourselves lacking the wherewithal to make a down payment on a home.

The first year in Forest City we occupied a house which belonged to Mr. and Mrs. Selmer Dahl. Mr. Dahl taught chemistry at the college, and they had bought the house as an investment. During that year the college decided to build a president's residence, but of course it was not ready immediately, so the school year 1952–53 we lived in rooms in Thorson Hall, a dormitory. The Dahls had decided to occupy the house we had rented from them.

In Thorson Hall we lived in four rooms at the end of a corridor on second floor. The rooms were over the college gymnasium, so at various times we had interesting entertainment, the thump, thump of basketballs. It proved to be a very good year for the whole family. Peter and Mary appreciated the opportunity to roam the building, frequently visiting student rooms. Our four rooms plus a gang shower were quite adequate if not especially convenient. We had a kitchen–dining room, a living room and two bedrooms. The four shower heads in our bathroom facility led Peter to boast to his friends that "our whole family can take a shower at the same time."

We ate most of our meals in the college cafeteria, having only a hot plate in our quarters. The food was good, being the product of veteran cook Tillie Rasmussen and her helpers. We had lots of contact with students and faculty, and thoroughly enjoyed that aspect of our life.

Waldorf was a junior college with an enrollment of 185 students in the two college years, plus about a dozen students in a high school program. The college was trying to offer a high school opportunity and had devised what was called a Rural Youth Program adapted to young people from the farm. The enrollment in that program was small, however, and in my third year at Waldorf we eliminated it.

Waldorf offered a general college program with special emphasis in two areas, business/commercial subjects and industrial arts. There was strong registration for courses in both those areas.

The faculty consisted of about twenty persons, some of whom had been at the college for many years. Odvin Hagen was the choir director and voice teacher. His wife Margaret (Muggy to everyone) did a little of everything. Only late in 1993 did Muggy finally retire after decades of service to the college in admissions, counseling and various other roles, for which she was given the honorary title, "Waldorf's Ambassador." Arthur Strand was business manager, and handled all building and facilities problems as well as the business office. Holger (Hap) Holmen taught industrial arts, Edith Quist taught piano, O.J. Johnson taught physics and math, Ingeborg Coltvet taught business subjects, Helen Asp taught physical education, as did Rolf Lund, who was also the basketball coach. We didn't have football the first year or two I was there. After that, Robert Bungum came to be registrar and football coach.

Among the very special people on the staff were Dr. Jacob Tanner, Evelyn Wolfs and Tillie Rasmussen. Dr. Tanner celebrated his ninetieth birthday while we were at Waldorf. He had retired from teaching at Luther Theological Seminary twenty years earlier and had grown restless in retirement. Dr. Nilssen had brought him to Waldorf as a temporary faculty member when he was eighty. He was still going strong at ninety, and lived until he was ninety–six.

Evelyn Wolfs was my secretary, but not only that. She also did all the bookkeeping for the college and acted as receptionist for Art Strand and me. Our offices adjoined each other in one corner of the Main Building and next to the famous Lobby, the real college center. Evelyn was and is one of the nicest and most efficient persons I have ever met or worked with anywhere. She did her work with seeming ease, always cheerful and treating students, faculty and visitors with gracious warmth and understanding. She had a good sense of humor which I appreciated in a very special way, and was an expert at sizing up people. She was a whiz at shorthand and typing, so I was soon spoiled.

Tillie Rasmussen was the old–fashioned kind of cook. She prepared food by hunch, never bothering with recipes as far as anyone knew. There was no dietitian or menu planner. Tillie just did what seemed appropriate, given the fact that she was feeding youngsters and that the market determined the availability of certain things. She and her helpers put out tasty food in abundance, and the students loved it. She was especially famous for her pies, cakes, bread and rolls. When we built a dormitory in 1953, we not only named it Tillie Rasmussen Hall, but also placed in the cornerstone two of Tillie's rolls. They are no doubt a bit dry by now.

Waldorf was like a family in many ways. Most of the students lived on or near the campus. Faculty and students knew each other quite well. All–college events were just that; there was a friendly spirit in the group. The Rands had a wonderful five years at Waldorf.

The college had inherited its name. In 1901, a group of Forest City businessmen, believing the town was destined for great growth and influence, built a rather substantial hotel one block from the main street and across from the courthouse square. In true hotel fashion, they named it the Waldorf, quite appropriate because the word in German means "town in the woods," or Forest City. There is a large stand of trees just east of the town, and that had no doubt given the community its name. Soon after the hotel opened, it ran into financial difficulties, and, complicated by the fact that the business group had split and a rival faction had built a second hotel, the building was put up for sale. A group of enterprising Lutherans, under the leadership of Pastor C.S. Salveson, purchased the hotel for $18,000 and opened Waldorf College in October, 1903. It started as an academy or high school, and the first two years of college were added in 1920.

I was the tenth president of Waldorf. Of special interest to me is the fact that four other Waldorf presidents had gone from Forest City to the staff of St. Olaf College. Lars Boe and Clemens Granskou became presidents of St. Olaf, Martin Hegland became a professor of religion, and Carl Helgen was for many years engaged in admissions work and the promotion of radio station WCAL.

Waldorf had established itself among the congregations of northern and central Iowa and the southern fringe of Minnesota, and most of the students came from that area. During my five years there, the enrollment grew from 185 to about 250 students. One building was added, Tillie Rasmussen Hall, a dormitory for women. It was built with the proceeds of a government–insured bond issue, a low–cost program begun in the early fifties and a boon to many colleges as they sought to accommodate the post–World War II increase in enrollments.

My days at Waldorf were spent largely in the general supervision of the program of the college. I was in my office much of the day dealing with all sorts of concerns, but I also spent quite a bit of time traveling among the congregations of the area seeking support for the college and preaching at services in many of them. We had a small staff and tried to operate on a lean budget. Salaries were low and we tried to keep student costs at a minimum. There was a general air of thrift and conservatism around the place, so innovation was not popular. Art Strand was a hard man to budge if someone wanted money, even for a quite legitimate expense.

The Board of Trustees was composed of pastors and business people from the area. Board meetings were, to a large extent, occupied with Mr. Rye, the chairman, telling the board what he thought should be done, punctuated by an occasional motion, usually in line with his recommendations. I soon learned that I needed to issue regular reports to the members of the board and to make specific recommendations for their action. In this way I exercised some of the initiative which I believed was proper to the functioning of the college, and responsive to my call as president.

The experience was good for me. I was a novice at college administration, but was bold enough to believe I understood fairly well both how an organization functions and how people engaged in such an enterprise interact with each other. My plan of action was to apply what I knew in these areas, and as time went on some constructive things were done.

Internally the college functioned quite well. The faculty members were diligent and dependable. There was some turnover in the five years we were there, but a core of veterans remained to give continuity to the program. While most of the students were from the farms and small towns of the area, we did have a few from Minneapolis, Detroit and New York. Student discipline dealt mostly with the expected student pranks, but nothing serious occurred. The college did not permit dancing, drinking or cohabitation of the sexes. Occasionally we faced problems related to those areas.

One day a group of students lifted a Volkswagen into the Lobby, a task that involved scaling about four steps. The feat attracted considerable attention, and I thought it was quite an interesting display of student ingenuity.

The Waldorf College Association was made up of 125 congregations. We asked each of them to make an annual contribution, and most of them did. This supplemented the annual grant the college received from the church at large. Once a year delegates from the member congregations gathered to hear reports, elect members of the board and transact other business.

My records show that I preached in some church of the Waldorf area every Sunday from September through December, 1951. After that I continued to preach regularly, but not every Sunday, in churches of the Waldorf constituency. Shortly after we arrived in Forest City, Arndt Halvorson accepted a call to Hope Lutheran Church in Minneapolis, and for several months after that I assisted at Immanuel Lutheran Church with weddings, funerals and some Sunday preaching. In 1952, I helped out for several Sundays at Grace Lutheran Church in Fairmont, Minnesota, and at Trinity Lutheran Church in Mason City, Iowa, in both cases during pastoral vacancies. I also did interim pastoral work one Lenten season at Zion Lutheran Church in Clear Lake, Iowa.

When I became a college president, I decided I should turn over to the college any honoraria I received for speaking. The college paid my salary and took care of my travel expenses, so I thought it was right that it receive any proceeds from my off–campus work. I have continued that policy ever since.

Waldorf didn't get rich from my travels. Some samples of my experience along this line were: preaching in Gilbert, Iowa, and receiving no honorarium, with expenses of $12.90; preaching in Roland, Iowa, where I was paid $25, with expenses of $11; preaching in Norway, Iowa, where I received $25, and spent $34.10 getting there. I spoke at Luther College, Wahoo, Nebraska, on one occasion and was paid $60, but spent $49 traveling there. One Fourth of July I was paid $100 for speaking at a community celebration in Clear Lake, Iowa. Expenses were small so I made money for the college that time. I believe it was the first time I had ever been paid as much as $100 for giving a talk. George Strum, pastor in Clear Lake, was responsible for my getting the invitation to give the $100 talk. He and his wife, Arline, became good friends and we visited often in each other's homes. Our usual entertainment was Rook, which all of us enjoyed. Our friendship has continued through the years.

In March, 1954, I accompanied the Waldorf Choir on a two–week tour which I had arranged. When I came to Waldorf, Tom Kilian was director of public relations and, among other things, arranged the choir tour. In 1952, he left for Augustana College in Sioux Falls, and I persuaded my college friend Jay Melberg to come to take that position. I thought that would be a splendid arrangement, but I learned that it doesn't always work to employ your friends. Jay wasn't happy at Waldorf, and after one year he left. It was then that I stepped in and became manager of the choir. The experience was worthwhile, but once was enough. I can't understand how anyone can make a career of tour management. There are dates to clear, travel arrangements to make, housing to be provided, local arrangements to check, and money to handle. But choir was an important part of Waldorf life. Odvin and Muggy Hagen were loved and respected by a host of Waldorf supporters, and they made the choir an effective public relations tool as well as a fine music organization. We found a new choir manager after my one year on the job.

Public relations and fund raising are important aspects of any college president's work. In a small college they are probably even more important in the sense that the president is seen as the chief embodiment and representative of the college. His presence is therefore required at numerous occasions and is indispensable in many cases. I was a neophyte in these areas, but I found I thrived on the work. I called on individuals and businesses and even a few foundations on behalf of the college. I learned a lot and we attracted a few gifts.

One of my most memorable fund–raising experiences took place in my office. Early in my time at Waldorf I received a telephone call from O.N. Gjellefald. I had heard of him; he was a successful engineer and heavy construction contractor who built water and sewer systems and airports throughout the midwest. He was not poor. He asked if he could come to see me, and of course I said he should. His office was only a block away. Before he arrived, Evelyn Wolfs coached me. He was a straightforward, plain–spoken man but a good friend of Waldorf.

As he entered my office, Mr. Gjellefald slapped a check down on my desk and said, "Rand, you can have this check on one condition, that you and I agree that it doesn't have a damn thing to do with my salvation." While I wasn't quite ready for that approach, I answered him to the effect that with that condition the college would be happy to accept any gift he chose to give us. The check was for $5,000, a magnificent sum in my early fund–raising career.

After that opening gambit, O.N., as I came to call him, sat down and we had a marvelous visit about Waldorf and about life. He was an alcoholic and had lived the rough and tough life of a construction engineer. He had stopped drinking, chiefly due to the influence of his pastor, Arndt Halvorson. He knew his theology, too. Though he was given to expletives, he shared with me his witness that Jesus Christ was his Savior. He and I had many a good conversation in the months and years that followed. I never called on him without coming away with a gift for the college, never less than $5,000. More than once it was $25,000 or $50,000. O.N. was a great encourager to a young college president. Incidentally, he placed us on his Christmas list and for more than twenty–five years sent an annual gift, usually an Amana ham or a turkey.

There were other Forest City businessmen with whom I became well acquainted. One was Ben Carter, editor of the local paper, the *Forest City Summit*. Herb Cleophas, president of the local bank, became a friend to one in need more than once. One day in 1953, when the call came that Mother was seriously ill in San Diego, he let me borrow enough money to make the trip to bring Mother back to Minnesota. Sid Reuben owned a store in town that sold everything. John K. Hanson, later to found Winnebago Industries and become a multi–million–dollar donor to Waldorf, was a furniture dealer and mortician. Henry Nelsen managed farms and became a representative in the Iowa legislature. He invited me to open one of the sessions of the House with prayer, an honor I appreciated.

Membership in the Rotary Club in Forest City put me in touch with many community leaders. I served on a committee that produced a history of Forest City, *Centennial Sketches*, in observance of the town's one hundredth anniversary. I wrote the copy with ample instructions from the other members. For a brief time I served on the Library Board.

The Waldorf days were important for our family. In spite of my frequent travels and busyness with college affairs, we enjoyed many family occasions. It was a special privilege to help plan and then live in a new house which the college built and into which we moved in 1953. Built on a hill that sloped away from the street, the two story house had a full basement that provided grade level entry at the back. On the first floor were a dining area and kitchen at the front next to the entry hall and half bath. At the back, the living room, which included a fireplace, overlooked a wooded area adjoining a small river. On the second floor were three bedrooms, a study and a bathroom. The basement was left unfinished at the time we lived there. The front was faced with brick up to the windows and above that wood siding painted red. We called it "deficit red" because the college had borrowed $12,000 from church headquarters in Minneapolis in order to build the house.

We used the house not only for family purposes but for college functions. It worked quite well as a public place.

Dorothy was active in church, community and college activities. The children had friends in various parts of town. Near us in a large old house were two faculty families, the Rolf Lunds and the Richard Moes. Moes came to Waldorf in 1953 from Mason City where he had taught in the high school. He and his wife Lila had been my students at Concordia. Dick later went on to Augustana College, Rock Island, and to Pacific Lutheran University, where he spent most of his career as a dean and vice–president. He was in charge of our teacher education program at Waldorf. We went back and forth with the Moes and Lunds for late evening coffee. Those two families inadvertently influenced us in the purchase of our first television set. Peter and Mary were invited to their homes to see various programs, so we finally decided to buy our own and not impose on the neighbors.

Peter entered second grade and Mary entered first grade when we came to Forest City. The school was convenient to our home, and the children had good teachers. It was a fine place for them to get a good start on their education.

One Christmas Eve, when we responded to a knock on our door, we met Stanford and Ruth Holtan, friends who lived on a farm near town. They had a puppy which they wanted to give to Peter and Mary. The children were overjoyed. We had had no plans to acquire a pet, but under the circumstances we could only accept and say thanks. We named the dog Nicky, remembering St. Nicholas and thinking that was appropriate to the Christmas season. Later we learned Nicky was a female, but the name remained. Nicky was a playful dog and for several months the children enjoyed her. One day Peter and I took Nicky to the veterinarian to have her spayed. Peter pulled her home in the wagon with a bandage around her middle and with a little new knowledge about dogs. When we were to move to Minneapolis in 1956, we returned Nicky to the Holtans.

One summer day, an especially exciting event took place in front of our house. Two men who had held up a bank in Crystal Lake, a nearby village, came through Forest City as part of their escape route. Mary was standing in front of our house when they came by with the police in close pursuit. The police fired on the getaway car as they passed our house. Mary was later questioned by the police as to what she had seen. It was one of her early moments of glory.

Mother died during the time we lived in Forest City. I got a call one day in February of 1953 from my sister Mary in San Diego, telling me that Mother had been diagnosed as having cancer and that she may not have long to live. She had gone to San Diego to spend several weeks with Mary and her husband Harold Miller. She had also done that one winter earlier. She appreciated getting away from Minnesota in the cold weather, because the home in Rothsay had never been fully modernized, and winter was the most difficult time to be there.

Mother had visited doctors quite regularly to check on her blood pressure, but there had been no hint of cancer. Now the doctor in San Diego, in a routine examination, had decided not only that Mother had cancer but that it was in its advanced stages. She wanted to return home; someone would have to go to accompany her. Lyman was unable to do it, so I decided I should. That's when

I went to the bank to float a loan from Herb Cleophas. I believe the amount was $250. The fact that I had to negotiate a loan in order to finance a $250 trip to California is some kind of indication as to how closely we managed our finances during Waldorf days.

I took the train to San Diego. Air travel was not even considered in those days, at least not by us. Mother and I returned to Minneapolis via Los Angeles, Denver and Omaha. We had a compartment with two berths. I slept above and Mother below. She was in physical pain and needed assistance with her toilet and bath. I did my best with that, and also brought her meals from the dining car so she could stay in her berth the whole trip.

It took about three days to make the return trip, and during that time Mother and I had several lengthy and satisfying conversations. She expressed a desire to continue to live, but also spoke of her readiness to die. She spoke of her life as having been good, even though I knew, as she must have, that much of that life had been difficult. She expressed gratitude to God for life, for family, for friends and for salvation in Christ. It was a wonderful few days in many ways, certainly the only time Mother and I had spent that much time together without distractions.

Lyman and Helen had made arrangements with a doctor in Minneapolis to have Mother admitted to the hospital when we returned. Interestingly, it was St. Mary's Hospital, where she had been for surgery on her leg at the age of seven. She had not been hospitalized since. Mother died on February 18, 1953, after only a few days in St. Mary's.

The funeral was held in Hamar Church in Rothsay on Sunday, February 22, and Mother's body was laid to rest in Hamar cemetery, not far from the grave of her sister Seline, Mrs. J.C. Serkland. The funeral was first scheduled for Saturday, but as Dorothy, Peter, Mary and I drove from Forest City to Rothsay on Friday, we were caught in a snowstorm in Clear Lake, near St. Cloud. Dorothy and the children went on to Detroit Lakes on a night train, where they stayed with Al and Inez Torgerson. I spent Friday night in a service station in Clear Lake watching poker games and hearing off–color stories. On Saturday morning, after the storm subsided, I drove to Detroit Lakes where I got some sleep before we went on to Rothsay for the postponed funeral service on Sunday afternoon.

At times during our stay in Forest City I was approached regarding other positions. One Sunday I was filling in at Trinity Church in Mason City and was visited following the service by a call committee from First Lutheran Church in Duluth. One member of the committee was Dr. Robert Bergan (not my relative of that name), a St. Olaf graduate who later became a good friend. I declined to be considered for a call. On another occasion, I think in 1955, I was attending a meeting of some kind, again in Mason City, and received a telephone call from Dr. Paul Empie, executive director of the National Lutheran Council. He wanted to know if I would consider accepting the position of director of public relations on the staff of the council in its New York offices. Again I decided not to be a candidate.

Our Waldorf days came to an end in a rather unusual fashion. One evening in February, 1956, Dorothy and I went to a concert given by the Concordia College Choir at Trinity Church in Mason City. Yes, it was Mason City again. It seemed those things never happened at home. Following the concert there was a coffee hour in the church basement, and we went both for the coffee and to see our friends, not least Paul Christiansen, the director of the choir. I fell into conversation with Dr. Arthur Tolo, pastor in Dows, Iowa, and a member of the Board of Christian Education of the Evangelical Lutheran Church. He was on his way home from a Minneapolis meeting of that board.

As we talked, Dr. Tolo looked at me a bit quizzically and asked, "Have you had any word from Minneapolis today?" I replied that I had not. Then he said, "I'm not sure I'm supposed to be telling you this, but yesterday you were elected by the board to be executive secretary, succeeding Dr. J.C.K. Preus."

Dr. Preus had been executive secretary of the board for many years and was planning to retire. The board was responsible for coordinating the education program of the church, including the colleges, so I was acquainted with its work. I had not heard, however, that Dr. Preus planned to retire soon, so the whole development was news to me. As it turned out, it was about two weeks before I received a written notice of my election.

The way this election had taken place seems quite strange now. In more recent times, there have been notices of vacancies in church positions, solicitation of interest or application, the sifting and interviewing of candidates, and considerable deliberation by committees and boards before positions are filled. But in the less complicated days of the 1950's, and in a church which was small enough so that persons were well known to each other, things were different. In this case, the board knew the college presidents quite well, because we met with the board annually and often had other contacts with individual board members. Also, the concept of the church calling a person to a position such as that with the board was part of the tradition that prevailed. This is in contrast with the idea that a person seeks the position, or that a board is simply filling a job. The process was seen as one guided by the Holy Spirit working through a responsible body.

At any rate, I was elected without interview, and without submitting a vita or recommendations of persons who knew me and my work. The salary was to be $9,000 per year, as compared with the $6,000 plus house which was then my annual compensation at Waldorf. After discussing the matter with Dorothy, Peter and Mary, and after giving it prayerful consideration in my own mind and heart, I accepted the call.

In correspondence with Dr. Morris Wee, chairman of the Board of Christian Education, it was made clear to me that the board wanted me to complete my doctoral studies. I would be given time off to do that, Dr. Wee wrote. He wondered how long it would take me, and I had to tell him I did not know. While I had completed all course work for the degree and had passed all the qualifying exams, I had not been admitted as a candidate yet. And, of course, the big job left was the dissertation. Dr. Sidney Mead, my Chicago advisor, had tentatively approved my dissertation topic, "Immigrant Norwegian Lutherans and the American Education System," and I had written what was to be the first chapter. But how long it would take to finish I could not say.

As time passed and I became more and more involved with the board work, the idea of completing the doctorate faded, and so, as I had done while at Concordia, I decided I was not going to do it. Instead, I invested my time and energy in the work at hand, which I found completely fulfilling.

Chapter 11

PART OF THE BUREAUCRACY

For the first time since I had entered the ministry, we now had to find our own home. Dorothy and I talked about where in Minneapolis we would like to live, and before June, 1956, we went house–hunting. Because we were somewhat acquainted in south Minneapolis and because we thought bus service to downtown would be convenient from that area, we set about looking at homes south of Lake Street and within the city. We thought the suburbs would be too far from my office. We expected to drive one car and be partially dependent on public transportation.

Through the office of the Board of Trustees of the church we were directed to E.B.L. Eckberg, a real estate agent. He and his family belonged to Bethlehem Lutheran Church at Forty–first Street and Lyndale Avenue, so he showed us mostly homes in that area. We decided to buy the house at 5000 Emerson Avenue South. The Eckbergs lived across the street. As it turned out, they became our good friends. Dorothy and Vi Eckberg belonged to a women's group that became very close and sociable.

We paid $19,500 for the house, which was a two–story, stucco–exterior house on a corner. Peter and I sometimes wondered about the wisdom of a corner lot as we shoveled the walks in the winter. It can't have been too serious a problem, however, because many years later Peter and his wife Nancy bought a house on a corner lot on Humboldt Avenue South.

Our house included a living room with fireplace, a dining room, a kitchen and eating nook on the first floor, together with a central entrance hall. On the second floor were three bedrooms and a bath. At a landing halfway upstairs at the back of the house, a sun room over an attached garage served as a study and TV room. The basement was unfinished and became a miscellaneous storage and play space. We were happy with our purchase and spent seven good years there. In 1963, when we were to move to Northfield, we sold the house for the same dollar amount as we had paid for it.

In order to purchase the house we needed to raise some capital for a down payment. We did that by using savings that had come to us from Mother's estate. I believe the amount was about $2,000. We took out a mortgage with Lutheran Brotherhood at five percent interest.

School and church considerations had played a part in our decision regarding the house. Mary entered sixth grade at Burroughs School, four blocks from our home, and Peter entered seventh grade at Ramsey Junior High School, ten blocks away. Both could walk to school. We joined Bethlehem Church, about a mile away and convenient to the bus line which passed our house. We found the congregation to be a fine church home. Pastor Maynard Iverson was a personal friend and an excellent preacher. Pastor Bill Smith was the very effective youth pastor, and Peter and Mary responded well to his ministry.

The Board of Christian Education of the Evangelical Lutheran Church was responsible for planning and coordinating work in both parish education and college education. Dr. J.C.K. Preus, my predecessor, had given distinguished service in both areas. His assistant was Dr. Orville Dahl, whose background and experience lay in the area of higher education. I made it clear to the board before I accepted the position of executive secretary that I was no authority in the field of parish education. Dr. Wee, chairman of the board, had assured me that this had been considered before my election, and that things would be worked out. There was general satisfaction, even enthusiasm, for the work of Dr. Dahl, and the board was not eager to lose him.

I visited with Dr. Dahl before I began my work in Minneapolis, and sensed that he did not believe it would be practical for him to stay on. He soon accepted a position in California and later became the founding president of California Lutheran College, where he made a major contribution to higher education in the church.

Dr. Dahl's leaving meant there was a place on the staff for a parish education specialist. I decided the person who should be called to that position was Dr. C. Richard Evenson, pastor of Woodlake Lutheran Church in Minneapolis. He had a doctorate in education and was a bright, enthusiastic young pastor whom I had come to know when he was an associate pastor at Trinity Church in Moorhead while we lived there. He proved to be an excellent choice and was an effective, if sometimes controversial, leader of parish education activities in the church, both while that work was part of the responsibility of our board and afterwards when it became a separate activity under a new board in The American Lutheran Church.

I was installed as executive secretary of the ELC board at Bethlehem

Lutheran Church on February 20, 1957. Dick Evenson was installed at the same time. Dr. Fredrik Schiotz, president of the church, was the installing officer and Dr. Morris Wee preached. My boyhood friend, Walter Ekeren, sang two solos, "Prologue" from *The Apostles*, by Elgar, and "God Be in My Head," by Clokey. His accompanist was his wife Lois. I was especially pleased that my boyhood pastor Emil Salveson came from Rothsay to be present at the service. My thoughts included Mother. She would have enjoyed being there, I'm sure.

A refugee from Latvia, Valija Jaunlinens, was my secretary much of the time I was in the Minneapolis offices. She was a devoted worker, not in good health but always willing to do her part. She had suffered both physically and emotionally prior to fleeing Latvia at the time of the Soviet takeover.

The fellowship with other persons in the church offices was also a special aspect of our Minneapolis stay. A sense of family prevailed, not least in noon–hour exchange in the lunchroom. Dr. Schiotz gave dedicated and personal leadership to all that was done.

I have mentioned that before the church merger my responsibility included parish education as well as higher education. After the appointment of Dick Evenson, my time was spent less and less with the parish education side of things. I did teach at some parish education workshops, in connection with which the family enjoyed trips to both coasts and to Texas. Dick was an excellent director of his area, so my attention more and more was concentrated on higher education.

I must recount an interesting incident related to our parish education involvement. One summer I took part in a workshop at Lewis and Clark College in Portland, Oregon. During a camp–type service, a pastor friend of mine from the area led the singing. After one stanza of a hymn sung by the group, he said he noticed the voice of Mrs. Rand as being especially beautiful. Would she sing the second stanza while the rest of us hummed? Dorothy never sang any solos and didn't count singing as a major talent. It was a woman seated behind her who had the beautiful voice. But good sport that she was, Dorothy sang the second stanza — with a bit of tremolo, I must say. She survived, but when we got back to our room she went into hysterics, laughing and crying uncontrollably for some time. Peter and Mary, who had stayed in the room during the service, couldn't understand. We all got through the evening, but it was a memorable event to say the least.

Another trip involving parish education work took me to the east coast. We decided to make it a family vacation, and Kent Olson, Dorothy's cousin, offered the use of his Airstream trailer on one condition. We would also have to use his car, which was equipped with proper clutch, brakes and lights for hauling the Airstream. We headed east by way of Chicago, and traveled on interstates part of the way, chiefly in Pennsylvania. We spent some time in Washington, New York and Boston. I was scheduled to conduct parish education training sessions, and I believe I did that. My chief memory of this trip, however, has to do with trying to maneuver the car and Airstream through traffic, into and out of camping places and on busy, crowded highways. We appreciated very much the fact that Kent let us use his equipment, but I became convinced that I didn't want to travel that way as a regular thing.

What Peter and Mary remember most about this trip is that at one point we parked the trailer and went on our way for a few days without it. One evening, I kept postponing our stop for the night, passing one motel after another. We finally did stop, and found a place for the night in what can best be described as an old–fashioned, non–modern cabin. I was not permitted to forget this.

Among Norwegian Lutherans, coordination was a more acceptable word than supervision or control. I knew I was not to run the colleges of the church. Each of them enjoyed a certain autonomy vested in them by their incorporation. They all appreciated the financial subsidy granted by the church, even though it was never large enough to satisfy perceived needs. Each of them saw itself as part of the work of the church, but was left pretty much to its own devices in determining its program and planning its future. I was to be the agent of a concerned church to encourage and assist all of them in the work they sought to do.

During the seven years I served the two church bodies, we did several things aimed at improving the relationship between the church and the colleges, and seeking to assist the colleges in their work. We established the practice of bringing together staff persons in various areas (admissions, public relations, business management, and academic and personnel affairs) for discussion, planning and mutual encouragement. We continued the practice, already in existence, of an annual meeting of the presidents of the colleges. We devised a program of financial awards for faculty and staff people and for future faculty members, which offered assistance toward the costs of graduate study and leave–of–absence projects. We worked hard to increase the financial support provided by the church directly to the colleges, but succeeded only modestly in that effort.

As the merger approached its 1961 fulfillment, much of my time was spent in meetings related to that development. This meant getting acquainted with the pre–1961 American Lutheran Church and the United Evangelical Lutheran Church, and especially their higher education work. The ALC colleges were

Capital University in Columbus, Ohio; Wartburg College in Waverly, Iowa; Texas Lutheran College in Seguin, Texas; and Luther College in Regina, Saskatchewan. The UELC had one college, Dana, in Blair, Nebraska.

In 1961, the Evangelical Lutheran Church had five senior colleges, namely Augustana in Sioux Falls, South Dakota; Concordia in Moorhead, Minnesota; Luther in Decorah, Iowa; Pacific Lutheran in Tacoma, Washington; and St. Olaf in Northfield, Minnesota. In addition there were Waldorf, a junior college in Forest City, Iowa; Augustana Academy, a high school in Canton, South Dakota; and two Canadian institutions, Camrose College, a junior college in Camrose, Alberta; and Saskatchewan Lutheran Bible Institute, a high school and Bible school, in Outlook, Saskatchewan.

In 1963, the Lutheran Free Church joined the new American Lutheran Church, and that brought into the program of higher education Augsburg College in Minneapolis, Minnesota, and Oak Grove High School in Fargo, North Dakota.

As one might expect, there were differences in policy and practice regarding higher education among the merging churches. The UELC had one college and one seminary, but no coordinating office for them. They were operated as the program of the church, but there was no executive in charge. Each institution had its faculty and administration, and the work was coordinated in the central church offices in an informal manner.

In the old ALC it was quite the opposite. The board of education of the church made key decisions for each institution in such areas as budgets, building plans, certain personnel matters and fundraising. The controls were quite tight.

The ELC practices were less centralized than those of the ALC. Individual colleges made decisions in financial, academic and personnel areas. The one limitation was that financial decisions involving debt were to be approved by the Board of Christian Education and the Board of Trustees prior to any commitment being made by a college.

As merger negotiations continued, one of the key issues was this one dealing with the degree of control by the church over its colleges. I advocated the ELC approach because I believed it was more in harmony with the idea that strong colleges must bear prime responsibility for their own destiny. That view prevailed, and the Joint Union Committee asked me to prepare a paragraph for the bylaws of the church describing the relationship. It was adopted as part of the basic policy of the new church.

The pre–merger talks led me into a close working relationship with Dr. William Young, who was executive director of the ALC Board of College

Education. He was a layman, a veteran of the faculty of Capital University in the field of education, and had been with the board for several years when I began to work with him in the 1950's. He and I became personal friends, and, though we disagreed on certain policy matters, he was always enjoyable to work with. I learned much from him and his shared wisdom coming out of a long career in higher education.

During the period from 1956 to 1961, the Evangelical Lutheran Church continued its practice not only of having both parish education and higher education included in the concerns of one board, but also some relationship between the board and the theological seminaries. This was a gray area, and I must say it was never completely clear to me. I was glad when the merger created a separate board for theological education.

But during that time I had some kind of relationship with the seminaries of the church in St. Paul and Saskatoon, Saskatchewan. I used to say that the seminaries were really run by their faculties and the Board of Trustees of the church, while the members of the Board of Christian Education and the staff watched. The presidents and faculties seemed to make all decisions regarding the curriculum, the admission and graduation of students and the size of the faculty, while the Board of Trustees not only made financial decisions but actually kept the books, issued paychecks, paid the bills and managed the property. A member of our education staff, E.C. Jacobson, kept the books for Luther Seminary in St. Paul, so we always knew what was going on, but we had no control over it. Dr. Alvin Rogness, president of the seminary in St. Paul, and Dr. Olaf Storaasli, president of the seminary in Saskatoon, were my longtime friends and I was in regular contact with them. But to say that I had anything to do with running the seminaries would be an exaggeration.

That somewhat removed relationship with the seminaries taught me something about having the right person in the right place. The seminaries had able persons in key places. That made them go. While it would have helped at times to have policies clarified and lines drawn, it was nevertheless true that people made the difference. Frequently since 1961 I have thought that fewer policies and better people would provide more satisfactory resources for institutional health and growth.

My contacts with the Canadian schools provided another different and interesting set of experiences. The schools there were very conscious of their church relationship. The church in Canada was smaller than that in the United States, and, as a result, the relationship of institutions to the church was more intimate and personal. In western Canada, where all the ELC and ALC institutions were located, the constitution of each province prescribed that all degree–granting rights were to rest in the provincial university. This meant that no church institution could grant baccalaureate degrees except in affiliation with the university. Before 1961, none of the Lutheran schools except the seminary was a degree–granting institution. Camrose College and Luther College in Regina have since achieved that status.

In dealing with the Canadian schools, my role was mostly advisory. I felt that Canada had its own history and its own environment for education, and didn't need (or want?) much direction from the States. I also knew that the churches in Canada were moving toward merger, as we were, and that this would also no doubt mean organizational separation from the churches in the United States. Both merger and separation have since taken place, and the Canadian institutions are doing well.

I enjoyed my contacts with the people and institutions in Canada. I was always warmly welcomed and invited to take part not only in board meetings but in chapel services, commencements and other special occasions.

One special experience connected with my visits to Canada had to do with an automobile trip from Minneapolis to Saskatoon. Olaf Storaasli, then president of the seminary in Saskatoon, found himself in need of a car he owned, which happened to be in St. Paul. Knowing I was coming to the seminary, he asked me if I would be willing to drive the car there. I agreed to do that, and it happened that I was part of a two–car caravan, because Dr. Mars Dale, then the president of the Canada district of the church, was driving from the Twin Cities to Saskatoon at the same time. We drove through North Dakota, crossing the border at Portal, and went to Moose Jaw, Regina, and on to Saskatoon. Not all of the roads were hard surfaced at that time, and the car I was driving was not the newest model. The trip proved to be an exercise in patience and a vibration treatment for my physique, but all went well and the Storaaslis were grateful that they had their car.

Campus ministry was also part of the responsibility of both the ELC amd ALC boards. The churches of the National Lutheran Council had joined together to conduct ministries on the campuses of non–Lutheran colleges and universities. A board composed of church representatives had oversight for what was called the Division of College and University Work. The office was in Chicago and was under the direction of Dr. Donald Heiges. Through that board, pastors and other campus workers were called, trained, assigned and supervised. The board also managed a capital fund from which grants were made to local campus ministry units for the purchase or erection of chapels, houses and other facilities.

The experience with DCUW was a fruitful one for me. I was one of the representatives of the ELC and then of the ALC, and served for a time as chairman. It was my first experience working in an organization with representatives of the United Lutheran Church in America, the Augustana Synod and two Danish– and one Finnish–background church bodies. Each had a distinct history and pattern of organization and procedure. The ULCA was, in many ways, a federation of synods, and its decisions reflected a high degree of respect for the area synods and their wishes. It was also eastern–dominated, meaning that its strength was in the eastern part of the country, and what prevailed there tended to become official policy for the church. The Augustana Synod was smaller and more cohesive, as were the Danish–background American Evangelical Lutheran Church and Danish Evangelical Lutheran Church, and the Finnish–background Suomi Synod. The formation of The American Lutheran Church in 1961 and of the Lutheran Church in America in 1962 reduced the number of cooperating churches to two and simplified many of the DCUW decisions.

Meetings of the DCUW were held in the Chicago office. Don Heiges was an efficient leader, always preparing a helpful agenda and leading us through it with skill and a spirit of good will. One of my memories of the Chicago meetings is traveling by train, usually an overnight trip. In the morning, before reaching Chicago, I would luxuriate in the dining car with a wonderful breakfast. For a boy from Rothsay that was really living! We also traveled on clergy passes in those days. Clergy could ride free; all we paid for was a berth. So my trip to Chicago probably cost about $15 each way, including breakfast. Incidentally, when I first began flying to Chicago instead of riding the train, the one–way fare was $25. Times change.

As I have already stated, my chief work with the boards in Minneapolis involved the colleges of the church. The presidents were a varied and challenging group. I was younger than they were and knew better than to try to be their director. I may not even have been their leader. Perhaps I was their colleague. I thought we got along well, had useful discussions when we met and tackled honestly the problems we faced together.

Lawrence Stavig was at Augustana College. He was a quiet, persistent man, conservative in his theology and in his manner of administration. At Augustana they used to say he made all the decisions, no doubt a stretching of the truth a bit. He was a man of sound judgment and he listened to the views of others.

At Concordia College, Joe Knutson reigned. I use that word advisedly. He was widely regarded as a prophetic preacher, a fearless leader and an almost messianic figure. He had come to Concordia when the college faced serious problems, and rallied everyone to the cause. Under his deeply pietistic but often slap–dash manner, Concordia grew and prospered. He was a delight to deal with, not least because you could never know for sure what he would say or do next. I once heard him address a district convention of the church where he reminded his hearers, a good number of whom were pastors, that if they heard stories about Concordia students misbehaving they should believe them, because they were most likely true. And the reason they were true, Joe said, was because "most of those kids come from your congregations." Joe Knutson could talk that way to pastors and others and be respected and loved for it.

At Luther College, the president was J.W. (Bill) Ylvisaker, a brother of my college professor, Carl Ylvisaker. Bill was a courtly, reserved and thoughtful man, in action quite the opposite of Joe Knutson. He was a member of what was familiarly known in Norwegian Lutheran circles as one of the first families of the church. He was also a dedicated churchman and a deeply loyal son of Luther College.

One of my distinct memories has to do with a meeting of the Luther College board in 1962 when Bill Ylvisaker found it necessary to report an apparently irreconcilable difference of opinion and doctrinal position between two factions within the Department of Religion of the college. One was headed by Dr. Gerhard Belgum, a bright and severely orthodox theologian; the other was led by Dr. Robert Jenson, also bright and also soundly Lutheran, but one whose self–confidence and style were abrasive to many. The two men and the colleagues who sided with each of them had actually come to the place where they could not work together. The Belgum group considered the Jenson group to be heretical regarding basic Lutheran doctrines.

Dr. Ylvisaker's natural leaning must have been to side with Belgum, but he didn't. He took the position that Belgum and his colleagues had gone too far in demanding that Jenson be dismissed from the faculty for false teaching. Ylvisaker advocated accepting resignations from the Belgum group, four in all, something they had threatened to do if Jenson were not relieved of his duties. The board backed Ylvisaker and approved his recommendation. I looked upon it as a great day for Luther, even though I felt badly that things had gone as far as they had. Academic freedom was the factor, but Luther lost some good faculty members. Belgum and his colleagues left immediately, and Jenson left soon thereafter. This incident together with a deterioration of Dr. Ylvisaker's health led to his retirement in 1963.

Pacific Lutheran College was headed by Dr. S.C. Eastvold. He was a legend around the church. He had been asked to accept the presidency of the college by Dr. J.A. Aasgaard, president of the then Norwegian Lutheran Church of America. It was 1942 and the college was struggling to stay alive. It offered a baccalaureate degree in education, but otherwise was a junior college. Eastvold came from a parish in Eau Claire, Wisconsin, and his reputation included the characteristics of effective preacher, decisive leader and church politician. He embarked on an aggressive program of fundraising, building of facilities and increasing enrollment. Soon the B.A. degree was added and the name changed to Pacific Lutheran University.

Dr. Eastvold inspired those around him, commanded the loyalty of faculty and supporters of the college, and became a spokesman for higher education throughout the church. He also served for several years as vice president of the church, and in that role gained exposure beyond the Pacific Northwest. Rumor had it that when Dr. Fredrik Schiotz was elected president of the church in 1954, Eastvold was disappointed because he had expected to be chosen. He was an ambitious man, ambitious for himself and for any cause that claimed his attention.

Through what some board members at Pacific Lutheran believed to be the unwise investment of college funds, disagreement with President Eastvold arose at a meeting of the board in 1962, and he was asked to resign. The college had shared in a program of grants from the Ford Foundation, given in order to endow an increase in faculty salaries at a time when all agreed college faculty salaries throughout the country were much too low. Without consulting the board of the college, Dr. Eastvold had invested the Ford funds in a development venture on the Pacific shore west of Olympia, Washington. Not only were board members irked by the fact the president had taken unilateral action, but they thought the investment was a risky one. Hence the opposition. I was present with the board on the sad day when Dr. H.L. Foss, president of the Pacific District of the church and chairman of the college board, had to tell his good friend Seth Eastvold that he should step aside. It had been my dubious privilege to attend a late night meeting of the executive committee of the board the previous evening when the fateful decision had been made. Such meetings were not the favorite part of my work.

At St. Olaf College, my friend Clemens Granskou was the president. I had gotten to know him and his wife Ella in 1941 when he was president of Augustana College and I was intern at First Lutheran Church in Sioux Falls. Granskou had been a missionary in China following his ordination in the 1920's, and had remained vitally interested in that nation and its people. He had succeeded Lars Boe as president of St. Olaf in 1943. Dr. Boe had been a legend in his own time as he led the college in a period of growth and maturing. He was a blunt and bold Christian leader. (I think Joe Knutson patterned his life after that of Dr. Boe). Boe stories abounded on the St. Olaf campus. Granskou carried on the tradition but not with the same personal flair or showmanship. He stressed academic quality and the building up of a strong faculty. He brought the college to a place of national recognition as a liberal arts college of the church. I enjoyed the board meetings I attended at St. Olaf. They were always well managed and efficient.

At Waldorf College, my successor was Dr. Sigvald Fauske, with whom I had shared teaching duties at Concordia College. It was always good to get back to Waldorf, and I did so frequently. Sig was a methodical and devoted leader, not colorful but faithful and hard working.

Augustana Academy and the Canadian schools claimed less of my time and attention, but I did try to visit each of them at least once a year.

I was frequently asked to speak at chapel services and to faculty groups during my visits to the campuses. That way I extended my acquaintance with the institutions. I got to know many faculty and staff members, as well as members of governing boards.

During the 1950's, a group of faculty and administrative staff people from several of the colleges formed a group which met with some regularity for about ten years. It arose out of a meeting of the Association of Lutheran College Faculties, where the perpetual question of how the liberal arts relate to the Christian faith was discussed. The group finally included persons from Augustana, Concordia, Luther, St. Olaf, Waldorf and Luther Seminary. We met at the various colleges and usually listened to and discussed a paper prepared by a member of the group. I was assigned the topic, "The Administration of the Christian Liberal Arts College." It became one of the chapters in the book, *The Christian Faith and the Liberal Arts*, published by Augsburg Publishing House. The experience was a challenging one for me. I grew in my understanding of what church colleges were all about. I am sure much of what was discussed found its way into my thinking as I went on to St. Olaf College in 1963.

As the merger of churches drew near, I found more and more of my time was spent on arrangements which had to be made to bring the higher education program into the new church. My visits at Dana College, at the colleges of the American Lutheran Church, and with Dr. William Young, grew more frequent especially in 1959 and 1960. Dr. Young and I worked closely to bring about the college involvement in the new church as smoothly as possible. He knew he was going to retire as the new church came into being, and kept saying to me that I should be the executive director of the new board. I thought that the board would probably want a different person, and wondered what I would be doing next. As it turned out, the whole thing was settled early. The Joint Union

Committee decided a rather lengthy lead time would be good if the boards of the church were to be up and running on January 1, 1961, so on July 10, 1959, seventeen months ahead of the new church's beginning, I was elected executive director of the Board of College Education.

I received a Memorandum of Election notifying me of that action, but I never did receive a letter of call. The salary and other conditions relating to the position were communicated to me later through action of the board. I have had some interesting and irregular experiences in getting elected to, or chosen for, positions during my career. I guess it has made life more interesting. The irregularity has not bothered me, but I am sure it would trouble some persons if they were fastidious about the way things ought to be done.

I met with the board during the weeks and months following my election, and at a meeting on October 14, 1959, I expressed to them my reservations with regard to one section of the Constitution of the new church.

Article IV, Section 1 (later to become Chapter 3.10), read as follows: "The American Lutheran Church accepts all the canonical books of the Old and New Testaments as a whole and in all their parts as the divinely inspired, revealed and inerrant Word of God, and submits to this as the only infallible authority in all matters of faith and life."

As I considered the statement, I became uneasy. I did not believe it stated what I had learned or had come to believe. So, following the October 14 meeting, I prepared a statement which I sent to Dr. Morris Wee, chairman of the Board of College Education, and to Dr. Fredrik Schiotz, president of the church and a chief negotiator in the Joint Union Committee. In this statement I said, "My chief concern...is based upon the fact that, as I read it, the phrase 'all the canonical books of the Old and New Testaments as a whole and in all their parts...' is synonymous with the phrase 'the divinely inspired, revealed and inerrant Word of God.' The Article continues by stating what the Church believes concerning the Word of God and its relationship to the confessional writings of the Church."

I continued: "I see two problems here. One is the omission that results. Instead of the Church's Confession of Faith being a declaration of faith in God and his redemptive work and thus a positive witness to the cardinal tenets of Christianity, it becomes a statement about the Bible and the Confessions. In other words, this Article in large measure is a confession of faith in other confessions of faith. Instead of confessing faith in the content and meaning of our faith, we confess faith in the instruments through which our faith is revealed and instructed."

"The second problem I see," I went on, "in the synonymous use of words which speak of the Bible on the one hand and the Word of God on the other, is that which arises when we reverse the sentence and say, 'The Word of God is the canonical books of the Old and New Testaments as a whole and in all their parts.' I believe it is not Lutheran or biblical to limit the Word of God to the status of being the same as the books of the Bible."

I continued by saying that I believed the Word of God also to be the person and work of Jesus Christ, and that the preached and the sacramental word are also the Word of God. I also said I could not accept the idea that the Bible is inerrant unless the word simply means that the Bible is the faithful witness to God's truth.

My statement was not well received by some who read it. Dr. Schiotz met with me and explained how the statement in the Constitution had been adopted after much discussion, and that anything less or other than saying the Bible is inerrant would have meant the end of the merger discussions. I can't remember that there ever was a resolution of our differences on this matter, except that I was told that my election to the position of executive director would stand. I was installed with other newly elected executives in January, 1961.

At the time of the formation of The American Lutheran Church, Norman Fintel, director of admissions at Wartburg College, was appointed assistant executive director of the Board of College Education. My title became executive director instead of executive secretary. We became well acquainted with Norm and his wife Jo, visited frequently as families and were often in each other's homes. He was an efficient and cooperative staff member, and succeeded me when I went to St. Olaf in 1963. He later accepted the presidency of Roanoke College in Salem, Virginia, and remained in that position until his retirement.

Shortly after the merger, Dr. Loren Halvorson, then pastor of Victory Lutheran Church in Minneapolis, became the second assistant on our staff. He was a specialist in conferences and ministry of the laity. He was an enthusiastic and provocative renewer for the church, sometimes criticized for his non-traditional ways, but effective as an encourager of adult programs and congregational renewal efforts. He later went on to a professorship at Luther Northwestern Theological Seminary. He and his wife Ruth were also good friends and appreciated associates. Ruth had been a student in my classes at Concordia.

As a result of the 1961 merger, I gained more clients. Capital University was viewed by the former ALC as its flagship institution. It was the oldest, and was located in the city where its church's headquarters were. It shared a campus and some facilities with a seminary. Its president, Dr. Harold Yochum, was a man of culture and dignity who had the respect of his colleagues and his church constituency. Capital was efficiently run, reflecting the emphasis of its parent church on balanced budgets and controlled growth.

Wartburg College was a bit different. Dr. Conrad Becker, the president, was a dedicated, quiet, persistent man. His board gave him problems. It was large, and composed of people who seemed to see their roles as either doctrinal or financial watchdogs. I always had the feeling that Connie Becker was under siege, but he was gracious and always a gentleman. Wartburg was the result of a merger of several institutions with varied backgrounds academically. These had been a normal school, a pre–sem type of college and a junior college. Since the 1930 merger creating the American Lutheran Church, Wartburg had been seeking its identity, and I believe in the 1950's and 1960's had not yet found it.

Texas Lutheran College was also the result of mergers. Three former junior colleges were represented in its history. It had been a senior college for about twenty years when I started going there. The president when I arrived on the scene was Ed Sagebiel, a Seguin businessman who had taken on the job at the persuasion of the board, more or less as a fill–in. He was soon succeeded by Marcus Rieke, formerly the youth director of the ALC, an enthusiast and natural leader. He gave the college several good years but died quite young. Texas Lutheran was just beginning a period of growth and effectiveness at the time I made my visits there.

Dana, the only college of the UELC, was located in Blair, Nebraska. The president, Dr. C. Clifford Madsen, was a soft–spoken, scholarly former professor of theology. He was a congenial and cooperative partner in the work. Dana College was struggling to maintain enrollment and to achieve fiscal stability. The college was eager to avail itself of the assistance of a church board of education.

In my new position, from 1961 to 1963, I found plenty to do as we tried to mesh the practices and traditions of the various colleges. Norman Fintel and Loren Halvorson were excellent assistants, as were the other staff members who were with us for longer or shorter periods of time.

Chapter 12

A TIME OF TRANSITION

During those years in Minneapolis, our family experienced some milestones and special events. Peter and Mary were confirmed in Bethlehem Lutheran Church, and both graduated from Washburn High School, Peter in 1962 and Mary in 1963. After high school graduation, Peter enrolled at St. Olaf, and the following year Mary entered Concordia. Perhaps as important as those events was the fact that the children got their drivers' licenses. We remained a one–car family, but when each of the children became licensed we had another set of car keys made. Each of us had a claim on the car. We never had serious trouble with this arrangement, even though occasionally there was some disagreement as to who should have it at a certain time.

My Aunt Nell lived in St. Paul, and we saw her frequently. Several of Dorothy's relatives also lived in the Twin Cities area, and we spent many special times with them. Pearl and Carl Olson, Dorothy's aunt and uncle, lived here, as did their daughter Elaine (Lanny), her husband Orv Seal and their five sons. Carl and Pearl's son Dr. Kent Olson and his wife Pat were in the city. My brother Lyman his wife Helen and their son Robert (Corky) also lived in Minneapolis. Lyman was a furniture buyer for Gamble Stores. We saw them occasionally, but were more often with Dorothy's relatives for times such as Thanksgiving, Christmas and birthdays.

Peter and Mary had many friends among their schoolmates. They seemed to be very good at finding things with which to be busy. They did well in school and required very little prodding by us to get their work done.

Dorothy developed numerous relationships with members of Bethlehem Church and persons working with me. She was active in church affairs, and at one time was asked to be a candidate for the presidency of the American Lutheran Church Women. She declined and was glad she did, because soon afterward we moved to Northfield and she found herself quite busy as the wife of a college president.

My work required a good deal of travel, because it was necessary to visit the colleges, attend board meetings and appear at church conventions. I shall always be grateful to Dorothy, Peter and Mary for not making an issue of that. I will probably never know how my absences may have affected them. I'm afraid I was so intent on doing my job that I didn't reflect much on what that might have meant in our family life. Whenever Dorothy and I talked about it, and we did do that, she was supportive of what I was doing and urged me to continue.

In the summer of 1962, an unusual opportunity was presented to Dorothy and me. Dr. Loren Halvorson, who had been in Europe during the post–World War II period working in ecumenical efforts, suggested to me one day that he would like to recommend me for the position of tutor at the annual five–month theological study term of the World Council of Churches Ecumenical Institute at Bossey, Switzerland. That sounded like a great idea, but could it be done? He did recommend me, and I was chosen. The Board of College Education granted me a leave of absence with salary, and we made plans to be in Switzerland from October 1, 1962, until March 1, 1963.

A few months before we were to go to Bossey, Dorothy surprised us all one day by finding a job as a counselor at an employment agency. None of the rest of the family knew about it until she announced it at dinner one evening. She explained that she had decided she would like to find a way to increase the family's income as a contribution to the costs involved with our going to Bossey. Peter, Mary and I all objected, saying she shouldn't feel obligated to do that. I may have practiced a bit of male chauvinism at that point. On the other hand, I was very much aware that Dorothy had a high blood pressure condition and that extra obligations tended to give problems. I thought a regular job would complicate matters for her. She turned the job down. So much for women's lib in 1962.

Peter and Mary were supportive of the Bossey opportunity. Peter had entered St. Olaf in the fall of 1962, and Mary was a senior at Washburn High School. As things worked out, a newly married couple, Elsa and Jim Hammond, agreed to live in our house with Mary while we were away. Elsa was the daughter of missionaries in South Africa, and had been a student at Waldorf College while we were there. She had become a nurse and had married Jim, whom she met while he was a patient in a Minneapolis hospital following an automobile accident.

So off to Bossey we went. It was the first trip to Europe for Dorothy and me. I flew to Geneva, and she chose to sail to London on the *Queen Mary* and then take a train to Geneva after some sightseeing in London. Two weeks after

I arrived, I returned to attend the biennial convention of the ALC in Milwaukee. That was a notable occasion, both because it was the first convention of the new church, and because the Cuban missile crisis occurred while the convention was in session. I remember wondering what would happen if war broke out, with Dorothy in Geneva and me in Milwaukee. Fortunately, the crisis was soon over when the Soviets removed missile silos from Cuba. Later, back at Bossey, we had an evening discussion regarding the Cuba events, and most of the persons there, Americans and others, expressed the thought that the United States had overstepped its rights in blockading Cuba. I spoke for moderation, claiming we didn't know all the facts, but basically defending the actions of President Kennedy as necessary in the circumstances.

I returned from Milwaukee later in October and we settled in for an enjoyable winter stay. Bossey is a conference center owned and operated by the World Council of Churches. It is located in a rural setting about fifteen miles east of Geneva, near Lake Geneva and on the outskirts of the small village of Celigny.

In 1962, Bossey consisted of the original chateau, a second chateau on an adjoining property, and a lecture hall, dining room and chapel which had been added to the older building. The main chateau housed offices, a small library, a common room, a conference room and several rooms for students. The second chateau, about a block away, housed students and provided a two–room apartment which we occupied. We ate all our meals with the students and staff.

The original Bossey property had been purchased and given to the World Council by the Rockefellers. Since 1962, a new library building, including a lecture hall and conference rooms, has been added.

My responsibilities were to counsel with students, lead in some worship services and give a few lectures. Forty students from more than twenty countries were enrolled. All had studied theology and could enroll in the Bossey term for credit at the University of Geneva. The semester had a theme, "Evangelism," and many of the lectures and several of the Bible studies explored that theme. Lectures were given by various theologians, some who were regular staff members and others who were visitors. Dr. Emil Brunner gave two lectures and participated in a discussion session one day.

Another day we all boarded the train and went to Basel, where we spent about three hours with Karl Barth. These were memorable occasions because I had read some of the writings of these men, and knew the influence they were having on theology everywhere. Incidentally, on the trip to Basel I learned what a Swiss lunch was. We were all given bags of food to eat on the train. Each bag included a piece of hard French bread, a piece of cheese, a chocolate bar and an apple. A sandwich was made by splitting the French bread and placing the cheese and the candy bar between the pieces. Quite a lunch.

We visited Geneva on several occasions, and also took trips to nearby Lausanne and Zurich. We celebrated Thanksgiving with our friends, Walt and Doris Schnackenberg from Pacific Lutheran, who were spending a year's leave at Heidelberg. The trip to Heidelberg took us through the Black Forest, Freiburg, Karlsruhe and Frankfurt.

Our travels were facilitated by the purchase of a Mercedes 190 before going to Switzerland. We picked it up at the factory at Stuttgart after our arrival. Peter was responsible for our doing that. We had been driving a Chevrolet, and Peter investigated the market to discover that we could trade in the Chevrolet, drive a Mercedes in Europe for several months, bring it back to the United States, and in the process spend about the same amount as for a new Chevrolet. That's the way it worked out. We bought a four–door sedan, covered the insurance while driving it in Europe, and paid $145 to have it shipped to the United States — all for $2,650. We drove the car until 1967, when we gave it to Peter and Nancy to take back to Germany where Peter was stationed in the service. They brought it back to the United States and finally sold it for $500 when it had 104,000 miles on it.

The Bossey experience was a positive one in every way. We associated with people from many cultures, we learned how the church functioned in other parts of the world, and we learned to appreciate various approaches to the Christian faith. Dorothy and I agreed that it was a true growing experience for us. I will always be grateful to Loren Halvorson for taking the initiative to get us the appointment.

We arranged to have Peter and Mary visit us in December. As soon as they had arrived and we had deposited their luggage in our rooms, we headed for a small restaurant in Celigny which specialized in "Fondue Bossey." This was a true Swiss cheese fondue, served with crusty bread and a glass of wine. Peter reminds me that this was the first time that we partook of any alcoholic beverage together as a family. When in Switzerland, do as the Swiss do!

We travelled to Rome for Christmas, where we visited Dorothy's cousin Barbara Boerger and her husband Frank, who was stationed in the Army there. They had a new addition to their family, and I had the privilege of baptizing her. She was given the name Patricia.

On the way to Rome, we drove through Avignon and Marseilles and along the Riviera. We stopped at La Spezia in Italy for dinner, and drove from there to Pisa on a winding mountain highway through a rainstorm. At Pisa we found the California Motel, where we stayed. The next morning the proprietor told us he had lived in the United States for several years, and so gave his motel an American name. We visited the leaning tower, of course. In Rome, we saw some of the famous sites — the Forum, the Coliseum, Trevi Fountain and St. Peter's. St. Peter's was impressive in many ways. It was then being readied for the Vatican Council.

On the return journey, we went through the Alps and central Switzerland, then on to Bossey. A few days later we again took off, this time to the north. We drove through southern Germany and into France. Our destination was Paris, where we spent New Year's Eve attending the Comic Opera. Late that night, Peter and Mary boarded the train for London, and Dorothy and I returned to Bossey the next day. Peter and Mary spent two days in London before flying home.

About two weeks before we were to leave Bossey, I drove our car to Rotterdam where we had made arrangements to have it shipped. When we returned to the United States in late February, 1963, we picked it up in Philadelphia and drove home to Minneapolis.

We brought back from Switzerland many fine memories, and also a fruit salad recipe which included wine as one of the ingredients. One day when we entertained the members of the Board of College Education at our home, Dorothy served that fruit salad, and it made a big hit with everyone. Of course they remained ignorant of the secret ingredient, which was not customarily a part of fruit salad served at church gatherings.

During the seven years I worked in Minneapolis, I received several inquiries about other positions. In 1962, when Dr. Eastvold resigned as president of Pacific Lutheran University, members of the board there urged me to permit them to elect me president. I declined, believing I had been too close to events at the university to be able to step in as president. Also in 1962, I was asked by the trustees of Augsburg College, not yet a college of the ALC, to be a candidate for the presidency there, but I also declined that offer.

On June 1, 1962, I was elected president of Luther College in Decorah, an action formalized by a letter of call, and publicized by a news release. However, in April, I had told a committee of the Luther board that I was not in a position to consider the presidency, and shortly after June first I declined. I had been quite close to the internal difficulties involving the Religion Department at Luther. I would not have been comfortable moving in to succeed Dr. Ylvisaker.

In early 1963, I had several weeks of discussion with representatives of the newly–formed California Lutheran College, which was jointly sponsored by the ALC and the LCA. In March, I notified Dr. Carl Segerhammer, chairman of its Board of Regents, and Dr. Gaylerd Falde, president of the California District of the church, that I should not be considered a candidate for the presidency of CLC. If there ever was a place where I had been close to the problems of the institution, it was there. I had not always agreed with Dr. Orville Dahl's recommendations as the college was begun; in fact, I had openly opposed some of the decisions taken. As a representative of one of the supporting churches, I had felt I must speak my mind. I was convinced the founders were moving too fast in wanting to start the college. For me to succeed the founding president would have been, in my mind, a mistake both for me and for the college. Now, after more than thirty years of history, California Lutheran University, as it is now known, is doing well, and I am glad for that.

Any of the positions I was offered would have given me the opportunity to grow professionally. All presented challenges and problems of a different magnitude than I had experienced at Waldorf. While I couldn't feel right about the possibility of accepting any one of them, I was compelled to think that perhaps I should consider moving on from my position with the church board. Maybe I was softened up by the time I was approached by St. Olaf. At any rate, the result was different.

In the summer of 1962, Clem Granskou had notified the St. Olaf board that he was ready to retire and would step aside as soon as a successor was found. This was not publicly announced, but I knew of it because I had been meeting with the St. Olaf board. In fact, the board had authorized its executive committee to proceed with a search for the new president. A search committee had been chosen, which included members of the board and of the faculty. Mr. H.P. Skoglund, chairman of the board, and Dr. Harold Ditmanson, professor of Religion, were the key members of the committee.

One day soon after our return from Bossey, I was at St. Olaf College in the course of my board duties. In visiting with Vice President David Johnson, I inquired how the search for a president was coming. Dave said he didn't know, but he had the impression that not much had happened. We agreed that with H.P. Skoglund in charge, things would happen according to his schedule.

Some time later, in early June, Mr. Skoglund invited me to lunch at the Minneapolis Club. Dr. Ditmanson was with him. We had hardly seated ourselves when Skog said, "Sid, we want you to be the president of St. Olaf." He then asked Dit to say something about how the decision had been made. It seems that the faculty members involved on the search committee had discussed various candidates, and that there was general agreement that they favored me over others. Skog said my election by the board was assured. Then he turned to me and said, "Sid, if you will come to St. Olaf, Margaret and I will build for the college the finest gymnasium on any college campus in the country." "Do you really mean that?" I asked. "Yes, sir," Skog said, "will you shake on it?" We shook hands, and I was destined to be the president of St. Olaf.

I went home and shared the news with the family. "Do I have to go to St. Olaf now?" Mary asked. No, we assured her; she could go to Concordia as planned. She started there in the fall of 1963.

Dorothy and I had talked about St. Olaf. Some friends had suggested to me earlier that I would be a candidate for that presidency, but I had not taken such suggestions too seriously. One dare not do that! But I must admit that I had long thought that St. Olaf was an excellent college, and that to be connected with it would be a privilege.

Skog carried through with his promise that I would be elected. On July 8, 1963, Dorothy and I drove to Northfield, entered the St. Olaf Center by the lower level loading dock, and went upstairs through the kitchen area to the hall near the Kings' Dining Room. At two o'clock, according to previous arrangement, we were ushered down the long hall to the Fireside Lounge where the Board of Regents and many members of the college staff were gathered. Mr. Skoglund introduced me as the new president of the college. We were warmly greeted by many people. A new chapter in our lives had begun.

Before leaving Minneapolis, I supervised the sorting of files in my office. Many records, some from ELC days, were sent to the archives at Luther Seminary. Norman Fintel was elected to succeed me. Our families had been close while we worked together, and that friendship was to continue.

In thinking about the move to St. Olaf, I am reminded of many things. One is how fortunate and truly blessed I have been. Few persons have had the privilege of serving in as many responsible positions as I have. I have been a pastor, a faculty member in one of the church's colleges, a church administrator, and the president of four church colleges, two in my career and two in retirement. I have continually been grateful to God for the way my life has been ordered and enriched. One day while I was a high school student in Fergus Falls, Pastor S.L. Tallakson of First English Lutheran Church, and a longtime friend of our family, said to me that when he thought of me without a father, but with a caring and able mother, he was reminded of the words in Psalm 16, "The lines are fallen unto me in pleasant places; yea, I have a goodly heritage." I have never forgotten that, and I heartily agree. I have worked hard, I have tried to be faithful in whatever task has been mine, but I can only say that it is the overwhelming grace of God that has guided my life.

In August of 1963, we moved to Northfield and into the president's residence at 1308 St. Olaf Avenue. It was a house built in 1920 while Lars Boe was president. It had been well cared for, and the college had provided new furniture for the living and dining rooms, two quite spacious areas which our furniture from Minneapolis would not have served very well. I was to be paid $18,000 per year, plus housing. In addition, I was to have the use of a college–owned car. I felt rich; my salary at the church office had been $12,000 per year, and we provided our own housing.

While speaking of money, I must report more fully. After all, money has played a fairly important role in my life. While a concern for money has not controlled me, I believe I have been quite aware of what money can and cannot do.

After Peter and Mary were born, Dorothy and I realized that, while we were always getting by, we also were not doing much in the way of saving or planning for the future. On the other hand, most of my moves had meant an improvement in our finances, so we seemed to live knowing that somehow the future would be taken care of. I remember Mother cutting corners and being thrifty. I don't believe I ever thought my life would be much different. Through childhood, I had enjoyed managing my own money. Income from Moen's Lumber Yard kept me solvent for several years. My first regular, fulltime job at O'Meara's in Fergus Falls had enabled me to live and to save money for college.

The move I had made from Nashwauk to Moorhead had not meant much change in income. The move from Concordia to Waldorf changed our income from $3,900 per year to $4,000 plus housing, a fairly good raise. When I went to Minneapolis, I received $9,000 per year, and my salary increased while there to $12,000. Then at St. Olaf, I started at $18,000 plus house, and through the years experienced increases which brought me to $60,000 per year plus house when I left in 1980.

A part of the arrangement at St. Olaf also included a tuition benefit for faculty children. Peter received a discount of seventy–five percent of the tuition and fee portion of the annual charge. Mary also received a discount at Concordia because of an exchange agreement among the colleges of the church.

When I entered the ministry in 1943, I entered the pension plan of the church. The congregation and I shared the premium cost, which I believe at that time was an amount equal to five percent of salary. When we went to Concordia, the college had no retirement program for faculty, so I kept my pension plan membership by paying a small amount annually. In 1947, Concordia joined the Teachers Insurance and Annuity program (TIAA), and I became a part of that. The college and the participant each paid an amount equal to five percent of salary. I then dropped out of the church plan for several years, because at Waldorf I continued in TIAA. The church Board of Christian Education required that I be a member of the church pension plan, so in 1956 I rejoined that and dropped my TIAA participation. When I went to St. Olaf, I continued in the church plan, and by that time the practice had changed so that the employer paid the entire amount. That meant I could again start paying into TIAA on my own, and this I did. I was involved with both plans until my retirement.

In addition, at the time I retired from St. Olaf, the college generously offered me a one–year terminal leave at full salary. Instead of taking that as salary, I agreed to have a trust fund set up and managed by the college in such a way that each year after retirement I would receive an amount equal to ten percent of the balance in the fund. The college has invested wisely, and the fund has grown through the years, even though we have received our payments. The trust is set up so that the payment will be made as long as either of us survives. I must say I have fared well financially as well as in other ways during my professional life.

The move to Northfield came at an appropriate time in our lives. With Peter already away from home, and Mary about to leave for college, our family had entered a new phase.

A PLACE CALLED MANITOU

1963–1980

Chapter 13

ANOTHER BEGINNING

Manitou seems like a strange name for the location of a college with Christian connections. However, that name had been given earlier to the promontory lying a mile west of downtown Northfield, no doubt inspired by the idea of the presence of the Great Spirit of the Native Americans. Enterprising Norwegians were not to be deterred if a beautiful setting had been associated with the god of another ethnic tradition. Besides, they had dealt earlier with places associated with Odin and Thor, with trolls and nisse.

I was forty–seven years old when we moved to Northfield. I remember wondering at the time if St. Olaf would be my last job. We had moved every few years since Dorothy and I had been married, and I believe both of us thought it would be nice to stay put for a longer period of time. Of course, being elected to a six–year term, I didn't share with others the hope that it would last longer.

When I became president of St. Olaf, the college was widely recognized as a quality institution. That fact was certainly a major attraction for me. More than some church–related colleges, St. Olaf had been able to maintain a visible and positive connection with the church while it grew in academic stature and reputation. I considered it an honor to be its president.

In the foreword I later wrote for Joseph Shaw's centennial history of St. Olaf, I stated:

> "My first conscious recollection of St. Olaf has to do with
> Carleton College! After graduation from high school in 1933, I
> received notice that I was the recipient of a scholarship at Carleton
> worth a semester's tuition. No such inducement came from St. Olaf,
> and I remember wondering about that. I later decided to matriculate at
> Concordia College, located only thirty–five miles from my home in
> western Minnesota. My arrival at St. Olaf was delayed for thirty years.
> By then the inducements were different, but led to what has now been a
> decade of satisfying association for me."
>
> (*History of St. Olaf College, 1874–1974,* p. ix)

My first official contact with St. Olaf had taken place in October, 1948, when I spoke in chapel during a meeting of the Association of Lutheran College Faculties. I don't remember what I said, and I don't expect anyone else does, either.

During the years I was with the boards of the church, I had visited St. Olaf regularly. I had attended meetings of the Board of Regents and of the faculty. Dorothy and I knew several members of the faculty, and had visited in the homes of quite a few of them. We arrived at St. Olaf in 1963 with considerable background knowledge of our new home and place of work.

The house into which we moved in Northfield was at 1308 St. Olaf Avenue, at the foot of the campus hill. From there to my office was a leisurely ten minute walk, including eighty–four steps up the hill. I got my daily exercise when I walked to the office. The house had been the home of the president's family since it was built in 1920 while Dr. Boe was in office. It is a story–and–a–half frame and stucco structure painted white. Since 1977, it has been a residence for students.

The first floor of the house included a large living room with fireplace, a dining room, kitchen, study, half bath, and a small room off the living room which became Dorothy's study and a TV room. On the second floor were four bedrooms and a bathroom. The basement provided a finished room with a fireplace, a laundry, furnace room and bathroom. What was lacking was a garage. Until 1968. when the college purchased the St. John's parsonage next door for student housing, we kept both our car and the college car in the driveway. The parsonage property included a detached garage, which after 1968 accommodated our car. Meanwhile, the college car remained outside; in the winter we plugged it in and cleared it of snow and ice whenever necessary.

Peter roomed in a dormitory and Mary was at Concordia, so the rooms assigned to them were not used regularly.

The house became a busy place. We entertained faculty and staff in groups of forty or fifty, and students in smaller groups. The college provided a person to assist with cleaning, and also took care of the maintenance of the house and yard, including repairs, snow shoveling, lawn mowing, screen and storm window changes, and such chores. I've often said that after seventeen years of that kind of treatment at the college, I was not of a mind to revert to being my own custodian, so in 1981, when Lois and I moved into our condominium in Minneapolis, we were glad that similar services were provided there.

I was inaugurated as the sixth president of St. Olaf College on September 16, 1963, a mild and sunny day. The ceremony was held on Manitou Field where football games and commencements were the regular events. The inauguration took the place of the annual opening convocation, a ceremony normally held in Boe Chapel.

Dr. Fredrik Schiotz, president of The American Lutheran Church and a St. Olaf alumnus, officiated at the inauguration. Dr. Harold Ditmanson, professor of Religion and "Mr. St. Olaf" to many people, gave the address. He had been chairman of the faculty committee which advised the board on the selection of a new president. He was my good friend, and I had suggested him as the speaker for the day. The inaugural is well described by Dr. Shaw in his history of the college. He has also told the story of my St. Olaf years in most complimentary terms.

My part in the inauguration was limited to a brief response following my induction. I received a medallion of office to be worn about the neck. In my remarks, I pointed out that the sign of office is not a mace or a scepter, symbols of authority, but a yoke to remind its wearer that the presidential office is one of service. I went on to state my creed "for working in this place:"

"I believe in God, present, powerful, kind and good,
known best to me in the life and world–redeeming
work of One who is called His Son, my brother,
Jesus Christ.

"I believe in people, the finest work of God in
this world, capable of desperate, evil things,
but also capable of greatness and contributions
of good to the lives of others.

"I believe in education by which men and women are
able to become what they are meant to be, wise
and committed to truth.

"I believe in work, hard work.
I believe there is no good life apart from work.

"I believe in the future. And I believe the future
is brightest in the care of well–educated and
dedicated young men and women.

"I believe in St. Olaf College. And I believe it
must ever be a community of those who together
seek to enrich the lives of one another and
leave this a better world."

The inauguration day ended with a dinner and a program of greetings. It was an exhilarating and wonderful time for the Rands.

The presence of family and special friends enriched the day. Lyman and Helen, Charlotte and Francis came. The Serkland cousins were there, as was Aunt Nell. Some of Dorothy's relatives were also with us: Al and Inez Torgerson, Lannie and Orv Seal, Kent and Pat Olson and Carl Olson. I thought how wonderful it would have been had Mother lived to see that day. Lannie Seal said she wished her mother Pearl could have lived to be there, also. Pearl was a great fan of St. Olaf, and she was the kind who would have reveled in the realization that her niece was the first lady of St. Olaf. Among the many friends who came were Walt and Lois Ekeren.

My office was in the Administration Building at the edge of the campus. It was connected with the St. Olaf Center and built at the same time. It had been completed in 1960, so I thought of it as a new building. The office consisted of a large room for me with an adjoining room for my secretary, Solveig Steendal, and Bonita Parker, David Johnson's secretary.

Solveig Steendal had been at the college for several years and was highly regarded by everyone on campus. She was efficient, patient, personable and understanding. She knew how to meet and deal with people whether on the telephone or in person, and she was skillful at protecting the president from unnecessary interruptions.

Before I came to St. Olaf, but after I had been elected, I made an appointment to talk with Solveig. I knew her good reputation, and I had decided I would like her to stay on. So I told her I had checked her out and found only good things. I asked her to continue. "But," I said, "before you give me an answer, you may want to check on me to see if you would like to work with me." Her immediate reply was, "I have, and I would like to stay." We got along fine as long as I was president, and Solveig stayed on to serve also during Harlan Foss's term. She retired in 1988, three years into the presidency of Mel George.

I believe in an open door policy, and announced that on campus. I encouraged people to come to see me whether they had a problem or not. Many did, and they helped me learn about the college and its people. I also made it a habit to go to coffee in the Kings' Room both morning and afternoon unless something interfered. While I like coffee, I also enjoyed that opportunity to meet and visit with college personnel, some of whom I seldom met with otherwise.

When I arrived at St. Olaf, there was a sink, refrigerator and coffee service in a small closet attached to Solveig's office. She and I agreed to remove those facilities, partly to gain additional storage space, but also to make it necessary for me to walk to the Center for coffee.

When I took office, there were three vice presidents at the college. Dr. Orin

Lofthus was dean of the college and vice president; David Johnson was vice president with a portfolio that included public relations, fundraising, radio station WCAL and alumni relations; and Maurice Knutson was vice president and treasurer.

I decided to call the three vice presidents and myself the Staff Council. We met regularly, usually once a week, to plan and coordinate college affairs. I also created a President's Council composed of the vice presidents and the chairmen of the faculty divisions. That group met on call, discussed overall college policy and made recommendations to me for change. It is interesting to note that in the 1970's the President's Council became less and less effective. The reason probably was a desire on the part of the faculty as a whole to exercise more direct control over academic affairs and college planning. The 60's had produced a wave of interest in "participatory democracy," implying that everyone on campus should somehow have a say in decisions affecting the college.

Not long after I arrived, it became apparent to me that Maurice Knutson was unhappy with our procedure of consulting together in the Staff Council. He had been a businessman most of his adult life, and was accustomed to acting unilaterally in matters for which he was responsible. He was, in a sense, the exact opposite of participatory democracy in his view of how a college ought to operate. I finally found it necessary to accept his resignation, which he had threatened to offer several times as a way to convince me that he must do his work in his own way. I appointed Stan Ness to succeed him. Stan was a hard–working veteran of the college staff and a jovial, cooperative colleague. Maurice Knutson returned to his business enterprises in Wyoming, but also became a consultant to several Lutheran colleges. I believe he was helpful to them in analyzing and strengthening the financial aspects of their operations.

I also accepted the resignation of Orin Lofthus, believing a change was in order to enliven the academic side of things. Albert Finholt, professor of chemistry, became dean and served for seven years. He had been a leader in the study that had produced the 4–1–4 calendar and curriculum change which went into effect in the fall of 1964, and later was to be one of the founders of the Paracollege.

The way had been cleared for me to make changes in staff positions because, prior to my coming, the Board of Regents had adopted a resolution which stated that when a new president took office all vice presidents were to submit their resignations. I saw that as a commendable action. While the vice presidents were elected to two–year terms, it nevertheless provided a way to clear the decks if a new president preferred not to wait to make changes until those terms expired.

There was considerable interest in strengthening the student affairs office. It was a responsibility of the dean of the college, with a dean of men and a dean of women in charge. Soon after Dr. Finholt became dean of the college, we decided to appoint a fourth vice president who would be dean of students. We selected Henry Helgen, a St. Olaf alumnus, who came to us from the student counseling staff of Dartmouth College.

I began my meetings with the faculty by announcing that, with the exception of the opening meeting each fall, I intended to limit the length of each monthly session to one hour. That announcement surprised some faculty members and horrified others. After all, there were those on the St. Olaf faculty, as there would be at any college, who believed unlimited debate was the key to successful determination of college policy. We did invoke the time limit, and it worked well. We even had some thirty– and forty–minute meetings. We adopted a motion stating that, if there was apparent need for an extension of time, the faculty would have to vote to do it each time. A few occasions in the famous late 60's required such an extension.

The first faculty meeting at which I presided, in September, 1963, had before it the report from a committee which had studied the possible radical change of the whole curriculum. The report recommended that we adopt a 4–1–4 calendar, which meant two terms of fourteen weeks each, and, between them in the month of January, a term of four weeks. The 4–1–4 meant that the student would normally take four courses in each of the fourteen–week terms and one course in the short term, which was called the Interim. The plan further called for a revision of all courses so that each would have equal credit value, thus getting rid of the one–, two–, three–, and four–hour variations which had persisted in the traditional semester system. After several hours of debate, the faculty voted, by an overwhelming majority, to adopt the recommendations, and as of September, 1964, the new plan went into effect. I was convinced it was a healthy change for the college. It has continued now for three decades, much longer than most such curriculum–calendar plans. It is not surprising to me that the college has recently adopted a major revision of the curriculum, but has kept the 4–1–4 calendar.

Academic packaging does not in itself assure quality education. A change may stimulate new life in courses which have become trite or stale, but it takes good people to make any program work well. So from the start I stressed the importance of recruiting the best possible people for both faculty and administrative positions. I made it a practice to interview every candidate personally. I looked upon it as my responsibility to guarantee, insofar as possible, the continuation of a strong academic program and a healthy relationship with the church. Dr. Granskou used to say, "A college lives by its appointments." I believe this to be true. The college is only as strong as those who are in charge of its day–by–day activity.

Chapter 14

AROUND THE CLOCK

The academic world lives its life in convenient annual cycles. The September to May pace and order are different from the routine of the summer months. In addition, vacation times during the school year offer variation in the way life is lived. It is not difficult to fall into the rhythm of such a calendar, although there are those who prefer the eight–to–five, five–days–a–week routine with one annual vacation. The academic calendar, in my experience, offers opportunity for reflection, planning and modification of working style which few other work environments do. There was always something exciting about the beginning and the end of a school year. Even though colleges have become more active in the summer with classes, conferences and other activities, it is still true that there is an interesting annual shift in working habits when June rolls around, and another when September comes.

Many of the activities in a college can best be understood in relation to this schedule. The college catalog, for example, is published in April. This means that faculty members must determine their offerings for the next school year shortly after the middle of the current one. Faculty appointments are normally made in the spring. The college budget must be ready for a board meeting which takes place several months before the beginning of the fiscal year during which it is effective. It is based upon the best guesses or informed judgment regarding enrollment prospects and the state of the economy. The college calendar records the dates for examinations, vacations and special college events, all of them determined more than a year in advance.

This means that the president must fit his schedule into whatever is the given routine of his institution. I tried to do this when I came to St. Olaf. Such things as fund–raising calls, alumni meetings, conventions, church responsibilities and personal vacations were scheduled in the best way possible, and it all seemed to work out quite well.

At St. Olaf I was a member of all twelve faculty committees. I decided early that I could not faithfully participate in all of them, so I chose to attend regularly the two I thought were most critical. These were the Curriculum and Educational Policies Committee and the Review and Planning Committee. The former dealt with courses, departmental affairs, off–campus programs, new departments or approaches to academic matters, student grading, and admissions and graduation requirements. The latter dealt with faculty personnel matters including tenure and promotion decisions, salary schedules and general college policies affecting the work of the faculty. Frequently there were interesting and determined debates in these committees, and I thought they often took more time to discuss and settle issues than should have been needed. Faculty members are specialists whose expertise is often seen by them to apply to fields beyond their scholarly accomplishments, and there is a tendency toward turf protection or empire building in college organization. No–one wants his or her department or course offerings to suffer setback or loss. Growth and increase in offerings are common goals for faculty members as they are for business people. I was an advocate of limiting the length of committee meetings as I had been for faculty meetings, but I succeeded only in part.

In the Staff Council, which was my own committee, we discussed and decided various administrative matters and shared information regarding our work. We conferred on the budget as prepared by Stan Ness, and gave advice freely to one another on every administrative area. The procedure was helpful to me, as it meant I had the benefit of the thinking of colleagues in whom I had confidence. It also meant I was kept abreast of what was going on generally, a necessity for a college president. One is sometimes in the dark regarding certain things, and needs continual briefing by staff members and others. I was fortunate to have Orin Lofthus, Al Finholt, Lloyd Svendsbye, Bill Nelsen and Harlan Foss successively as vice president and dean of the college; Maurice Knutson and then Stan Ness as vice president and treasurer; Hank Helgen as vice president and dean of students; and, certainly not least, Dave Johnson as vice president for college relations. Dave was the one I conferred with most. He had been at the college so long and knew so much about every aspect of its life that I found him a tremendous resource and a great help. He had also been a friend for many years, and, contrary to what many say regarding the danger of having friends together in a close working relationship, I found that we got along fine. Dave's knowledge of the college, and his experience in fund–raising and the management of investments, made him an extremely valuable partner in the work.

I spoke regularly in chapel and at other college occasions. My files bulge with copies of talks given at opening convocation, opening faculty meeting, parents day, alumni gatherings, college anniversaries and special observances. Copies of most of these are housed in the college archives. Someone has said that a college president is a person who is paid a generous salary for shaking hands and bringing greetings. I've enjoyed both of those reponsibilities, but I can assure everyone that there is a little more to the job than that.

I like to appear before a crowd. It's a challenge and opportunity I've always enjoyed. It gives me the chance to perform a bit, and there is enough of the ham in me so that I feel good about public speaking. As a college president, I appreciated the opportunity to be an emcee or to make impromptu remarks, and there were many occasions for both in my schedule. Many people have told me they have liked hearing me speak; thus, my ego has been fed sufficiently to cause me to continue and to feel I am fairly good at doing it. It may be in the genes. My mother told me that my father had relished being in similar roles and seemed to rise to the occasion whenever he was up in front.

With regard to hand–shaking and greeting people, I was fortunate that both Dorothy and Lois have been willing participants in that phase of the presidency as well as in many others. We would together shake hands with all the new students in the fall — up to 900 in an evening — and with hundreds of people at alumni gatherings, Christmas concert receptions, commencements and other events. Many people have commented to me that they appreciated the fact that the president's wife was a participant in college functions. A college such as St. Olaf has grown up with that kind of social interaction. More and more in recent times, the spouses of college presidents have their own careers, and, as a result, it becomes impossible or at least inconvenient for them to be involved in college affairs. I know that during my time at St. Olaf such involvement was an important, and I would say expected, part of college life. I appreciated the participation of Dorothy and Lois in those activities.

As I reflect on the social aspects of the presidency, I am reminded that the college enjoyed visits from many important and interesting people. None was more enjoyable and challenging to welcome to campus than Vice President Hubert H. Humphrey. He came to speak at commencement and was accompanied by an entourage of personal staff and secret service agents. We had received firm instructions as to how we were to entertain the Vice President and Mrs. Humphrey. I had corresponded with him and reminded him that the time for our commencement program was limited, and that we would appreciate a commencement address of not more than twenty minutes. This would hardly be adequate for a normal Humphrey address. About ten minutes into his talk, the Vice President looked up from his manuscript and out at the audience, and announced, "This is pretty good stuff, isn't it?" It made me wonder if he had seen the manuscript in advance. At any rate, he completed his address in nineteen minutes, and as he sat down next to me he said, "We did it!" At the conclusion of the program, he said, "We have time now to visit with the people. Let's go!" And he moved into the crowd while I stayed at his elbow as I had been instructed to do by the secret service. He was in his element.

There were, of course, off–campus activities which were significant in the conduct of the president's role, and which increased year by year. It was always necessary to ask which of these were important, and to avoid becoming too entangled in peripheral activities. I will tell a little more about these in the chapter titled "The College Is Everywhere."

There were problems to be dealt with. Some of them involved structural or procedural matters. The pressures to do more or to find more money while keeping a lid on expenses and student charges are a constant in college life.

Personnel problems also required attention. I was occasionally involved with student behavior, but most of those issues were taken care of by the student personnel deans. I was called upon to approve decisions they had made, rather than being the one to decide. However, I was often the one who heard from parents when there had been difficulty with a son or daughter. So I played the role of diplomat or explainer or arbitrator or peacemaker on several occasions. After Carol Johnson joined the staff in 1968 as Dean of Women (later to be Vice President and Dean of Students), she handled much of the direct counseling with students as well as meetings with parents. She was a capable and always cheerful college representative.

The personnel decisions which involved me the most were those related to faculty and staff. Sometimes a person would need to be terminated for poor performance or for unacceptable conduct. Such matters took time and patience. There were days when I felt more like a pastor or a counselor than anything else. Decisions regarding promotion or tenure of faculty members, or the appointment or reappointment of staff persons, often gave rise to problems that went beyond the life and career of one person. Department personnel or personal friends would often become involved, and matters would become sticky, to say the least. The president was often the court of last resort.

I've been grateful that, with a few exceptions, I have been able to be objective about decisions affecting the careers of other persons. It is never easy to tell a person that his or her work is not satisfactory, or that another kind of work would seem to be more suitable, or that age and its effects have begun to interfere with job effectiveness. Judgments regarding such situations are often called for, and the president is frequently the one both to decide and to inform the person involved. This was not my favorite activity.

I was elected to a six–year term as president in 1963 and re–elected for a second term in 1969. Prior to my re–election, I suggested to the Board of Regents that there should be an assessment of my work. The board chose a committee of faculty members to assist in an evaluation, but it didn't amount to much. I believe the board had no intention of doing anything other than re–electing me. When my second term was about to expire, I strongly urged a thorough evaluation of my work, and even suggested to the board that twelve years of a Rand administration might be enough. A somewhat more organized critique of my work than in 1969 resulted. Division chairpersons were consulted, and they, in turn, met with the faculty members in their divisions. The result was that there were negative observations regarding my work as well as positive ones. Some suggested that I had become more strict and inflexible as time went on, and that I was not as accessible as earlier. The board weighed these comments among others, and I was elected in 1975 to a third six–year term. When that term neared its end, I told the board that I definitely would not consider continuing. I would be sixty–five years old in 1981, and I had been a strong advocate of that being a proper retirement age. Some board members suggested that I could be re–elected and then resign before another term ran its course, something I did not agree to do. Life was made simpler for all of us when I was asked to accept appointment as United States Ambassador to Norway later in 1979. The board not only did not re–elect me, but graciously awarded me the last year of my third term as a leave with full salary.

The above indicates that I worked with a board which appreciated my work, and with whose members I got along well. They would frequently compliment me on my work both in formal meetings of the board and in personal contacts. Evidently I didn't accept those compliments as graciously as I should, because one day after a board meeting Daryle Feldmeir, an alumnus member of the board and editor of the *Chicago Daily News*, took me aside and said, "You know, Sid, you don't know how to take a compliment. Why don't you accept what we say about your work and not always try to deny it?" I've never forgotten that wise word.

The Board of Regents treated me in a most generous way. Under the leadership of H.P. Skoglund, Leonard Hoeft and Oscar Husby, the board operated on the principle that the president was in charge of the operation of the college, and the board was to be the policy maker and guardian of the institution's assets. The board operated with a minimum of committees and with four one–day meetings per year. It was a happy and productive relationship, as far as I could tell.

One example of the concern the board showed for me and my family was the fact that the subject of a new home for the president was brought up with some regularity, beginning not long after I arrived. I kept saying we needed a lot of other facilities more, and held them off until 1976, when Mr. Skoglund again brought the matter up. Soon a motion was passed that a house be built. At that point, Leonard Hoeft, owner of the Ziegler Company in Minneapolis and vice chairman of the board, spoke up. I had reminded the board that we had no money for a house. Mr. Hoeft said that the board had decided to build, so the board members should pay for the house. He said he would match dollar for dollar the gifts of other board members for this project, and would personally call on each board member for a gift. Within a few weeks, the cost of the house had been pledged in the amount of $300,000. Mr. Hoeft gave half of it.

The board recognized my work in another way after I left the college. A new dormitory was named Rand Hall. I have already made mention of the terminal leave arrangement the board voted for me, another indication of the generous way I was treated by St. Olaf.

I see these actions by a governing board as an indication of the quality of its membership. My working assumption has always been that a successful college needs a board whose members are committed to the purposes of the institution and are willing to invest their time, energy and resources in its program. That's the kind of board we had at St. Olaf.

It was a pleasure to work with the board. Before each meeting, I prepared an agenda which was mailed to the members a week or ten days in advance. Most board members studied the agenda before coming to the meeting, and that tended to make our discussions quite informed and probably briefer than might otherwise have been the case. Mr. Skoglund was always eager to get decisions made, and when he was chairman he saw to it that discussions were to the point and not extended.

The board elected five of its members to be the Executive Committee. That group met when necessary between plenary meetings, which occurred in March, May, August and December. Other committees were chosen as needed, but there never were many standing committees. During the 60's, the board decided to create two new standing committees, however: the Regent–Faculty Conference Committee and the Regent–Student Conference Committee. These groups usually met the evening before the board meetings in March, May and December, and provided opportunities for faculty members and students to have regular contact and conversation with board members. In addition, we had a faculty member and a student who met with the board as observers, and in the 70's a new position was created. A recent graduate was elected by the board to serve a two–year term as a regular voting member. That gave assurance that the voice of youth was being heard and taken seriously.

The Articles of Incorporation of St. Olaf state that the President is a member of the Board of Regents. I favor that principle because it means that the chief administrator of the college participates fully in all policy discussions and decisions. It was my experience that my being present in board meetings was welcomed by the other members, not least when matters of consequence required board decision. I also served as Secretary of the Board. While that was not prescribed by the Articles of Incorporation, I was glad to have the college follow that practice. It meant that Solveig Steendal, my assistant, was present at board meetings, and that she and I were responsible for producing the board minutes.

It is impossible to satisfy the desires of all campus groups for participation in the governance of a college. During the 60's, participatory democracy was the goal of many faculty members and students who believed that board members and administrators were removed from a true understanding of college life. The problem was, of course, that participatory democracy often meant that "no–one else can represent my views." As a result, unless every interested person was somehow directly a party to college policy decisions, the advocates of the principle were unhappy.

My position has been that while faculty members and students have ideas about the operation of the college that are worth consideration, it is impossible to merge all of them with those of the board responsible under the law for the governance of the institution. My goal was to try to listen carefully to all ideas, make use of all possible structures within the college to winnow and sort suggestions, and then to glean as many constructive ideas as possible to pass on to the board for its consideration. As long as I was president, certain people on campus regularly told me that their ideas never got a fair hearing. There were others, both faculty members and students, whose counsel was "to ignore all those folks and let the board make the policy decisions." A college is nothing if it is not a forum for the free exchange of ideas.

Members of the Board of Regents became friends as well as colleagues, and several invited us to their homes and made us feel welcome in their close circle of friends.

The Skoglunds often entertained us at their home and at the Minneapolis and Minikahda Clubs. I attended several Vikings football games as a guest of Mr. Skoglund, one of the team's owners. He also had me elected to the board of his business, North American Life and Casualty Company. Except for my time as ambassador, I remained a member until 1989, long after the sale of the company by Mr. Skoglund, and several years after his death. This position, by the way, paid an honorarium, and Mr. Skoglund insisted I accept it. I asked the board of the college if I should turn that in to St. Olaf in accord with my earlier decision not to accept such payments, but they endorsed his position. It was a few thousand dollars per year.

Mr. Husby took it upon himself to see that I got some exercise. He regularly organized tennis matches including David Johnson and others we could draft. Among them were Jennings Feroe, Hoover Grimsby and Ray Schweigert. That continued until 1989, when age seemed to suggest we call a halt. The Husbys also entertained at a board party for Lois and me before our marriage.

My experience tells me that the work of a college president can be pretty much what one chooses to make it. I have known presidents who spend most of their time in the office, and others who are hardly ever there. Some are chiefly fund–raisers, others are business managers, a few are academic leaders. Some write books!

I adopted the point of view that the president must do a little of everything if he or she is to serve the college best. The time of a college president is not entirely subject to personal scheduling. There are demands from students, faculty, administrators, alumni, parents of students, community organizations, educational groups, government agencies and, in the case of a college such as St. Olaf, the church. The day involves a balancing act as competing interests vie for attention.

I usually went to the office at 8:00 a.m. and tried to look at the mail and do some dictation before chapel, which was at 10:00. Sometimes we would have a Staff Council meeting first thing in the morning, even as early as 7:30 if there were several important issues to discuss.

Each day brought mail of all kinds. There were letters from friends of the college, often including gifts. There were also letters of criticism or recommendation. Much was routine business correspondence or mail that was unimportant, such as advertisements and solicitations. During the years I was at St. Olaf, the largest single increase in mail volume was in the area of advertisements of conferences. Holding a meeting is the chief sport of academics. Each ad made it seem that, if you didn't attend, your college would immediately fail. I ignored most of them.

My practice was to go through the mail as soon as it appeared on my desk. Solveig did some pre–sorting and referral to others, and that helped. I replied to letters as soon as possible, but I did follow one rule regarding letters of criticism or complaint. I would wait at least a day to reply, in order not to answer out of anger or uninformed reaction to what was said.

Following the Christmas Festival in 1965, I received a letter from a man in the Twin Cities who, together with his wife, had attended the concert in the old gym, which was the site of the Christmas Festival until the Christmas of 1967. The letter was a full–page, single–spaced, typed complaint relating this couple's experience coming to the concert without tickets and being told that they could look for a place to sit in the balcony. The balcony was a running track with slanted floors where temporary bleachers were placed for the Christmas Festival. It was of course less than ideal seating, but was the only way to accommodate the large numbers of people who wanted to see and hear the concert. My correspondent told of the difficulty in finding seating, the fact that his wife had snagged her hose on a sliver in the bleachers, that the temperature was uncomfortably warm, and that the orchestra had played off key!

My problem was how to answer such a letter. I replied, thanking the gentleman for writing, and then told him not to plan to come to the concert the next Christmas, but to wait until 1967, when we would have a new building. I told him that if he would write to me shortly before that concert, I would see that he got tickets on the main floor, and that he and his wife would sit in metal folding chairs, so there would be no danger of snagging hose. I went on to say that if he would let me know the cost of his wife's hose, we would send him a check. A few days later, I received a three–line reply. The man thanked me for my letter and added, "My wife told me I should never have sent my first letter."

Solveig and I had a simple way of taking care of correspondence. I did not use a machine, but she took oral dictation very quickly, and the important mail was done that way. Sometimes I would jot a brief reply on a letter received, and Solveig would put a response in proper form.

I have what may be called a fetish for a clean desk. This was aided by a rather large "out" drawer in my desk, regularly filled by me and emptied by Solveig, and by a good–sized round file which was usually quite full by day's end. I am remembered by many of my friends for my clean desk. I consider it a compliment to be so regarded, even though some have reminded me of the saying, "Clean desk; empty mind."

I have always been able to leave my work at the office and not let it monopolize my time at home. There were times, of course, when I took things home to catch up on reading or to do special preparations such as talks or sermons, but the bulk of the college business stayed at the office. I usually lost no sleep over college problems, but I must admit there were a few exceptions to that in the late 60's and early 70's when the Vietnam war brought all sorts of problems to the campus.

Chapel was scheduled for Monday through Friday mornings, and I tried to attend whenever I was on campus. It not only refreshed me as I worshiped and heard inspiring messages from colleagues, but I would often see and greet persons I did not regularly contact otherwise. After chapel I would usually have coffee in the Kings' Room or the Cage with faculty and administrators.

During the rest of the day I would meet with college personnel and visitors, and try to do whatever desk work presented itself. Some evenings were free, but often there would be meetings, concerts, athletic events, lectures or other programs. The job was demanding and certainly full–time, but I thrived on it.

There were aspects of the work I liked more than others. I especially enjoyed the one–on–one contacts with people. These included folks at the college, and others such as donors, business people in Northfield, associates in the work of higher education, and government officials. I enjoyed presiding at faculty meetings, speaking in chapel and experiencing the give and take in board meetings and Staff Council sessions. I enjoyed somewhat less the meetings of faculty and student committees, because it seemed to me that too often time and energy were wasted with posturing, partisan debate and side issues. But I realized that it wasn't what I enjoyed that should determine my activity. Every job I've known has involved aspects less rewarding than others. It's part of the process. It is interesting to observe, however, that many of us behave differently in a group than we do as individuals. Maybe we play up to others. Maybe we have egos to defend. For whatever reason, some of the nicest people are not at all pleasant to have on a committee.

While I had the background of teaching at Concordia, being president of Waldorf and administering a program for a church board, I realized when I came to St. Olaf that it would be good for me to broaden my horizons and learn something about college administration in a larger setting than I had known. So in the summer of 1964, I spent three weeks at Harvard University in a course designed for new college presidents. That proved to be a stimulating and altogether worthwhile experience. I rubbed shoulders with men and women from such places as Stanford, West Point, Franklin and Marshall, Emory, St. John's (Annapolis) and several state universities. We were exposed to the Harvard case study method, which gave opportunity for lots of debate and exchange of ideas. While not all the issues were new, there were enough angles and nuances regarding administration to keep one thinking for a long time. I took home with me many useful ideas.

A part of the routine of college life in our day is the need to gain and maintain accreditation for a variety of programs. This includes general accreditation by the regional group (in our case the North Central Association of Colleges and Secondary Schools) and recognition from the specialized accrediting groups in various fields where the college offers programs. For St. Olaf, this meant the National Council for the Accreditation of Teacher Education, the National Association of Schools of Music and the National Association of Schools of Nursing.

Each of those groups makes a visit every five to ten years, and prior to the visit massive amounts of information must be submitted to the agency. I suggested to the specialized groups that they should accept the material required by the North Central Association with regard to the college program in general, and then supplement it with specific information relevant to the area with which each was concerned. I failed to achieve anything along that line. Each group chose to start from the beginning, devising its own categories of information, and would accept nothing prepared for another group. This represents one of the problems of higher education. We are plagued by a certain provincialism which results in a kind of empire building among departments, interest groups and professional associations. Few of us are able to maintain the perspective that sees the education of students in some whole or unified manner. If not from a sound academic point of view, then on the basis of sheer efficiency and cost–saving, we should make changes such as I mention.

St. Olaf was successful in its various accrediting inspections while I was there. The programs were well organized and educationally sound, and were so recognized. I was glad of that and grateful to the many faculty members who did the good work. They prepared for accrediting visits and also maintained high quality in their daily work, which became the basis for favorable action by the accrediting agencies.

There is a bit of irony in all of this. In 1990, in my retirement, I was asked to serve on the National Architectural Accrediting Board. I accepted, and that put me on the other side of the fence. In 1995, I retired from that activity and must admit that my five years on an accrediting board have resulted in no revolutionary ways to do the job.

Chapter 15

GREAT PEOPLE

In *Christian Faith and the Liberal Arts*, I had written that "it is quite important to understand that the faculty is the indispensable heart of the college. Without teaching there is no college." (p. 78). Throughout my career I have been convinced that the successful college is one which has a faculty that is strong and has within it a sizeable contingent of outstanding teachers. By outstanding I mean persons who know their subject, enjoy teaching, relate well to students and are personally committed to the goals and program of the institution. The administration and support staff also need to be committed in the same way as they carry out their responsibilities. St. Olaf has been fortunate to have been served by many such committed and able persons through the years.

When I arrived in 1963, I knew that the day of outstanding faculty and staff was not over at St. Olaf. That's one reason I was interested in being connected with the college. I am fearful of trying to make a list; there are so many I should include, both from the past and from my period of service. However, several come to mind in connection with special events and experiences during my presidency.

The spirits of many well–remembered former faculty members were very much present on campus. One heard regularly of the significant contributions made to the life of the college by, for example, Ade Christenson, F. Melius Christiansen, E.O. Ellingson, P.M. Glasoe, Erik Hetle, Theodore Huggenvik, Karen Larsen, Agnes Larson, C.A. Mellby, Ella Hjertaas Roe and O.E. Rolvaag. It is interesting to observe that this list includes three persons in the sciences, two each in history and music, one each in religion and literature, one in physical education and athletics, and one in "everything." Doc Mellby, as everyone called him, taught Greek, Latin, sociology, philosophy and art at various times during his career. There are three women and eight men. Others of course could be included, but the significant thing to me is that this truly broad cross–section of disciplines (and, one might add, personalities) tells much about the strength of the St. Olaf tradition.

Administrators were also fondly remembered, and college myths and traditions clustered around them. There were Lars Boe, long–time president; P.O. Holland, his able business manager and assistant; Halvor Ytterboe, man of many talents as admissions officer, fund–raiser and teacher; P.G. Schmidt, loyal aide to Dr. Christiansen in building the choir tradition; Gertrude Hilleboe, long–time dean of women and instructor; Hank Thompson, dean of men; and Sam Bye, treasurer and manager of farms and livestock.

And one must not pass by John Berntsen. He retired shortly after I arrived, but left behind him a trail of stories connected with his work as director of physical plant, sometime campus security officer and counselor to everybody. One fall day he and I sat together in the bleachers watching a football game on Manitou Field. As we looked across to Thorson Hall and the grove of trees surrounding it, John said, "Not too many years ago there wasn't a tree there. I thought there should be, and I talked to Art Lee about it. He said there was no money to buy trees. So I went and bought some trees and planted them myself." Art Lee was the business manager and was properly concerned about college finances. That action by John Berntsen, however, was typical of the way he carried on his work. He was responsible in great measure for beginning the extensive tree–planting which continues on the campus to this day. He was truly a legend in his own time. I am glad to hear that a garden being developed on the campus is dedicated to him.

It was to be my good fortune to work with many who represented the same characteristics as the former greats. One day a senior came to my office to tell me how grateful he was for his St. Olaf education. He went on to say that the faculty member who had most influenced him was Harold Ditmanson. "I believe I am a Christian today because of Dr. Ditmanson," he said. "I came here intending to leave behind the connection I had with the church from my childhood, but Dr. Ditmanson's lectures changed all that." Dit, as he was called, was probably the most highly regarded member of the faculty. He was a careful scholar, competent teacher and faithful college spokesman. His life and work were appropriately honored when the addition to the library was named for him in 1992.

Lloyd Hustvedt of the Norwegian department was a regular favorite with students. He drew large enrollments for his classes, and his chapel talks were gems of both solid content and beautiful expression. His charming Norwegian accent, sense of humor and thorough scholarship characterized the work in his classes and as secretary of the Norwegian American Historical Association, which is housed on campus.

Dr. Elaine Tracy, professor of education, was a St. Olaf veteran when I arrived. She was devoted to the welfare of the college and the students, and committed to a Christian life of witness. She was also something of a character, always herself, boisterous in her approach to life and enthusiastic about everything she did. Once when she visited my office, I thought she was going to make a pitch for additional faculty or additional something for the department of education, of which she was the chair. Instead, she sat down and very seriously said to me, "Sid, I think I need to trade cars. What do you think about that?" We had a good conversation about cars, and I think she did make the trade. She made a name for herself buying cars, houses and dogs.

Arnold Flaten, the highly regarded founder of the art department, was still teaching when I came to the college. He told me that he had not been appointed to the faculty; he had been drafted. Dr. Boe had sent him a letter while he was serving as a pastor in Montana telling him that it was time he became a teacher of art. Flaten obeyed, which is what most people did when Dr. Boe gave the orders. Flaten became a masterful sculptor in wood and stone. He stopped at my office one day and placed a wood carving on my desk. "This is for you," he said. "I think of a college president when I look at it." It was a human figure pressing at a barrier that bends but does not give way. He called it "The Pusher." For Lois and me it remains a treasured reminder of a dear friend and a marvelous artist and teacher.

Olaf Christiansen carried on the great choir tradition started by his father. Early in the 1967–68 school year he came to me to talk about his retirement. He had been the director of the St. Olaf Choir since 1941, and now felt he should step aside. "I don't hear well anymore," he said, "and if you can't hear you can't direct a choir." I had to agree with that, so we proceeded to talk about the future of the choir. Olaf was straightforward and said, "It is not my business to pick my successor, but if you want my advice I believe it should be Jennings. He's an able musician and he has proved himself." I had thought that the selection of the next director of the choir might be a difficult problem, knowing the reputation of the choir and its key place in the life of the college. As it turned out, we appointed a committee to advise the dean and the president, and with no difficulty Kenneth Jennings was the one recommended. It proved to be one of the easiest faculty appointments I was to make. Jennings was a graduate of St. Olaf and had been a faculty member since 1953. He continued as director until his retirement in 1988, and enhanced the already distinguished reputation of the St. Olaf Choir.

When Orin Lofthus resigned as dean and returned to the biology department, I appointed Albert Finholt, professor of chemistry and one of the outstanding members of the faculty, as his successor. He served with distinction as dean for seven years, fostering an overall enhancement of the academic program. Together with philosophy professor Bill Narum and others, he led the college into the 4–1–4 curriculum, and spearheaded the planning and implementing of the paracollege, both of which made major contributions to what we could offer students.

Olaf Millert, professor of psychology, was one of several transplants from Europe to join the faculty. He never lost his love for his native Estonia or neighboring Finland. He and his wife, Juta, with unfailing European charm, hosted Woodrow Wilson scholars who visited the campus year by year. One of the most memorable of these was Lord Caradon, a retired British diplomat. He had been one of Britain's negotiators in working out the status of Jerusalem at the end of the British mandate. The students were captivated by his British accent, his impressive credentials and his charismatic personality. By popular demand, he was invited to return to the college, and the editors of the student newspaper published a headline, "The Second Coming of the Lord."

In my day–to–day work, I had frequent contact with Carol Johnson, who came to the college as dean of women to succeed Lavinia Anderson, and later became vice president and dean of students. She has given outstanding leadership in an area of campus life that is constantly changing because of shifting patterns that prevail in the lives of young people. I also found myself frequently in conversation with the college pastor, Cliff Swanson, who brought solid preaching and creativity to his challenging area of work. Especially in the years prior to 1974, I worked closely with Joe Shaw, professor of religion, as he wrote the history of the college in preparation for its centennial. He always entertained those around him with repartee born of a delightful and droll sense of humor.

An unusual pleasure for me was to have as colleagues some of my former students at Concordia who were now St. Olaf faculty members. Miles (Mity) Johnson, was band director at St. Olaf for thirty–seven years of distinguished music making until his retirement in 1994. Rod Grubb and Jack Schwandt are long–time members of the political science department.

The St. Olaf faculty has always included those whose influence has reached far beyond the campus. This includes those associated with the college's strong music program, and others as well. Among them were Kenneth Bjork, immigration historian; Stewart Hendrickson, research chemist; Howard Hong, philosopher and Kierkegaard scholar; E. Clifford Nelson, church historian; and Lynn Steen, creative mathematician and national leader in his field. One of the more interesting appointments I made was that of James May to the department of classics. He brought not only fine scholarship but an infectious enthusiasm that rejuvenates everything he touches. This characterizes both his work on campus and his leadership nationally in the field of classics.

Some specialized areas of the college's program experienced strong growth during the 60's and 70's. I cannot forget the many visits I had with Howard Hong regarding the Kierkegaard Library. Howard's strong interest in the Danish philosopher brought to us a major collection of books, some directly to the college library and others belonging to Howard and his wife, Edna. An area on the top floor of Holland Hall had been preempted for this collection, and, through the years, grew into a major holding attracting the attention of scholars from around the world. There was always need for funds to provide additional space, to purchase books, and to manage the collection. The Hongs regularly went to Denmark, where they discovered additional material and returned with the results of their quest. One summer day I received a telegram from Howard, who was in Copenhagen. He had found some volumes which we "must have," and he needed funds to purchase them. After some discussion in the staff council, we sent him the money, which came from "somewhere," but not necessarily a budget line designated for the library! The Hongs were busy translating and editing a major edition of Kierkegaard's works, and the college tried to do as much as possible to encourage them in that endeavor. However, it was not until the Ditmanson addition to Rolvaag Library was built that a major new space for the Kierkegaard Library was provided. The collection is now housed in quarters quite adequate for research and study as well as for the proper care of the volumes.

Something similar happened in the area of international study. There, too, the initiative and drive of individual faculty members made the difference. St. Olaf had international connections from its beginnings. The Norwegian heritage had resulted in at least occasional traffic back and forth with Norwegians coming to the college to study or teach, and St. Olaf students going to Norway. Also, the foreign mission program of the church had resulted in the college hosting, from time to time, students from China, Madagascar and South Africa. But it was the initiative of a post–World War II student from Norway which brought the foreign study program into major focus at the college. Reidar Dittmann, a native of Norway who had been imprisoned at Buchenwald during World War II, taught in the department of Norwegian while he was a student, and joined the faculty following his graduation in 1947. During his career at St. Olaf he taught not only Norwegian language and literature but also art history. In 1964, he became director of international studies. He and Ansgar Sovik, the son of China missionaries and a member of the department of religion, took the lead in organizing programs for St. Olaf students to study abroad. Since the 60's, this program has grown to include opportunities in a dozen or more locations around the world and involves nearly two–thirds of the students before they graduate. Increasingly, the faculty has become involved; many of them accompany student groups for terms abroad or enroll students from other countries in their classes.

Another feature of St. Olaf life which grew without much planning or promotion was the practice of appointing both husband and wife to positions on the faculty or in the administration. When I came to the college, the unwritten practice, with a few exceptions, was that we should not employ two members of the same family. This was a common policy at most institutions. The problem, if that's what it was, seemed to take care of itself in the 60's and 70's, when we faced a shortage of well–prepared persons to teach in certain fields of study. Frequently, persons married to one another were both highly qualified; often both had earned the terminal degree. So little by little, husbands and wives joined the staff and the result has been beneficial to the college. Difficulties sometimes arise when one person leaves and two vacancies suddenly occur, or when one person receives tenure and the other does not. But in the majority of cases the experience has been positive.

Related to this development was the growth in the number of faculty and staff who lived away from Northfield. Frequently a spouse was employed in the Twin Cities or was involved in a graduate study program at the University of Minnesota. Burnsville, Lakeville and other suburbs became attractive as compromise homesites. This practice has meant that the faculty does not have the strong sense of cohesion and fellowship which was the case in earlier years.

I tried to become acquainted with as many of the persons working at the college as possible. I visited faculty offices, administrative offices, the kitchen, the dining room, the heating plant, the carpenter shop and the radio station. I did not visit classes, believing the dean was the one who should do that.

One day I stopped by the newly installed boilers in the heating plant (enlarging the heating plant was the first building project I was involved with after my arrival), admired them and the excellent housekeeping done by the engineers in charge. A man who obviously didn't know me approached and made a remark about the area not being open to the public. I told him who I was, and he was embarrassed and apologetic. I found out he was newer to the college than I was, but he was doing his job.

This reminds me of an experience I had shortly after we returned from Norway in 1981. Solveig Steendal left a letter for me at the information desk in the St. Olaf Center, and I went there to pick it up. "What is your name?" asked the young woman in charge. "Rand," I said. She looked around and under her desk, and then turned to me and said, "How do you spell that?" I told her, and she found the letter. As I left, I thought to myself, "How soon you are forgotten." It's probably good for one's ego.

I have commented earlier about faculty meetings and committee organization. In addition to those contacts, I met irregularly with departmental groups and with faculty divisions, both socially and in matters of business. As the size of the faculty grew, I realized, however, that it was increasingly difficult to get to know all of them or to have meaningful professional give–and–take with each one. During my second and third terms, some faculty members became concerned about that, and were occasionally critical of my way of working. It seems to me that the way a college is organized, with the demands placed upon both faculty and president, it is next to impossible to answer that criticism satisfactorily. The day of close personal relationship between the president and each faculty member was one where the numbers were smaller and the pace of life slower. I do not offer this as an excuse for any failures on my part, but as a realistic assessment of what goes on in a busy college world.

The chief change in president–faculty and president–staff relationships during the time I was at St. Olaf was the growth of formal rather than informal ways of meeting together. I have referred to the trend toward participatory democracy. This was a very real change. Formerly, faculty members taught, staff members did their jobs and the president handled all contacts with the board. The 60's and 70's brought to the fore the need to encourage faculty, staff and student input into the decision–making process. This was done in various ways, but one structured way was to organize committees, hearings and other methods for various college groups to speak and listen to each other. This was a positive development overall, but it also had one flaw. It could never satisfy all persons. There were always those who felt they had not been heard, or who believed the system was inadequate to produce favorable results.

On the social side, Dorothy and I, and later Lois and I, did what we could to cultivate a spirit of fellowship and participation by campus groups. Each fall we entertained new faculty and staff members, with spouses, at an evening sit–down dinner in our home. As numbers grew, it became necessary to do this in shifts. We would have thirty to forty persons at a time. During the year we entertained each faculty division for an evening meeting with refreshments. These meetings also included most of the administrative personnel. At

Christmas we had a brief afternoon program and party for all administrative and staff personnel, and in the summer a picnic which featured ribeye steaks cooked on large grills.

It was a special privilege to succeed Clemens Granskou as president, and to build on the strong foundation he had provided. He had been in office from 1942 until 1963, and during his years of service the college had grown in size, prestige and financial stability. He insisted that appointments to the faculty and staff were the chief responsibility of a college president and the source of the college's strength. He was a congenial, open–hearted man with a delightful sense of humor. He and his wife, Ella, built a home near the college following their retirement, and they retained their interest in college affairs during the post–retirement years. While Clem never interfered with official college decisions, he was available to me for consultation and friendly reflection on what was happening.

Clem used to tell people that every morning he would go out on the balcony of his home, across the street from the athletic field, shake his fist in the direction of the campus and shout, "Down with the administration!"

Dr. Granskou died in 1977 after a fall in the Lavender Inn at Faribault. We have in our kitchen an oak cutting board which has a label on the back saying, "Made by Clem." He loved to work with wood, and had made that cutting board from a tree in his yard. We are glad to have this reminder of his friendship.

There were literally dozens of other faculty members, administrators, custodians, secretaries, cooks and engineers who made impressive and consistent contributions to the life of the college. Some of them displayed those quirks or enhancements of personality which made them special people, unforgettable to those who knew them. I wish I could list them all one by one. They made my life enjoyable and the college great.

Chapter 16

THOUSANDS OF TEACHERS

I have said, as have many college presidents, that college life would be fine if it weren't for the students! None of us really meant that, but I must admit that there were days in the late 60's when my work was made less than enjoyable by student activity.

St. Olaf College has been fortunate in that it attracts a large number of not only bright but also highly motivated and socially conscious students. When I came to the presidency in 1963, students were relatively peaceful. We had our expected debates regarding dormitory hours, intervisitation in dorm rooms, and car permits. St. Olaf had separate dormitories for men and women, the hours for women's dorms to be locked were defined, and the college did not allow students to have cars on campus without a special permit. Soon after I arrived, the debate about single–sex dorms became heated, and as a result we converted some of the dorms to coed housing. That meant there were men on one floor, women on another. For several years we kept two dorms as single–sex for those who preferred, or whose parents preferred, that lifestyle. The car rule remained, but exceptions were usually made if the student was disabled, had an off–campus job or lived away from campus and commuted. We had few commuters. This system of control simplified campus parking problems and strengthened campus life. Occasionally I also emphasized with parents the economies for the family that resulted from this policy. We initiated regular bus service between Northfield and the Twin Cities to serve St. Olaf and Carleton students. Later we established a shuttle service between the two campuses on a frequent schedule.

One of the first decisions I made after arriving at St. Olaf had to do with smoking. The college permitted men but not women to smoke. Cigarettes were sold in the bookstore. Students raised the issue of sexual equality, and Mark Almli, the dean of men, presented me with the problem. After giving the matter some thought, I decided that on the basis of equal treatment for all students, women would be allowed to smoke. Then, because I really wanted to discourage smoking, I decided that the college should no longer be in the tobacco business, so we discontinued the sale of cigarettes in the bookstore. That inconvenienced some people and drew some criticism. I remember a special sequel to this decision. One day in the fall of 1963, Mr. Skoglund was on campus for a board meeting. As we passed the bookstore on the way from my office to the Presidents' Dining Room, he said, "Just a minute, I need some cigarettes." "I'm sorry, Skog," I replied, "you can't buy cigarettes there any more." He was gracious about it and we sent someone down the hill to the Ole Store to get him some. It is encouraging to note that the late 80's brought a push to make the entire St. Olaf campus smoke free.

One day a senior student, Phil Voxland, came to my office to have a talk before he graduated. He expressed gratitude for his St. Olaf experience and then asked me a rather straightforward question, "How long do you plan to be president of St. Olaf?" I wasn't quite ready for that. I was in my first six–year term and had no plans for leaving or being terminated. So I explained to Phil that I served at the pleasure of the board, and that I might be around a few more years. I inquired why he had asked, and he replied that he would be interested in the job. So we talked about what a president does and how a person might prepare for the position. Phil went on to do graduate work in computers and has been on the staff of the University of Minnesota. We've had several enjoyable visits through the years, and I always ask him if he is getting ready to be president of the college.

Another day two junior counselors stopped to invite Lois and me for an evening visit at Kildahl Hall. One of them was Blake Grangaard. I have known his father, Don, since we were kids together in Rothsay. Blake was a good student who went to the seminary after college and became a pastor. As they left my office that day, Blake turned and said, "When you come to Kildahl, would you tell us a bedtime story?" "Sure," I said, not knowing what I was talking about. I went home and asked Lois what she thought he meant. She supposed he meant what he said. We perfected an act by choosing the book, *The Romance of the Dot and the Line*, and prepared a flip–chart which we could use as we read. The performance seemed to be a hit. We were asked to come to other dorms, and we developed a repertoire of stories for Halloween, Christmas and general use. Students would come in their pajamas carrying their stuffed animals. Once when we came to Mellby Hall, we saw on the bulletin board a sign reading, "Come and hear Ma and Pa Rand tell bedtime stories." These were happy experiences and a little surprising for us. Kids aren't always as sophisticated as they try to be.

Sometimes I was invited to dorms to lead in devotions, or just to talk. Once I was asked by Blue Key, a men's honorary service society, to speak on "How My Mind Has Changed."

Each fall Dorothy and I, and later Lois and I, greeted the freshmen in the Fireside Lounge. They came in groups with their junior counselors, and we shook hands and welcomed each one. In some years there were more than a thousand of them, and it took three hours on those occasions. It was both tiring and fun. We could talk with students individually, and often there were children and grandchildren of people we knew.

Often the pace required that we meet many people or deal with demanding occasions when we were weary and felt like resting. But duty called, and the contacts with people were interesting. Lois often reminds me that I have always lived by the motto, "We can be tired a week from Tuesday."

I was often asked to meet with groups of students or with individual student representatives to discuss some issue of college policy or student government. Students are always interested in acquiring greater freedom from college regulation, and the right to govern their own lives. As has been true of all church colleges, St. Olaf has had rules and regulations which have limited students in various ways. The trend has been toward greater freedom, and some of that took place during my time. I was glad that Dr. Granskou had settled the dancing issue before I became president. Dancing was allowed on campus as of 1962. The problem we had during my time, according to my student informants, was that "nobody comes to the dances."

As long as I was at the college, students continued to press for more freedom and greater options for determining how they lived on campus. In the 60's, students also campaigned to secure more of a voice in the determination of college policy. After much discussion, the faculty decided to include students on key faculty committees, and we also added a student (and a faculty) observer to the Board of Regents. These actions had mixed results. Some students took their duties seriously and made helpful contributions to the groups with which they served. In other cases there was laxity of attendance and a failure to keep informed on issues. But such student involvement soon became accepted as the norm, and it is doubtful that the college will alter the practice. The challenge instead is to try to emphasize the importance of such involvement, and hope that truly interested students will be chosen.

One spring, toward the end of my time at the college, a student committee visited me and proposed that instead of a junior–senior prom there be a President's Ball. Proms had failed to attract students for several years, and finally they had been discontinued, casualties of the Vietnam War furor, I believe. Now students wanted a social affair again. Lois and I consented, and invitations went out in quite formal style with "President and Mrs. Rand" inviting people to the ball. It was held in the cafeteria portion of the St. Olaf Center (no carpet there) and Lois and I danced the first dance. Those readers of this chronicle who know me will wonder how all of this could happen. Since I had never learned to dance, Lois took me in hand and tried to teach me. She did the best she could, and I did my part the evening of the ball, but I know I spent more time watching others dance than doing it myself.

The students were pleased, and the President's Ball has now become a spring tradition at the college.

Some of my most distinct memories of students have to do with the school years 1968–69, 1969–70 and 1970–71, when the anti–Vietnam fever reached its height. I would judge that between fifty and a hundred students during each of those years were vocal, committed and effective leaders of an anti–war effort on campus. They succeeded in rallying the support of a large portion of the student body for their cause. They were aided and abetted by a number of faculty members who felt as strongly about the war and American involvement in it as did the students. The campus generally was kept in a state of unrest much of the time.

To the anti–war campaigners, the issues were quite simple. It was argued that the United States was mistaken to be involved in the Vietnam War. If we would get out the war would soon cease. It was our continued provision of troops and materiel that kept the war going. The presidents responsible for our involvement (Kennedy, Johnson, Nixon) were all at fault, as was the Congress. As a result, some St. Olaf students took the position that the college should take a firm stand deploring the war. This could be done by getting rid of ROTC and by closing the college so that students could be free to demonstrate against the war.

My position, which had the support of the board as well as most administration and faculty, was that the college had a contractual relationship with students to continue our normal academic work, and that the college, as a college, fulfilled its obligation best when it provided a forum for debate on the issues rather than by closing down. I also felt strongly that the college should debate the issue of ROTC and make a decision only after such debate. As it turned out, the ROTC issue solved itself when the Air Force withdrew its program because we had not been producing enough candidates for commissions.

I met regularly with students in my office and in groups around the campus to discuss the war issue. I'm not sure I convinced any of those who disagreed with me, but we usually had lively debate.

One day in the spring of 1970, a group of twenty students came to tell me they were going to take over my office and the entire Administration Building. After some discussion, during which I asked them not to disturb unlocked personnel files in the office, I left and led other staff people out. For twenty–four hours the student group stayed, with chains securing the doors to the building. Then they sent emissaries to ask to meet with me. I met with two of their leaders in a conference room in the Center. They had planned well; a Twin Cities TV station was there to record the meeting. The students said they were "giving back" the Administration Building, and they asked me to provide them with buckets, brooms and mops. They proceeded to clean the building. This illustrates the bittersweet experience of the anti–war effort.

A leader of the group of occupiers was Richard Hordern, an excellent student with a deep concern about ethical issues. After graduating from St. Olaf, he went on to the seminary and later earned a doctoral degree in theology. He became a faculty member at Luther College in Regina, Saskatchewan, and in 1995 was elected president of the college. I wrote to congratulate him, and couldn't refrain from suggesting that it served him right!

Our students were decent and well–intentioned. Beyond some graffiti on sidewalks and buildings, they did not damage anything. I kept telling them that they were free to protest and free to demonstrate, but there were two things they must not do. They must not destroy property and they must not interfere with the rights of those who disagreed with them. By and large, they did not violate those limitations.

In early May of 1970, there was a community assembly in the old gymnasium. A series of these had been called by the leadership of the student protest. These meetings included talks by students, St. Olaf and Carleton faculty and others, which served to rally support for the anti–war movement. I was present at this particular May assembly, trying to be inconspicuous in a far corner of the room. Gary Hartke was the student in charge. After an hour or so of debate (it was quite one–sided), Gary took the mike and asked, "Is President Rand here?" I came forward. As I did, Gary told the crowd that as they, the students, skipped classes and demonstrated, there was one person on campus who had to work all the harder answering letters and calls from parents wondering, "What's going on around here?" "That person is President Rand," he continued, "and today is his birthday. I think we ought to sing Happy Birthday to him." So they did. Not only that, they brought in a large cake iced with the greeting, "Happy Birthday, President Rand." As many as could shared the cake, Gary hung a peace symbol around my neck, and then brought the group back to order and to further discussion. I was deeply moved and grateful that such a strange combination of events could take place.

One of the students who gave me a bad time was a pastor's son, a B+ student who seemed to do well in his studies without spending all his time at it.

He was heavily involved in the anti–war effort. He came to my office more than once to bang the desk with his fist as he scolded me for my immoral and unchristian behavior in not supporting the anti–war cause. He was one of our long–haired, unkempt students, and his eyes radiated fierce feeling. I've said I thought I knew all "those words," but he taught me some new ones. I'm afraid Solveig heard more than she wanted to, also. My way of dealing with him was to let him talk and then quietly remind him of my position that the college was properly a forum for the discussion of the war issue, and could not officially take a partisan position. We didn't convince each other, of course.

There is a sequel to this. A few years after this student's graduation, Lois and I were in Washington, DC, to attend a St. Olaf Choir concert at Kennedy Center. We were in the lobby greeting people when up to us walked a young couple beaming and obviously glad to see us. The young man was well–dressed in a vested suit, shirt and tie. He was nicely groomed with a fresh haircut and shaved face. The young woman with him was also nicely dressed and all smiles. He greeted me heartily and then said, "You don't know me, do you?" I admitted I did not. It was my old friend, and he proceeded to give me another lecture, this time in proper English. He complimented me on all he had heard about the college. He was glad it was being true to its heritage and faithful to its Christian principles. That was all–important, he insisted. My mouth must have been agape. I could hardly believe what I was hearing. But he meant it. Since that day, he has become an attorney and is a grateful alumnus of St. Olaf College.

To witness such a change in a student is one of the great rewards of being a college president.

All in all, I would say my dealings with students were profitable and positive for me. One can always regret that the shortage of time and the press of business keeps the president from getting to know most students well. I see no way to solve that problem. But it is a greatly rewarding thing to be in a college where there is some regular and close contact with students, and I have had the privilege of such relationships through my years not only at St. Olaf, but also at Concordia, Waldorf, Augustana and Suomi.

Those in leadership positions and those who caused problems became well known to me. But I often think of the hundreds, even thousands, of students who tended to business, got an education and graduated without fanfare — and whom I didn't know. I'm grateful that to this day I meet them — in the Minneapolis skyways, at meetings I attend, and even on planes and in airports — and they stop me, tell me who they are, and usually have some kind words for their college experience. So the rewards of the presidency go on, and for that I will always be thankful.

Chapter 17

THOSE MUNDANE THINGS

No matter how much one tries to keep firmly in mind that a college is chiefly the academic program and the teacher–student relationship, the reality is that money and buildings play a major role in the success or failure of a college presidency as well as of the college itself. They are the necessary tools of the business.

When I arrived at St. Olaf, I realized that what the college had stressed in the years since World War II was growth in enrollment. Eight hundred students registered in 1945 and about two thousand in 1962. In order to accommodate that increase, the emphasis had to be on building student housing. In 1945, Ytterboe, Mohn (the one razed in 1965) and Agnes Mellby Halls were the three dormitories on campus, with a total capacity of about four hundred. By 1963, Thorson, Kildahl, Ellingson, Kittelsby, Hilleboe, Hoyme and East (now Flaten) Halls had been added, for a total dormitory capacity of about thirteen hundred. Larson Hall and a new Mohn Hall were under construction, and they would add another four hundred spaces. In addition, students lived in college–owned homes near the campus and in other Northfield homes. Off–campus study programs had begun, so some students were involved in these each semester. The Administration Building and St. Olaf Center also had been added in 1960 and, after the tower dorms were built, Flaten Hall became a classroom and art studio building.

What the college urgently needed in 1963 were additional classrooms, library space, faculty offices, science classrooms and laboratories, and more adequate physical education and athletic facilities. This would involve a total cost of several million dollars.

The centennial of St. Olaf was to be celebrated in 1974. That meant we could capitalize on the decade preceding it by trying to improve facilities. The college had approached the Ford Foundation for a major grant a year before I became president. The foundation had announced a program through which it would make grants to sixty colleges considered especially strong and promising.

Carleton, St. Thomas and St. Catherine's had already been chosen in that program, and it was doubtful if another Minnesota college could qualify.

But soon after I came to St. Olaf, I received a call from James Armsey, vice president of the Ford Foundation, asking if I would be in New York any time in the near future. Of course I would! We began to plan in all seriousness. The grapevine reports told us that the Ford grant might be in the neighborhood of $2,000,000 — if we got it. We decided to ask for $2,500,000, knowing that the grant would require a match of two–and–a–half times that much to be raised from other sources. We therefore decided to launch what we called the Forward Fund, with a goal of $11,500,000 to be raised in the decade from 1964 to 1974. Mr. and Mrs. Skoglund had pledged a gift of $1,750,000 to build a new gymnasium, so we thought our goal was realistic if we could secure the Ford grant.

I went to New York soon after receiving Mr. Armsey's call, and told him that if we received their grant we would use a substantial part of it to build an addition to the library, and that the balance would be placed in the endowment fund. We asked for $2,500,000 from the foundation. Mr. Armsey had studied the fund–raising history of St. Olaf and said he was doubtful that we could make the match. We tried to convince him that we could, and he promised to think about it. At least it sounded as if we were going to get something.

Some time later, we scheduled a meeting of the St. Olaf Board of Regents at Bankers Trust Company offices in New York, the bank where Roy Reierson, a member of our board, was a vice president. I had another meeting with Mr. Armsey and told him of the Skoglund pledge. He was impressed, but thought the Ford grant should be $2,000,000. We talked some more, and finally he said they would make it $2,200,000. That meant we would need to raise $5,500,000 as the matching amount. I reported to the board. The members were elated, and voted to accept the Ford grant and proceed to make the Forward Fund the emphasis for the centennial decade.

We had another problem. If we were to add any buildings to the campus, we would need to replace or add to the heating plant which was operating at capacity. We decided to use the first money received in the Forward Fund to double the size of the heating plant, and then go on to build the library addition, to be followed by the gym, or athletic center as it came to be known. When those projects were completed in 1967, we decided to build a new science facility. And we kept on raising money. By 1968, the Forward Fund had exceeded its goal.

The library addition was popular with everyone. Both stack and study space had reached capacity. We decided to name the new addition for O.G. Felland, the first librarian and the one who had gathered the initial collection in a room of Old Main. The first library building had been a gift of alumni and friends and was named for O.E. Rolvaag, professor of Norwegian and author of several immigrant

198

novels including *Giants in the Earth*, which had gained wide fame on both sides of the Atlantic.

When the Skoglunds made the offer to build a gymnasium, it was the second time individual gifts would provide the total cost of a building. Harald Thorson, one of the founders, had left most of his estate to the college, and it had made possible Thorson Hall at a cost of approximately $1,000,000. The Skoglund gift enabled us to plan an athletic complex which included basketball and handball courts, a field house, swimming pool, weight room, classrooms, offices and dressing rooms. It was quite adequate for an enrollment of three thousand. The basketball floor was in a space large enough to seat four thousand people, and it became the site for the traditional Christmas concert. For the dedication of what we called Skoglund Athletic Center, the well–known coach, Bud Wilkinson, was the speaker. Mr. Skoglund, one of the owners of the Minnesota Vikings, had used his influence in the athletic community to persuade him to come.

Next on our building agenda was the science center. Holland Hall, which was being used for sciences, had once housed the administration and several academic departments other than science. Now it was no longer adequate even for the sciences. Chemistry, physics and biology had grown to be among the most popular majors, due not least to the strength of the faculty in those areas. St. Olaf had become known for producing graduates who became physicians or research scientists. In 1965, we began planning for a new building, and the first step was to decide on a site. We determined to use the location of Mohn Hall, a building which had deteriorated and was not considered adequate for student housing any longer. That building was razed and the new science facility was completed in 1969. It included classrooms and laboratories for chemistry, physics, biology and mathematics, together with faculty offices and research space. In addition, the science library was housed there, and two large lecture rooms added desirable space not only for the sciences but for general college use.

We chose the Sovik architectural firm to plan all of these buildings. The lead architect was Ed Sovik, a St. Olaf graduate who also taught part time in the art department. He had gathered a group of able partners, and they were cooperative and effective in their work for St. Olaf. The buildings harmonized with the total plan of the campus, using the same limestone exterior which had been used for all buildings since the late 30's. The location of buildings and roadways was done in such a way that automobile traffic was slowed as it passed through the campus, and the total effect was pleasing to the eye as well as being well–adapted to the many relationships of campus life.

As the centennial of the college approached, we planned another fundraising effort. This time it was the Centennial Fund, with a goal of $9,500,000. It was completed in 1977, having produced about $12,000,000.

With the proceeds of our fund–raising, we added to the college endowment, strengthened the current operating budget and provided student aid funds in addition to physical improvements on campus.

One of the special events of the centennial celebration was the groundbreaking for a new music building. The new Christiansen Hall was dedicated in 1976. It provided studio, classroom and practice space, together with a music library, rehearsal rooms for choir, band and orchestra, and a recital hall which is called by some "the most beautiful room in Minnesota." The former Christiansen Hall was connected to the science center and continued in use, serving both music and mathematics.

While a building may be considered mundane, what goes on in connection with it is quite another thing. Several special events highlighted the opening of the music hall. The Polish composer, Krzysztof Penderecki, came to the campus for a week and conducted a choir and orchestra concert of one of his own major works. The students were challenged as they learned and performed his extremely difficult contemporary music. A month later, the well–known conductor, Antonia Brico, came to rehearse and perform with the St. Olaf Orchestra. She had been Lois's conducting teacher at Colorado College, and was a forerunner in orchestral conducting among women. She took the campus by storm and endeared herself both to the orchestra and to those who heard the concert. Her electrifying style pulled from the players more than they knew they had. At the end of the first run–through of the first rehearsal piece, she quietly laid her baton down and the students sat with bated breath awaiting her verdict. Very quietly she said, "I hope you children realize how well you have been trained." That was a great tribute to their regular director, Donald Berglund.

On the same visit she gave a convocation address, and with the zeal of an evangelist she roused the audience with a stirring message about life and careers that echoed and re–echoed with the challenge, "I will not be deflected from my course!" Several students who were present have quoted her challenge repeatedly in the years since.

Brico visited St. Olaf more than once. She always came loaded with more baggage than she needed, and was only partly organized. Once when she arrived to stay in our home for a few days, Lois asked if she had laundry to do. "No," she said as she unpacked her voluminous bags and covered every available surface in the room. A few minutes later she called for Lois; she did have laundry to do after all. Years later, she visited us at the Embassy in Norway and that proved to be an equally unforgettable time.

When the music building was completed, we converted the old gym to a speech–theater facility, which included a main theater, an experimental theater, and several classrooms and offices. The exterior was red brick, and the architect recommended that we paint it gray to match the color of the stone buildings. I proposed that we leave it red, because I had seen other brick buildings which had been painted, and had never seen one where the paint lasted for any length of time. The board took the architect's advice, as I'm sure they should have, but I'm sorry to report that after a couple of years the gray paint began to peel, and for several years left the building looking increasingly shabby. I am glad to report that it has now been restored to its original red brick exterior.

After the various buildings were in place and several roadways moved, I was taken to task more than once by older alumni who said, "I can't find my way around campus any more."

Fund–raising goes on all the time at a college, and I was fortunate to have as vice president in charge of such activity my good friend David Johnson. He is a take–charge person with lots of know–how in such matters. While he is an expert in all phases of that activity, he is a specialist in deferred giving. That means bequests, trusts, annuities and insurance. The college continues to benefit from his work. He began his employment during his student days, and since his graduation in 1938 has been on the staff in various capacities, with time out only for service in the Navy in World War II. He engaged and trained a staff of able assistants, planned our fund–raising and public relations programs, and directed all activities with a sure hand. The fact we raised as much money as we did is testimony to his hard work and skill. To this day we meet on a regular basis to talk about the good old days and enjoy the continuing success of the college.

Dave also directed the work of WCAL, the college radio station. Melford Jensen and, later, Paul Peterson gave able management to the station, but Dave and his staff were in charge of fund raising to support it. The station had been started in the physics lab of the college in 1921, and has been continually on the air ever since.

We tried to operate on a balanced budget during my years at St. Olaf. Between 1967 and 1970, however, we accumulated a current fund deficit of about $300,000. The Board of Regents passed a resolution that we were not to run deficits, and within two years we had eliminated the accumulated amount. From then on we always ended the year in the black. The power of a board resolution is awesome.

Student charges continued to rise each year. In 1963, the comprehensive fee (tuition, fees, board and room) was $1,800. In 1980 it was $5,500.

College presidents are responsible for the successful fiscal operation of their colleges. I believe I spent a fourth to a third of my time in fund–raising. I made calls on prospects, but in addition I wrote letters, attended meetings of alumni and friends of the college, and accompanied staff members as they made calls on donor prospects. Acknowledging gifts was important, too. I've always believed that a prompt and personal thank–you is one of the most important aspects of fund–raising.

During the Forward Fund's beginnings (1964–65), I spoke at fifty–two meetings over a twelve month period, giving the same talk, or a reasonable facsimile thereof, at each place. The meetings were from coast to coast and places between. Dorothy accompanied me on many of those trips, and David Johnson attended every meeting. How bored he must have been! At the conclusion of the campaign, the staff had a party and gave me a specially printed copy of my speech. It serves yet to remind me of a strenuous but satisfying year of activity. I must admit, however, that I seldom read it. One unfortunate outcome of all that speaking and the stress that went with it was a permanent sore throat. A doctor told me that I had simply strained my voice beyond recovery. It has improved somewhat since that time.

One special memory of those fifty–two Forward Fund meetings is that at forty of them we ate green beans almondine. There must have been a great crop that year.

Money is not only raised; it is spent. We tried to keep a watchful eye on expenditures while also offering as competitive and high quality a program as possible. The faculty usually thought salaries should be higher and teaching conditions improved. Students and their parents wanted fees and charges held as low as possible. I have always believed in what may be called internal fund–raising. Every organization tends to grow, and seldom do people voluntarily cut expenses affecting their own work. In a college there can be a kind of empire building where departments and offices grow in costs and numbers of personnel without much thought to the effect on the total program. The president is frequently called upon to be an umpire to decide where and when cuts and limitations should be employed to keep the operation lean and strong. In this way the health of the institution over the long period is insured. Thousands of dollars can usually be shaved from first estimates of any budget.

Some of our liveliest discussions in Staff Council had to do with budget matters. Each vice president made a case for the work in his own area, and together we tried to reach a consensus, which meant that there had to be compromises and that everyone couldn't win all the time. The fact that we did work as a team meant that we could usually solve our problems without hard feelings or carry–over to discussion of other matters. Favorable reports from many students and their parents, and the visible signs of progress on campus, made all of this worth while.

Chapter 18

THE COLLEGE IS
EVERYWHERE

In the early days of my career I thought travel at any time and to any place was a grand and welcome experience. The passing of time and lots of travel seem to change that point of view.

As I saw it, there was no way to be successful in a college presidency without traveling. I knew that before I arrived at St. Olaf, and I accepted it as part of the job. I even enjoyed most of it.

One of my first trips as president remains unforgettable. On November 22, 1963, I was scheduled to speak to the Milwaukee St. Olaf Club. I flew there in the morning, and as I stepped from the plane shortly after noon I was met by a St. Olaf alumnus whose first words were, "Did you hear that President Kennedy has been shot?" I had not. We gathered members of the local committee to discuss whether we should cancel our meeting. We decided not to, and as it turned out we had a good crowd and spent a somber, thoughtful evening together.

St. Olaf had done a good job of building loyalty among alumni. There were about fifty places around the country where we could count on a sizable crowd for a St. Olaf affair. People like David Johnson, Virgil Foss, Jack Laugen and Chet Lacey had worked hard on alumni relations, and I was to enjoy the fruits of their efforts. We regularly held meetings in key cities of the middle west, but also in New York, Boston, Washington, D.C., Los Angeles, San Francisco, Denver and Seattle. During the days of the Forward Fund and the Centennial Fund, I was especially involved with meetings around the country. St. Olaf made it a practice to include parents of students and other friends of the college in these meetings, and I thought that was a good thing to do.

There was other travel, too. Academic life is as guilty of organizing groups as is any profession or occupation. So I became involved in state, regional and national organizations of colleges, college presidents, church colleges, and so on. For a longer or shorter period, I served as a board member and officer of the Council of Protestant Colleges and Universities, the National Association of Independent Colleges, the Association of American Colleges, the National Lutheran Educational Conference and the Associated Colleges of the Midwest. The Minnesota private colleges were quite active and there were many meetings each year involving that group.

In 1964, I was appointed by Governor Karl Rolvaag to be the chairman of a newly created Higher Education Facilities Commission. It was called into being by a program of the federal government through which funds were provided for grants and loans to colleges and universities for the purpose of building or renovating facilities. Each state was required to have a commission to administer this program. We started without a staff and in a modest way, but, as with almost all government programs, we grew. Soon we became the Higher Education Coordinating Commission, with responsibilities for coordinating the work of all higher education institutions in the state. I continued as a member until 1973. Among other state bodies on which I served were the Board for Continuing Legal Education (1975–80) and the Judicial Planning Committee (1975–80).

I was a member of the board of the Wheat Ridge Foundation from 1975 to 1984. This is a pan–Lutheran organization that receives gifts from individuals and churches for the purpose of making grants to health and healing ministries in the church.

Closer to home, I served on the board of the Northfield National Bank (1964–80) and the board of North American Life and Casualty Company (1967–79 and 1981–89).

All of those were worthwhile experiences. I met many new people and gained knowledge in the areas of education, government and business that broadened my horizons and generally enriched my life.

One interesting sidelight regarding travel is the fact that much of it took me to Washington, D.C. While there I would often visit the Congress and call on our representatives. During much of the time I was at the college, Congressman Albert Quie, a St. Olaf graduate, represented the district in which Northfield is located. He became the ranking Republican on the House Education Committee, so his influence was great, and it was therefore of importance to the work of the college to keep him informed and let him know our concerns. Walter Mondale, who later became Vice President, was a Minnesota Senator, and I called on him regularly, also. Our paths crossed in a very important way for me when he was Vice President.

In March of 1968, on our way to Pascagoula, Mississippi, for a meeting of the Associated Colleges of the Midwest, Dorothy and I stopped at Gulfport to visit my uncle, Clayton Rand, and his wife, Mae. We watched the evening news on television and heard President Lyndon Johnson announce his decision not to run for re-election. A few days later in Pascagoula, we heard the report of the death of Dr. Martin Luther King. I began to wonder if all important historical events took place when I was away from home.

I was not a world traveler at the time I became president of St. Olaf. Dorothy and I had spent five months in Bossey, Switzerland, and we had seen a bit of Germany, France and Italy. But there were lots of places we hadn't been. Perhaps for a St. Olaf president, the most serious lack was that I had not been in Norway.

Dorothy and I sought to remedy that in the summer of 1965. St. Olaf had maintained its ties with Norway through the years. The founder of the college, Rev. B.J. Muus, was buried in the churchyard at Nidaros Cathedral in Trondheim. Since its beginning in the fifties, the International Summer School of the University of Oslo had maintained its American office at St. Olaf. The choir and band had toured Norway on several occasions. There also had been academic visits and exchanges involving both faculty and students of St. Olaf and personnel of the universities in Norway. King Olav V, then Crown Prince Olav, had visited the college in 1939, and had received an honorary doctorate.

Dorothy and I spent two weeks in Norway in the summer of 1965. We visited the International Summer School, saw the Oslo tourist sites, traveled to Bergen and on through the fjord country to Trondheim, then back to Oslo via Gudbrandsdal. Mary was at the summer school, as Peter had been the year before, so she accompanied us on a visit to Sigdal, the birthplace of my Pedersen grandparents. It was a highlight of the trip to have an audience with His Majesty King Olav, a privilege I was fortunate to enjoy several times in the years that followed.

I was impressed by many things in Norway. Certainly the scenery is some of the most beautiful in the world, with the combination of mountains, fjords, rivers and streams. The mountains are covered with trees and crowned with year-round snow and dramatic plateaus. The cities, in charming contrast, are combinations of old and new. But most impressive to me was the opportunity to visit the farms where my grandparents had been born. These are located about seventy-five miles west of Oslo in a secluded and forested valley where farming is difficult. Seeing these farms gave me a new understanding of why so many Norwegians left their homeland for America. Certainly this was true of my grandparents.

Succeeding trips to Norway came in 1967 with the college orchestra, 1968 and 1973 (when Dorothy accompanied me), and 1974 with the college band. Lois and I traveled in Norway and the British Isles in 1975. Each of these trips gave me the opportunity to reinforce St. Olaf's ties with the royal family, various government ministries and officials, and leaders in church, education and business. During the 1973 and 1974 visits, I persuaded the government of Norway to assist St. Olaf in establishing an endowment to fund a chair in Scandinavian studies. The initial grant was $220,000. Since that time the government has made an additional gift, and the college, together with the Norwegian American Historical Association, has secured other funds to complete the endowment. In 1986, I accompanied President Mel George on a visit to the birthplace of Pastor Muus, the founder of St. Olaf College, at Snåsa, north of Trondheim.

In December, 1968, I went to the Orient to visit the sites of our student programs there. St. Olaf had developed an extensive program of foreign study opportunities in the Orient, Europe and Africa. On the 1968 trip I visited universities in Japan, Taiwan, Hong Kong and Thailand on a rather fast–paced tour. I gained valuable insight into the way educators in those lands viewed exchange or visitor programs, heard comments about our students, and received suggestions for certain improvements. It was all very helpful to me.

On the way home from that tour I met Dorothy in Hawaii. The Board of Regents had kindly offered to fly her there. We spent the week of Christmas at the Kauai Surf Hotel on Kauai. That was a special treat even though we both caught a flu bug, and as a result spent much of the week lying around our hotel room. We did go to Christmas worship at a small Lutheran church on the island. We had given Mary and Gary a trip to Germany to visit Peter and Nancy. They had a more enjoyable time than we did — no flu bug and lots of skiing and sightseeing.

In 1972, Dorothy and I enjoyed the luxury of a trip around the world. The Danforth Foundation in St. Louis (Ralston Purina money) sponsored a program by which the foundation selected college presidents from around the country and offered each of them $5,000 to do with what they chose, provided they could secure a paid leave of not less than three months' duration. They selected presidents who had been in office several years and therefore were in need of respite. I was glad they made me the offer.

Dr. William Nelsen, later to become our dean, was the foundation officer who called me to explain the program and ask if I would be interested. In typical generous fashion, the Board of Regents approved a leave for me, and in January, 1972, we left for what was to be a three–month journey.

We decided to begin with an ocean voyage. We flew to San Francisco and boarded ship on January 11. The next day we stopped at Los Angeles, and then set sail for Auckland, New Zealand, where we arrived on January 26. There was one stop on the way, at Tahiti, where we spent a day exploring the island and enjoying the tropical weather. While in Tahiti we took a taxi ride around the island — around is the right word; Tahiti is a round volcanic island. As we traveled, the driver told us about places we passed. We asked him if he had ever been away from the island. "No," he said, "when you are already in heaven, why should you leave?"

Our ship was the *S.S. Monterey*. We had no sooner left San Francisco than we met a couple from Albert Lea, Minnesota. "Aren't you the president of St. Olaf College?" Mrs. Martell Severson asked. She and her husband, a businessman in Albert Lea, were on their first ocean cruise, and came prepared. They had several pieces of luggage, and it seemed that each time we saw them they were wearing different clothes.

I've often said that I will always behave when I travel, because someone will recognize me. I had had a similar experience on my 1968 trip to the Orient. In the Bangkok airport, as I waited for a plane, a man came up to me and said, "Aren't you President Rand of St. Olaf College?" He was a dentist on his way to New Guinea to do volunteer work in a mission hospital. His home was in Hudson, Wisconsin, and he had a son who had graduated from the college the previous spring. It is a small world.

The ocean trip was a delight. The food was delicious, the ship rode smoothly in the sea, there was time for resting or reading or whatever we chose to do. Entertainment of various kinds was provided, including the appearance of King Neptune as we crossed the equator. We even crossed the date line and lost a day!

We sailed as far as Auckland. The ship was going on to Sydney, the Philippines, Hawaii and back to the United States. Several on board were going the whole way, a six–week trip.

In Auckland we visited Sylvia Mollard who had taught at Waldorf one year on the Fulbright program while we were there. We took side trips to Rotorua to see the hot springs, to a Maori village and to Rothesay Beach, a suburb of Auckland named for the same place in Scotland as my home town, only in New Zealand they spell it correctly.

We flew to Sydney, Australia, and spent three days there including a side trip to Canberra. We then flew to Manila where we spent two days sightseeing. Our next stop was Tokyo, and we spent several days there and in Kyoto. We visited missionaries, held a St. Olaf alumni meeting and saw many of the tourist sights. I preached at the American church in Tokyo and at a missionary retreat in the mountains outside the city. We rode the bullet train from Tokyo to Kyoto where we visited shrines and beautiful Japanese gardens. In much of this, our missionary friends, Lyle and Melba Larson, were our guides. He is a St. Olaf grad and Melba had been a student at Waldorf when we were there. We also spent time with Phil and Judy Hyland and Carl and Elaine Westby.

From Japan we went to Taiwan, where we met Merle Metcalf, a missionary who had been helpful in coordinating the study program for our students who came to Taipei as part of the Global Semester. We also met Brynhild Rowberg, a St. Olaf graduate who was a foreign service officer stationed in Taipei. We were taken one evening to a Mongolian barbecue in the Ghengis Khan Restaurant. That meant that we went to a table of raw meat and vegetables, selected what we wanted and then had it cooked on a large outdoor grill.

In Taipei we attended a Sunday worship service where Dr. Arne Sovik preached. He is a St. Olaf graduate and was my classmate at the seminary. We also were taken for a tour down "snake alley" where there was snake soup and snake meat for sale.

Our next stop was Hong Kong, and we arrived to find most shops closed for the Chinese New Year observance. We stayed in the Peninsula Hotel, a grand palace of a place in the nineteenth century hotel tradition. (Reidar Dittmann had suggested most of the hotels we stayed at on that trip.) We were glad to be in such a place, because the first night we were there I became ill, and in response to Dorothy's call to the front desk a nurse appeared almost immediately. She gave me some medication for an upset stomach. That helped, at least for the time being. We were glad to be in a hotel where there was a nurse on duty twenty–four hours a day. I think this illness was the result of eating at the Mongolian barbecue.

In Hong Kong we visited several friends. Cora Martinson, a St. Olaf graduate and long–time missionary, showed us some of the sights. A St. Olaf couple, David Lee, pastor of a church there, and his wife Lorraine also entertained us, as did Luthard Eid, a seminary classmate of mine. We also visited with Dr. Peng Fu, the former president of the Lutheran Church in China.

While there, I had what I believe is my only professional manicure. I went to get a haircut, and the manicure came with it. The total bill was $2.75.

From Hong Kong we flew to Thailand, where we visited briefly in Bangkok and Chiang Mai. One day while we were in Bangkok, Roger Serkland, the son of Alvin and Clara Serkland, came to have dinner with us. He was stationed at an army base south of Bangkok and had been alerted to our presence by his aunt, Alice Serkland.

We traveled on the picturesque canals, or klongs, of Bangkok, visited shops where jewelry, silks and lacquer work were abundant, and saw many temples. In Chiang Mai we were taken to the teak forests where we saw elephants at work hauling logs, and to a village where hill–country people lived in their traditional style. We were entertained at rather lavish dinners with shark fin soup, egg white soup, bird's nest soup, pork and chicken. We were guests of university officials in both Bangkok and Chiang Mai. St. Olaf students regularly studied at Chiang Mai and occasionally at Chulalongkorn University in Bangkok.

In Chiang Mai we had another of our small–world experiences. As we entered the dining room of our hotel one morning, I looked across the room and there eating breakfast was a man in an American military uniform. It was Art Erickson, a chaplain on duty in Thailand. He had been a student in my classes at Concordia College.

In all of the places we visited where St. Olaf students were involved, we learned that the university authorities took our students seriously and offered them solid programs of instruction. There were problems of logistics, payment schedules and credit standards, but all in all we were satisfied that our overseas programs were worthwhile for our students, both in terms of general impressions gained and in the content of courses studied. Occasionally there was a comment by a host director or faculty member indicating that the freedom and even brashness exhibited by some American students was not appreciated.

Our foreign study program was, to a great extent, the result of the dreams of two faculty members, Reidar Dittmann and Ansgar Sovik. Dittmann had traveled the world and had become convinced that American students tended to be provincial in their outlook, and that they would benefit from contact with others. Ansgar Sovik, with his missionary background and experience, was interested in foreign study as a particular way for a church college to assist students in their knowledge of the world and the far–flung work of the church. The foreign study program grew steadily, and by the end of the 80's about 60% of each graduating class had experienced study abroad for an interim or more.

From Thailand we flew to Nairobi, Kenya, with a twenty–four–hour layover in Bombay, India. In Bombay we stayed at the Taj Mahal Hotel, arriving at 2:00 a.m. after a five–hour flight from Bangkok. During the brief time we had there, we visited the Prince of Wales Museum (jade, paintings), the aquarium and the home once occupied by Mahatma Gandhi when he practiced law there. We saw an outdoor laundry with clothes hung out to dry in a block–size area. There were many beggars on the street and others in the hotels and restaurants, where everyone was looking for large tips. The streets were filthy. The general impression was one of overcrowding and lack of sanitation. I shall not forget this experience. One is deeply moved by the sad plight of so many people, and at the same time frustrated knowing that there is little one can do, especially while being a tourist. It evokes both sympathy for those who suffer and a desire to advocate policies which on a global scale can begin to attack such problems.

In Nairobi we stayed at the New Stanley Hotel, evidently a favorite place from which to start a safari. I've never seen so many clothes appropriate to such treks, unless it would be in a Banana Republic store. Wild animal parks surround Nairobi.

We took a trip out about fifty miles to Treetops Hotel, a building on stilts near a watering hole for wild animals. At twilight we watched as large numbers of animals of many kinds gathered at the watering place to drink, bathe and play.

Treetops is an attraction for tourists who want to see wild animals but not hunt them. It has also a measure of renown because it is where the Queen of England was staying when, as Princess Elizabeth, she received the news that her father had died and that she was Queen.

Our next stop was Addis Ababa, Ethiopia. There we were met by Mr. Fit Baissa, a member of the Parliament and a leader in the Mekane Jesu Church, a partner of The American Lutheran Church. We stayed at a modern, western–style hotel, the Hilton. We were entertained at the Baissa home and were taken to an Ethiopian restaurant where we ate a traditional dinner, seated at a round wicker table in wicker chairs. A table cover, gray in color, was spread before us and bowls of food were poured out on it. We soon discovered that the table cover was a kind of bread, and the trick was to pinch off pieces of bread, dip them in the food, and hope that everything came out even. We did wash hands both before and after.

In Addis we saw the government building, called the African Building, where the Organization of African States meets, the city market, the church headquarters and radio station RVOG. That station, whose initials stand for Radio Voice of the Gospel, had been set up by the Lutheran World Federation. It broadcast regularly in fourteen languages for twenty–four hours a day, and into many time zones. The station could reach two billion people, almost half the population of the world. Since we were there, the communist government has taken over the station, and its gospel voice is stilled. But it was great while it lasted.

From Ethiopia we went to Israel, staying from March 3 to March 10. I believe most Christians hope that they might visit the land of the Bible. Dorothy and I had eagerly awaited this part of our trip. We stayed at the King George Hotel in the eastern (Arab) section of Jerusalem. We took tours to Jericho, Bethlehem, Hebron, Bethany and the Dead Sea. We spent many hours walking in the Old City only a few blocks from our hotel. It was a moving and thought–provoking experience to be in the land where our Lord had lived, and where so much history has been and is being made.

Our next stop was Athens. There we checked in at the Royal Olympic Hotel, and as we did I noticed a sign in the lobby which announced, "Welcome Fargo Elks." Sure enough, it greeted a group from Fargo, North Dakota, and during the next two days we met several persons we knew from our Concordia and Moorhead contacts. We ate with them and visited with them. During our Athens stay we climbed the Acropolis. There we met a travel group sponsored by Luther Seminary and including our friends, President Al Rogness and his wife Nora. We invited Al and Nora to come to our hotel the next evening for dinner.

We had a good visit with them, and as the meal concluded I asked the waiter for the check. He gave me a sign that it was taken care of, which I interpreted to mean he had charged it to our room. After all, we had eaten there several times and he probably knew us. The next day we were to leave. We came down to the dining room for breakfast and were served by the same waiter as the evening before. He expressed surprise to see us, and said, "I thought you were with that Fargo group. They left this morning." We explained that we were traveling by ourselves. Then, with a puzzled look on his face, he said, "You know, I charged your dinner last night to the Fargo Elks." We have since told the story to Al and Nora, and we have seen some of our Fargo friends to thank them for dinner.

Athens is a great city to visit. We couldn't manage all the antiquities, but in addition to those in Athens we did get to Mycenae and Epidorus. We passed Corinth, that great commercial city of former days, now a rather insignificant town.

From Athens we flew to Dubrovnik, Yugoslavia, where we spent a delightful three days taking it easy. Our hotel was located just outside the wall of the old city, and looked out on the Adriatic Sea. We attended a chamber music concert in the Rector's Palace, an old castle, and visited shops and city squares just to appreciate the history of the place. While in Dubrovnik we received news that Peter had been struck by a car as he crossed a street in downtown Minneapolis. Fortunately he had not been seriously hurt.

Then it was on to Munich with a six–hour layover in Zagreb. In Munich we were met by Gertrude Sovik, a St. Olaf faculty member spending her leave of absence in Germany. We drove south to the Bavarian Alps, saw the impressive mountain scenery and visited Berchtesgaden, Hitler's retreat, now an American Army base. We drove on to Strasbourg where Gert was living during her leave. After a day of sightseeing there, she joined us as we went on to Vienna for a three–day stay. Vienna is a special city, and Gert had planned a busy few days there. We toured the city, attended a concert in the opera house and visited the Lippizaner Stallions.

In Vienna, I developed an eye infection which turned out to be iritis. I didn't know it then, but I was to learn later that I had Reiter's Syndrome, a rare disease of the arthritis family. It was diagnosed only after we returned to the United States, and the doctors surmised that I had picked up the bug at the Mongolian barbecue in Taiwan. The symptoms are an eye infection, swelling and pain in one or more joints and a burning sensation when urinating. Chiefly because of the last of these, and because it was first diagnosed among sailors in the Orient, it had also been classified as a venereal disease. Great news.

The various symptoms came on at different times while we were in Vienna, and the iritis was treated by a doctor there. The other symptoms weren't too troublesome, so we decided to continue our journey. We said goodbye to Gert Sovik and flew to Moscow.

It was exciting to visit Russia, the land which embraced so much history, but which had become an almost forbidden and shadowy place for Americans. We were in Moscow for three days and Leningrad for two. Our visit was cut short by my increasing discomfort. We had intended to visit Norway and then spend several days on the Costa del Sol in Spain, but all that was abandoned in the face of my growing discomfort.

I think gray when I think of Moscow in March of 1972. It was cold and cloudy. The buildings were mostly gray stone or concrete. One exception was the Kremlin, located a short distance from our hotel, the Intourist. Its red brick exterior and crowning onion domes made it stand out from other buildings.

Our hotel room was satisfactory, much like what we would call second class in America. A woman was stationed on each floor. She was the custodian of our room key and, I suspect, general watch–person of all who came and went.

We were guided in our sightseeing by an Intourist guide. We saw what she selected, not what we might choose. She showed us mostly the exterior of buildings — the University, the Kremlin, the Bolshoi Theater, some apartments. One day we escaped and went to the GUM department store a block from our hotel, and learned how to shop Moscow style. You first find what you want, then you take it to a clerk who writes out a slip. You go to another counter and have your purchase wrapped, then on to another counter to make your payment. Each step includes standing in line and waiting. It seemed to me an effective way to employ lots of people and to occupy the time of many others as they shopped.

Each time we went to the dining room in our hotel, we were seated by a host at his pleasure. The system called for all tables to be filled. One evening we were at a large table with eight other persons, all Russians, I think. Another evening we were seated at a table for four with a young couple. We learned how to visit with them by the use of gestures, smiles and a few words of Latin derivation. The young man was an Italian going back to Italy after having been employed in Moscow. The young woman was a Georgian, from the south. They were vivacious, demonstrative and happy, even though this was a night of parting for them. He had bought a bottle of champagne which they insisted on sharing with us. At the end of the meal the man gave Dorothy a quite proper kiss and me a big hug. We gave each of them one of the Eisenhower silver dollars, several of which we carried for just such times as this.

In Leningrad we stayed at a fine old hotel in the Victorian tradition — large room, high ceiling, ample wardrobe space and ancient plumbing. We had a delightful time, except for my troublesome pains. Leningrad seemed to us to be a brighter, freer and more charming place than Moscow. Unfortunately the Hermitage was closed, so our sightseeing lacked one of what we thought would be the highlights of our trip.

In Moscow I had bought a cane because my ankle was swollen and painful. My other symptoms were present and becoming more painful each day. I was reluctant to be hospitalized in the Soviet Union, having heard stories about leeching and other less–than–modern medical practices. So we decided to go home. We got our tickets changed, flew to Helsinki for an overnight stop and then on home by way of Copenhagen. I entered the hospital, was there a few days, and then stayed home for a while before going back to work. It had been a great trip despite the abrupt ending.

Before leaving Leningrad, we decided to give some things away. We had traveled through various kinds of climate and had with us clothing for every temperature. Dorothy decided she could do without two dresses and a pair of overshoes. She summoned to our room the ever–present matron on our floor, and indicated to her that she was to have those articles of clothing. The reaction was immediate — the woman gave Dorothy a big hug and a smile of joy. She also said what must have been, "Thank you very much."

Other trips Dorothy and I took, though not as grand as the one I've just described, were a trip to England in 1965 when we also visited Norway, and a Caribbean cruise with the directors of North American Life and Casualty Company in 1969.

In February, 1970, I participated in a conference of educators at Ditchley, a conference center housed in a country estate near Oxford, England. In January and February, 1973, I spent a week in Beirut, Lebanon, as a member of the Scholarship Committee of the Lutheran World Federation. As I've written earlier, I attended another meeting of that group in Stuttgart, Germany, shortly after Dorothy's death. In June, 1977, I was in Dar es Salaam, Tanzania, for two weeks as a delegate to the Assembly of the Lutheran World Federation.

In all of these travels I gained much in terms of understanding other people and other cultures. I always returned home glad to be an American, but at the same time I believe I grew in appreciation for the way other people live. Travel also persuades me to be cautious in the judgment of other countries, knowing that my brief contacts have not made me an authority on any of them.

A college presidency involves participation in many official and semi–official groups. I served on the boards of several education–related organizations, such as the Association of American Colleges, the Lutheran Educational Conference of North America (which included schools in Canada), and the Council of Protestant Colleges. These groups charged themselves with the responsibility for lobbying members of Congress on behalf of understanding and granting fair treatment to the private sector of higher education. These contacts broadened my knowledge of private higher education as a whole, brought me into contact with many knowledgeable and influential persons, and led me to think through my own views regarding the way colleges function and are supported.

I cannot forget one unusual experience in connection with the Lutheran Educational Conference of North America. In January, 1970, the group met in Houston, Texas, at its usual time in the month of January. I was the outgoing president, and, as such, obligated to give a speech on some supposedly relevant subject at one of the sessions. The schedule called for me to speak in the early afternoon on Sunday during the time when the Minnesota Vikings and the Kansas City Chiefs were to play in the Super Bowl. The attendance at our meeting had been about one–hundred at one of the Saturday sessions. When I arrived to speak, about fifteen of my colleagues were present. I chose to believe it was because of the football game, not their assessment of the quality of speech they would hear. I suggested that my remarks be included in the report of the conference, and that I not deliver them in person. My suggestion was hardly made when everyone rose in agreement and left the room.

There were many meetings in Minneapolis and St. Paul involving the private college group, visits to the legislature, meetings with donors and alumni, and sessions of some of the countless boards and commissions I served on from time to time. Not infrequently I went to the Twin Cities twice a day, and on a few occasions I made three separate trips in the same day, heading back to the office to work between meetings scheduled at mealtimes.

Some of the challenging and satisfying involvements I experienced were related to groups and boards not directly involved with higher education. For several years I was a member of the Minnesota State Board for Continuing Legal Education, appointed by the Minnesota Supreme Court. We proposed regulations to govern a program of legal education required of all attorneys in the state in order to maintain their licensure. It was a learning experience for me. Most of the other members were attorneys, and our meetings resembled faculty groups discussing requirements for majors or for graduation. The program continues as such programs do these days in many of the professions. I believe it is a wise policy for the state and for the protection of the public. During another period of time, I served on the State Judicial Planning Committee, part of the time as its chairman. This group recommended to the Supreme Court policies which would govern the manner of judicial appointment or election and the tenure and discipline of judges. This, too, was an education for me, and, I believe, a valid public service.

Off–campus also meant Carleton College. It is my firm belief that St. Olaf has benefited in many ways by its proximity to Carleton. Carleton is a well–known and highly regarded liberal arts college, and St. Olaf cannot but be mindful of that. I think St. Olaf has been prodded to be as good as it can be partly because Carleton is across town.

When I came to St. Olaf, John Nason was president of Carleton. He proved to be a good neighbor and friend. Dorothy and I were in the Nason home on many occasions, and both John and Elizabeth were always cordial and welcoming. John's successor was Howard Swearer, and he was followed by Robert Edwards. They, too, were good neighbors and friends.

I was once asked to give a convocation address at Carleton. I titled it "Carleton College — Near or Distant Neighbor," and tried to talk about the rivalry between the schools but also the ways in which we worked together. In May, 1980, while we were back in the States during our Norway stay, Carleton honored me with the degree Doctor of Laws. I was grateful for that; to me it meant our relationship had been a good one.

Several efforts had been made to increase cooperation between the two colleges before I came to Northfield. Academic departments had worked together on occasion, and a modest coordination of libraries had been effected. During the years I was at St. Olaf, some further steps were taken. The libraries adopted a common catalog, and students at both colleges were permitted full use of both. (Citizens of Northfield were also welcome in the college libraries and could make use of the collections). We jointly appointed a science librarian, and made several joint faculty appointments. We established a common health service located at the Northfield Hospital. We initiated bus service between the two college campuses and also between the colleges and the Twin Cities. We could not agree on a common calendar (Carleton had a three–term calendar) so class sharing and cross–registration remained minimal. There was brief conversation regarding the building of a concert hall, with the colleges and the community sharing ownership, but nothing came of that.

Twice during my stay at St. Olaf, the two colleges contributed to the cost of city improvements. When there was need for a new safety center in the 60's, each college contributed $75,000 toward its cost. The city had long provided fire and police protection for the two campuses, so this seemed like the proper thing for us to do. When the Northfield City Hospital was to be expanded, the colleges each contributed $75,000. The colleges, as educational institutions, pay no real estate taxes, so special contributions such as these seemed both practical and politically wise. Incidentally, a Northfield city well and water storage facility had long been located on the St. Olaf campus, near Hilleboe and Kittelsby Halls. That was another gesture by the college toward good will in the community.

Off–campus activity included other Northfield involvements. We were members of St. John's Lutheran Church and appreciated that relationship for several reasons. It brought us into contact with many non–St. Olaf people, and helped us know the community as a whole. We benefited from the ministries of several fine pastors — Boral Biorn, Loyal Golv, David Thompson and Delmar Jacobson. All of them were our friends as well as our pastors. Lois had been employed by David Thompson's father in Thief River Falls when David was a youngster. Delmar Jacobson had worked part–time in the Board of Education office during my days there when he was a seminary student.

I maintained a semi–official relationship with some other college presidents. Oscar Anderson of Augsburg, Elwin Farwell of Luther, and John Bachman of Wartburg were friends as well as colleagues. The four of us, together with our wives, decided to meet occasionally both to discuss our common tasks and to enjoy each other's company. We met in rotation at our colleges on a schedule of about twice a year over a period of eight or nine years.

We invented a name for ourselves, SLAW, using the first letter of the name of each of our colleges. During the late 60's and 70's it was encouraging and helpful to be able to share ideas and concerns. All of us were faced with special problems related to the Vietnam War and its effects on society. Our wives also seemed to welcome the opportunity to be together. Our meetings were informal, unplanned, and usually lasted from a Friday afternoon until Sunday. After our retirements, which came close to one another's, we have occasionally gotten together using the light–hearted designation BARF, an acrostic formed with the first letters of our last names.

216

Chapter 19

A PRIVATE LIFE, TOO

While the college provided plenty of opportunity for every waking hour to be occupied, we nevertheless found it possible to be a family, too.

Dorothy was an admirable president's wife. She entered into the spirit of things, being as committed to the college as I was. Without hesitation she gave of herself in whatever way she could. She entertained, traveled with me, gave talks, served on committees and also tended the home fires.

We ate most of our meals at home when we weren't occupied with college affairs. As nice a community as Northfield is, it wasn't known for its restaurants in the 60's and 70's. As time went on we developed a certain fondness for the Lavender Inn in Faribault, only fifteen miles away, and quite frequently went there for dinner in the evening.

I had a study at home and, while I did not as a rule take work home from the office, I did often prepare talks and sermons at home. Most of that was done when I could find a free evening. Dorothy was an avid reader and also did quite a bit of knitting. I remember her ripping up an afghan after she had made it, not liking the way it had turned out. She immediately knitted another one. She also enjoyed playing the piano. We had realized a small bonanza when we sold our Minneapolis home for the same amount we had paid for it seven years earlier. We decided to use those funds to buy a Baldwin baby grand piano when we moved to Northfield. I used to like to tell Dorothy that we had now redeemed the inheritance of $2,800 we had received when her father died, which we had used to help with the expenses of our 1947–48 stay in Chicago.

In addition to a car provided by the college, we always had one of our own. After we gave Peter and Nancy the Mercedes we had bought in Germany, we drove Chevrolets and Buicks.

Peter lived in Ytterboe Hall his freshman and sophomore years, and then moved to Thorson Hall. His protests in favor of staying in Ytterboe fell on the deaf ears of Mark Almli, whose office decided where each class was to be housed.

Peter majored in art and philosophy. He had decided on architecture as a career several years before college, I believe. The seeds of that choice were probably sown in Forest City, where we were good friends with Norman Madson and his family. Norm was a partner in the Thorson architectural firm there, and welcomed Peter's observation of the work. Peter worked one summer during his high school years in the office of the Sovik–Mathre firm in Northfield, and that seemed to solidify his interest in architecture.

By interesting coincidence, Norm Madson had joined the Sovik–Mathre firm shortly before Peter entered college, and several years later I appointed him to the position of staff architect and superintendent of buildings and grounds at St. Olaf. It has been wonderful to have this ongoing contact with him because he is such a fine person, excellent architect and Christian gentleman, dedicated to the highest standards in all that he undertakes.

Dorothy and I were pleased when Peter began to date Nancy Straus, a classmate whose home was in Madison, Wisconsin. His first date with her was shared with us. We had purchased four tickets for one of the Metropolitan Opera performances at Northrop Auditorium at the University of Minnesota in May of 1964, and suggested to Peter that he find a date and go with us. As an alternative we said we would invite Aunt Nell, my elderly aunt living in St. Paul. Peter asked Nancy.

Nancy was a biology major who planned to go into physical therapy after college. She was a delightful young woman and we were pleased that they chose to go together. By the time of their graduation in 1966 they were engaged. Peter then went off to answer the call of his draft board, and Nancy went to Iowa City to study physical therapy.

In the spring of 1967, Peter was commissioned a second lieutenant in the Army, after taking the officer training course at Ft. Belvoir in Virginia. During his time there, I had spent a few hours with him one cold, rainy evening when I was in Washington for a meeting. We later went to witness his commissioning, and Nancy was there also. We were glad Peter was to be a commissioned officer, and not least that he was going to Germany rather than Vietnam.

The most memorable part of the trip to Ft. Belvoir for Peter's commissioning was the return. Nancy rode back with us, and we drove from Ft. Belvoir to Iowa City, and then on to Northfield with only restroom and restaurant stops. I don't do anything like that anymore. A short time later Peter left for Germany, and returned in October for their wedding.

In the fall of 1963, Mary enrolled at Concordia, a decision she had made without much direct participation by Dorothy and me. She has since said that she felt some pressure from us to go to Concordia, but I believe at the time she preferred it to St. Olaf, where both her father and her brother might interfere with her experience. We had told Peter and Mary that we wanted them to go to one of the church colleges, and that we would assist them in securing whatever education they chose to pursue. We also had said that we would probably not leave them much of any other inheritance when we were gone.

While at Concordia, Mary majored in English and prepared to teach secondary school. She made good use of that training for several years. Early in her college career, Mary began to go with Gary Williams, a classmate from Kerkhoven, Minnesota, and a football player. They seemed well suited to each other. Both did well in their studies. Mary continued to be her independent self and, unlike most Concordia students, did not join one of the societies which were the focal point of much organized college activity. She was homecoming queen her senior year. We attended her coronation and brought her a sporty fur coat as a gift. After the ceremony I gave her a hug and kiss as I congratulated her and said, "We're proud of you, Mary. You've been a wonderful daughter and you've never given your mother and me anything to worry about." Quick as a flash Mary replied, "There are lots of things you don't know, Dad." We let the matter rest there.

Both Peter and Mary were married in Boe Chapel at St. Olaf. Mary and Gary were married on August 12, 1967, and Peter and Nancy two months later on October 21. Both days were beautiful. The weddings were well planned and quite simple. The receptions were in the St. Olaf Center, and Mike Simione, director of the food service, did himself proud in catering the meal. I officiated at both weddings, with Dr. Morris Wee assisting at Peter and Nancy's. Dr. Wee had been Nancy's pastor at Bethel Lutheran Church in Madison during her childhood and teen years.

Nancy and Peter had decided to be married in Boe Chapel because Nancy's mother had died before she came to college, and she felt no desire to return to Madison for the wedding. Dorothy assisted her in the planning. In Mary's case, the decision was based on the fact that she had been in Northfield very little and did not feel at home in St. John's Church, the congregation where we belonged. The college chapel seemed the ideal solution in both cases.

Mary and Gary were married shortly after their graduation from Concordia. Gary entered the graduate school of the University of Iowa at Iowa City, and Mary secured a teaching position at North English, about twenty miles west. They lived near the University campus for two years and then moved to Coralville, a suburb of Iowa City. Mary then got a job at a school just south of Cedar Rapids, closer than her former school. Gary completed a Ph.D. and then was admitted to the medical school. He completed work for the M.D.

degree in 1973, and they moved to Rochester, New York, where he served his residency at Strong Memorial Hospital. After two years there he went to the National Institutes of Health in Bethesda, Maryland, and did research on lupus for two years. Then he received an appointment as a rheumatologist on the staff of Scripps Clinic in La Jolla, California. He and Mary bought a home there and settled into what we expected would be a long–time pleasant experience in southern California.

While Mary and Gary lived in Iowa City, their first child, Luke Rand, was born on August 20, 1971. We were happy to be grandparents, and I had the privilege of officiating at his baptism. His sister, Leah Alice, was born on July 3, 1974, six months after the death of her grandmother. I traveled alone to Rochester to perform that baptism, a bittersweet trip. I was glad that their parents had chosen the name Rand for Luke and Alice for Leah. There had been many Alices in our family, and Leah was to carry on that tradition. Luke was not very old when he gave me a special name, Bop. He still calls me that, and so does Leah, at least some of the time.

Following their wedding, Peter and Nancy were off to Europe. Many gifts remained with us until they returned. Dorothy and I visited them while they were in Germany. They lived in an apartment over the garage of a home in Wiesloch, a village not far from Heidelberg, where Peter was stationed at Army headquarters for Europe. The owner of their place was a wholesale grocer who also sold wine. I believe Peter and Nancy enjoyed a special price on wine while in Germany. Nancy worked as a physical therapist while they were there, so they were two busy people.

Following their return from Europe and Peter's discharge from the Army, he attended the School of Architecture at the University of Minnesota in Minneapolis for three years. Nancy worked as a physical therapist at Northwestern Hospital during that time. They bought a house on Eleventh Avenue South, near Powderhorn Park, where they lived for several years.

Amy Elizabeth, their first child, was born on May 13, 1972, while her grandmother Dorothy was still living. Red–haired Dorothy Alice (named for her grandmother) was born on March 4, 1976. I had the privilege of baptizing both girls at Bethlehem Lutheran Church.

After his three years at the University, Peter took a job at the firm of Setter, Leach and Lindstrom in Minneapolis. Later he became manager of the Twin Cities office of the Architectural Design Group headquartered in Rochester. Interestingly, two of the principals in that firm were former Forest City architects, Gordon Gjelten and Willis Schellberg. Later Peter joined the staff of AIA Minnesota, and in 1982 became its executive director. He has enjoyed his architectural work, but I believe he prefers the mix of responsibilities offered by an office management position. Nancy has continued her career as a physical therapist.

Our Northfield life, so enjoyable, busy and satisfying, was not to continue without interruption. Dorothy suffered from high blood pressure and had been under a doctor's care much of her adult life. At the time of Peter's birth, and again prior to Mary's birth, Doctor Harris in Hibbing had warned us of possible problems with her pregnancy. In both cases he induced labor to insure birth at a certain time and under what he believed would be optimum conditions. In 1946, Dorothy had been pregnant again, and that pregnancy was terminated early on the advice of our doctor in Fargo. I remember consulting with our pastor, Roy Harrisville, before our decision to terminate the pregnancy. His advice was that if Dorothy's life was in danger it was proper and right that the pregnancy should not go full term.

On January 3, 1974, we decided to go to Faribault to do some shopping and to eat our evening meal. As we left the restaurant at about 6:30 p.m., Dorothy said she had a very painful headache. I knew she had suffered from such a symptom before, and that it was serious. I said we would hurry home. About halfway to Northfield Dorothy vomited and then passed out. I tried to talk with her, but she could not respond. We hurried to the Northfield hospital where the emergency staff took over. Dr. David Halvorson, our physician, was called. He arrived within minutes, and after examining Dorothy he recommended that she be taken to Fairview Southdale Hospital in the Twin Cities. I remember wondering if she would recover and thinking she probably would not. I prayed for strength and for peace of mind.

Once at the hospital I called Peter and Mary. Peter came immediately and Mary arrived the next day. Dorothy's brother, Elmer Holm, came from Chicago.

By morning it was clear that, barring a miracle, Dorothy would not recover. She had suffered a massive cerebral hemorrhage. The doctors assured us that she could be kept alive by intravenous feeding and other means. We called a family conference. In addition to Peter, Nancy, Mary and Elmer Holm, there were the doctors and Loyal Golv, our pastor. We decided not to keep Dorothy alive by the special means required. She passed away soon thereafter.

She and I had talked about a condition such as hers. We knew of its possibility for either of us. We had agreed that our choice would not be to be kept alive under those conditions.

It is difficult to describe exactly what one thinks or feels at a time like that. I remember I thought of all the good days and the wonderful experiences we had shared. Since that day in September, 1934, when I met Dorothy at the freshman mixer, she had tolerated my idiosyncracies and had shown me only wonderful love. She had been willing to let me pursue professional interests that did not always seem supportive of family life, and she had been a marvelous mother for Peter and Mary. I remember how thrilled she was when Luke, our first grandchild, was born. We went to Iowa City and stayed for a few days after Mary and Luke came home from the hospital. She also lived to welcome her first granddaughter, Amy, into the world. Together we were grateful to have two wonderful grandchildren. Sad to say, Dorothy did not live to know her other two grandchildren, Leah and Dorothy.

After thirty–one years of blessings in our life together, there was bound to be grieving and a terrible sense of loss. But somehow the presence of family and friends, together with the assurance of the strong grace of God, came to my aid. I knew I was not alone.

Dorothy's funeral on January 7 drew a host of friends and relatives. I remember being saddened in a special way by the fact that Al and Inez Torgerson had moved to Northfield less than a year earlier, I am sure because they chose to spend their twilight years near such a favorite niece. Now she was gone, and Al and Inez must have missed her almost as much as I did.

The college did what it graciously does when a member of the St. Olaf family dies, offering to serve a luncheon prior to the funeral. On this day the Kings' Room was filled. Strangely, or maybe not so strangely, as we took our places, there was a vacant chair next to me. I invited a last–minute arrival to be seated there. It was Lois Ekeren.

The service at the church included music by the St. Olaf Choir and a sermon by Pastor Golv. Dorothy's remains were later buried in Oak Lawn Cemetery.

Life goes on, of course. I remember how good it was to have my work at the college. I also remember how lonely it often was in the evenings or other times I was alone. The college arranged for Marion Pinc, who had been our regular cleaning woman, to come more frequently than before. She did my laundry as well as the cleaning. I've never been in love with household chores, so I appreciated that service very much.

In late January I was scheduled to go to Stuttgart, Germany, for a meeting of the Scholarship Committee of the Lutheran World Federation. I thought of skipping that, but my friends and colleagues urged me to go. I did, and I believe it was good for me. I served on that committee a short time and also remember attending one other meeting, earlier than 1974, in Beirut, Lebanon.

In May, 1974, I spoke at the Downtown Rotary meeting in Minneapolis. A member of that club, Roland Minda, was president of Minda Public Relations, the firm of which Lois was vice president. After the Rotary meeting, Roland told me Lois would like me to stop at the office. Lois had been widowed in December, 1972. Her husband Walt had died suddenly while visiting a friend in the lobby of the Curtis Hotel. I can't remember why it was that Lois wanted to see me. We talked, and as I rose to leave her office, I took her in my arms and kissed her.

Upon my return from Leah's baptism in July, I called Lois and we went out to dinner. We began to see each other with increasing frequency. She lived at the Towers in downtown Minneapolis in a condominium she had purchased following Walt's death. Soon we found ourselves talking about getting married.

It was of course easy to drive to Minneapolis, so I often would go in late afternoon and we would have dinner together before I headed for home. On one of my first visits to her home Lois cooked a delicious dinner. That certainly did not discourage me.

I experienced an increasing desire to be with Lois. I was attracted to her physically; she is a beautiful woman. I admired her various accomplishments and capabilities in fields as diverse as music and public relations. But a relationship of the kind we developed is not based on some coldly rational assessment of a person. There is that other something, a feeling of warmth and affection. Lois seemed to return my feelings, and I grew to believe that she would love me as I loved her.

Our relationship grew. The more I saw of her, the more I was convinced that she was the person with whom I wished to share my life. I considered her truly a gift which God had provided for me at a special time in my life. The years since have confirmed that for me.

The interesting coincidences in our lives going back to 1941 seemed only to enhance the love which grew up between us as we saw more and more of each other and planned our life together.

The pastor for whom Lois had worked when she went to Thief River Falls, Minnesota, as a parish worker in 1946 was G.S. (Jerry) Thompson. He and his wife, Agnes, had moved to Northfield in retirement, and they welcomed Lois and me to their home several times. They certainly encouraged our courtship. Lois stayed with them on a few occasions when she came to Northfield.

As the opening of school approached in late summer, 1974, I told Lois that I thought I would not ask her to attend the opening faculty dinner at the college. I don't know if that was because I thought it was too soon after Dorothy had died, or what the reason was. Anyway, I changed my mind and invited her after all. She accepted, and I introduced her to lots of folks as "my friend, Lois

Ekeren." It was fun to watch the craning of necks and to imagine the conversations which no doubt speculated regarding what was going on between us.

That fall was a busy one because it was the culmination of St. Olaf's centennial celebration. Lois came for many of the events, including the occasion when the Norwegian Ambassador to the United States, Søren Christian Sommerfelt, on behalf of King Olav V, made me a Knight First Class of the Order of St. Olaf. Soren also announced at that time that he shared my birthday. We were twins, both born May 9, 1916. We have since become personal friends, and he always signs letters and birthday cards, "Soren Twin."

Lois and I were married on November 23, 1974, in the Fireside Lounge of Central Lutheran Church, the congregation where she belonged. Jerry Thompson officiated. Lois has not let me forget that I suggested to Jerry that there be no meditation, and that the whole service should be brief. This also meant no music, and for those who know Lois, it will always remain a mystery how she ever agreed to a wedding under those conditions. I wonder at that, too!

It was a challenge to decide who should be the guests at a small wedding. Besides our children, we included representatives of our families, our former spouses' families, our places of work, and our friends. We had a wedding brunch at the Northstar Inn, with special touches courtesy of a friend of Lois's who was sales manager there.

Then we were off on our honeymoon! I had once visited the Wigwam, a resort hotel near Phoenix. We decided to go there for a week. As we boarded our plane in Minneapolis, we discovered that Joe Shaw of the St. Olaf religion faculty was on the same plane, headed for a speaking engagement with an alumni group in Phoenix. He told one of the flight attendants that we were newlyweds. After some hesitation, no doubt due to the fact that she thought Lois looked a lot younger than I, the attendant brought us a congratulatory bottle of champagne. We have since teased Joe fairly often about going along on our honeymoon.

A trip to the Wigwam provided a convenient way for me to get acquainted with Lois's parents, Art and Emelie Schiager, who lived in Phoenix. At the Wigwam we loafed, ate, slept and had a wonderful time together. It was a good way to begin our married life.

Just as Lois yielded a point in not having music at our wedding, so I made a concession, also. When Lois and I started seeing each other I was a pipe smoker. I asked her one day if she minded my smoking. Her reply was, "Of all the types of smoking, I mind pipe smoking the least." That told me something. I went home and threw all my pipes and my tobacco in the garbage can. I haven't smoked since.

Lois's former husband, Walter Ekeren, had been my best friend in childhood. I had stayed in contact with him — and Lois — through the years. Lois likes to tell the story of how she first heard of me. A cousin of hers in Sioux Falls, Kathryn Brende, was one of the young people I mentioned earlier who had assisted me on Sunday afternoons in bringing devotional services to First Lutheran shut–ins. During that year she had written to Lois telling her of the fabulous intern in their church. Lois says that she heard so much about me that she decided she would just as soon not hear the name Sidney Rand again.

In 1946, Lois became the parish work–secretary–organist–choir director at Trinity Lutheran Church in Thief River Falls, Minnesota. She had received her B.A. and M.A. degrees from Colorado College, both in the field of music. In Thief River Falls a member of her choir and a tenor soloist was Walter Ekeren, a pharmacist in business with his brother. To make a long story short, in 1947 they had decided to be married. They made a trip to Fargo to buy wedding clothes, and before leaving Walt suggested they stop in Moorhead to see his friends, Sidney and Dorothy Rand. Sure enough, it was the same Sidney Rand Lois had heard quite enough of five years earlier! They stopped, and Dorothy and I became acquainted with Lois. Our families continued to see each other off and on through the succeeding years.

Walt decided to enter the ministry after several years in pharmacy, and attended Luther Theological Seminary from 1953 to 1956. He and Lois served parishes in Wells, Minnesota; West Salem, Wisconsin; and Springfield, Illinois until 1969 when they moved to Minneapolis. Walt's health had not been good while they lived in Springfield. In Minneapolis he worked part time as visitation pastor at Woodlake Lutheran Church in Richfield, and part time on the pharmacy staff of Miller Hospital in St. Paul. One of his duties at Miller was to teach classes of heart and diabetes patients and their families, and to set up a program on death and dying. It was an interesting way to combine his two careers. Lois worked for a time at the Minneapolis Society for the Blind and then for Minda Public Relations, where she was an account executive and later vice president.

Walt and Lois had two children. Sarah Beth was born on March 16, 1948, in Thief River Falls, and Mark Harold was born on March 17, 1951, in Denver, Colorado. Through the years following 1947, the Ekerens and Rands had visited each other on several occasions and our children knew each other. It seemed quite natural for me, and I believe for Lois also, that we should be married.

Another connection between the Ekerens and the Rands seemed to make our relationship even more a providential one. My mother's sister, Seline, was the first wife of Dr. J.C. Serkland in Rothsay. Following her death, Dr. Serkland had married Anna Langeland, who was the sister of Walt's mother. So Walt and I grew up sharing the Serklands as relatives. We would be together through the years at family affairs such as weddings and funerals.

It was also an interesting coincidence that Walt and Lois had been married in Shove Chapel at Colorado College, where Lois had done her organ study. This was a building given to the college by a distant relative of mine who had been in the lumber and mining business. In view of all these connections, I have often said to people that we had to get married.

I have also said that I married Lois for her big black chair and her condominium. The chair was a large recliner which I liked to occupy when I would come to see her. She had purchased a two–bedroom condominium in the Towers in downtown Minneapolis after Walt's death in 1972. That seemed like a nice place for us to live when I retired, which wouldn't be too many years hence. Of course I loved Lois and married her for that reason. But those other factors were certainly not discouragements.

Lois fit right in at St. Olaf. She was quick to become acquainted with people and had a knack for remembering names and faces. On the evening of the September faculty dinner, we were invited after dinner to two faculty homes where there were departmental groups gathered. In each case there were between twenty and thirty persons present. I took her around the room and introduced her. When we left and got in the car, she went around the room in her mind and named all the people! I couldn't get over that. Her first test, five days after returning from our honeymoon, was to co–host with me the many guests who came to campus for the Christmas dinner and concert. We greeted guests for three hours before the concert, and again at a reception following it, each night for three nights. Lois was warmly received by college people immediately. The rhythm of the life of a college president and spouse easily moved again into high gear.

Lois was a gracious and thoughtful hostess at college functions. She stood in many a reception line with me and traveled extensively as we met with groups of alumni and friends. As the years went by, she also added to her activity through the teaching of courses in business writing in the Continuing Education program.

In the summer of 1975, we traveled to Norway and England. Lois had not been in Norway, and I was willing to go there any time. Lois found many relatives and built a solid base of contacts for our future trips. We took a well–traveled tourist route, mapped out for us by Reidar Dittmann, from Oslo to Bergen to Trondheim and back to Oslo, seeing fjords, experiencing ferries and mountain roads, and being fascinated by the beautiful scenery. I had been in Norway the previous year with the band as we celebrated the college centennial, but it was quite enjoyable to be back again.

In England, we visited many historic places and, in addition to London, saw Coventry, Stratford, Stonehenge and the Lake Country. We were in Edinburgh for several days, sightseeing and eating haggis. We made a swing through Wales and stayed at the Prince of Wales Hotel in Caernarvon, not one of the better hotels in which we have stayed.

Lois and I took other pleasure trips as well; we didn't travel only for the college. In January, 1977, we went on a week–long Caribbean cruise, and in July, 1979, we had a delightful time touring the American and Canadian Rockies, visiting Glacier Park, Banff and Lake Louise.

One of the highlights of the years from 1974 to 1980 was the planning and building of the new residence for the president's family. I have mentioned that development in an earlier chapter. The house is in what we called Scandinavian Modern, designed by the Sovik–Mathre firm of architects. They first proposed a house of stone to match other college buildings in material and style. We rejected that idea as too pretentious and out of keeping with what a house of today should be. We believed we got an attractive and functional residence, although not everyone liked the rather severe lines of its basic shape. They could easily see how well it worked as a president's home, though.

A spacious entry hall leads to a large living–dining room area in one direction, and to a study, the kitchen and the rest of the house in another. A family room, guest bedroom with bath, and another half bath are located on the entrance level, with a screened porch attached off the kitchen at the back of the house. Up a half flight of stairs at the end of the house away from the living room is a wing with three bedrooms and two baths. Below this wing are the garage, a utility room, and the furnace and air–conditioning room. There are 4,200 square feet of living space, quite ample for any use.

Lois spent uncounted hours helping to plan the house. She got along fine with the architects, and I think they enjoyed working with her. In fact, the Minnesota Society of Architects had been one of her clients at Minda Public Relations. She deserves the credit for the fact that the house turned out pretty much as we had hoped it would.

The move to the new house was an interesting one. It is across the street from the old house, so on the appointed day several persons from the college crews came and proceeded to carry things across the street. At one point a line similar to the old–fashioned bucket brigade was formed, and articles were passed from hand to hand the 150–or–so feet from one house to the other. A college truck was used to move such items as the piano. It all took only a few hours.

Two weeks after we moved in, I went to Dar es Salaam, Tanzania, as a delegate to a two–week meeting of the Lutheran World Federation Assembly. Lois stayed home getting us settled in the new house. Fortunately for us, Mark was with us at that time and helped Lois with those responsibilities.

Both of our homes in Northfield involved more than the houses. Our yards were large and included beautiful trees and other plantings. They also included Johnny and Tinky Squirrel, two friends which I identified originally many years earlier for Peter and Mary when they were children in Moorhead. In Northfield, Johnny and Tinky liked to play in the oak trees and gather acorns. When our grandchildren began to visit us, I made it a point to introduce them to Johnny and Tinky, and told them stories about the two little creatures. This seemed to fascinate them, and there was no end to the adventures which could be concocted.

The Ole Store, a block down the street from our home, is famous in St. Olaf College history. One of its claims to fame is the Ole roll, a sweet, sticky piece of bakery goods popular with college students of many generations. We introduced our grandchildren to Ole rolls, and Amy likes to recall trips we took with a little red wagon to get a supply for breakfast or lunch.

We tried to arrange family gatherings with our children and grandchildren as frequently as possible, but as the families grew and scattered that became more difficult. Peter, Nancy and their girls were in Minneapolis, but Mary, Gary and their children were settled in California. Sarah married Ben Buck of Ames, Iowa, in 1975, and I had the privilege of officiating at their wedding. We gained a wonderful son–in–law. Ben is a dental technologist, and Sarah continued her work on the staff of Mary Greeley Hospital in Ames. Her son David Boosinger lived in Springfield, Illinois, with his father Ray but I was happy to have another grandson. Ben had three children and they were all in school.

Mark was home from a less than happy experience in Vietnam, and after trying several things had decided to go back to school. He attended Inver Hills Community College for two years and then surprised us by announcing that he would like to complete his college work at St. Olaf. He entered the paracollege program and did very well, graduating in 1981. That year he married Katherine Rush from Cottage Grove, whom he had met at Inver Hills Community College, and I officiated at that ceremony, also. Mark had worked in construction to put himself through college. We admired him for going back to school after several years away from his studies.

Our grandest family gathering took place at Christmas time in 1979. We were in the midst of preparing for our departure for Norway, as a result of my appointment as ambassador. We knew that when we returned we would be moving into our condominium in Minneapolis. We had kept that when we were married, and rented it out, with Peter as our agent, from the fall of 1974 until we returned from the Embassy in 1981. In anticipation of our leaving for Norway and the need to dispose of many of our possessions, we invited all the children and grandchildren to come home for Christmas. I guess we even threatened them a bit, because we said we were going to divide up much of what we had, and they had better come to claim what they wanted.

Everyone appeared and we had a wonderful time. In preparation, we had wrapped certain family heirlooms — dishes, glassware, silver, with notes attached explaining their origins and importance — as Christmas presents to give each family under the Christmas tree. Then there were various pieces of furniture from which we let them choose. We disposed of three bedroom sets, a dining room set and several individual pieces. Mary got the grand piano as her mother had wanted. We loaded the shelves in my study, where we had already packed the books, with all sorts of things, and told the kids that was the country store where they could shop "without money and without price." They cleaned it out quite well. Finally, we had wrapped some items we thought the grandchildren would like, and color–coded them for the various children. Then we conducted a fish pond by way of the laundry chute from the upstairs hall to the basement utility room. I was down below ready to attach a gift to a string of color–coded yarn we had given each child. A good time was had by all.

We were left with only a little more than we could squeeze into the condominium. That went into storage to await our return from Norway.

Chapter 20

A SURPRISE ON THE WAY

During the 60's, David Johnson and I used to wonder how much longer we should stay at St. Olaf. The Viet Nam War, with its student reaction of unrest and protest, made some days less than enjoyable.

Dave had been at St. Olaf longer than I. He had played many roles. One he played well while I was at the college was to be a counselor, guide and friend to the president. I appreciated him very much.

As the war issue passed, we moved on into the 70's, and I came to the end of my second term in 1975. I agreed to stay on, as I have recorded earlier, and I was glad that Dave agreed to stay also. I was re–elected to a third six–year term, to expire in 1981.

During 1979, I tried to make it clear to the Board of Regents that in 1981 I would be sixty–five years old, and I would then have been president for eighteen years, quite a bit longer than the national average. So, I reasoned, the board should get busy with a search for my successor. There were those on the board who asked that I consider being re–elected to still another term with the understanding that I could step out prior to the completion of that term. I appreciated such comments and the confidence they reflected regarding my work, but I noticed that such thoughts simply diverted the board from planning for a presidential search.

I also knew that there were at least some faculty and staff members who believed a change in the presidency would be a good thing. I didn't want to overstay my welcome, so I insisted that I would not consider re–election after my third term. The board took me seriously and set up procedures for a search. Not only that, they voted to grant me my last year as a terminal leave at full pay. This meant I would complete my work at the college in the summer of 1980.

The board not only voted the terminal leave, but offered me the option of receiving my salary for a year after I left the college or of placing that amount in a trust fund from which I could receive income as long as I, or Lois, lived. We chose the latter, and have been grateful to the college for the generous addition to our other retirement income.

As is so often the case, things did not work out as planned. They worked out better!

One day in September of 1979, Dr. David Preus, presiding bishop of The American Lutheran Church, called. As was often the case, I was at a meeting, this time in Denver. Dave told Lois it was quite important that he speak to me soon, so the two of them agreed that Lois and I would meet Dave and his wife Ann for lunch at the Minneapolis Club the next day, a Saturday. When I returned home, I called to confirm the meeting. Within a few minutes, Dave called back to say that Vice President Mondale wanted him to talk to me about a possible appointment as ambassador to Norway.

So we met with the Preuses. The idea of an ambassadorship had of course never been in my plans. Again, my life was faced with one of those strange and wonderful twists of fate, or Providence, which I had known before. I had not planned to teach in a college, nor to be a college president nor a church board administrator. All of these opportunities seemed to appear before me as gifts of a gracious God. That's exactly what I think each of them has been.

As we talked, Lois and I agreed that we should not dismiss the idea of an ambassadorship. Dave Preus evidently reported back to the Vice President that I was open to consider it, because a few days after our Minneapolis meeting I got a call from Mr. Mondale. "Sid, how would you like to be United States Ambassador to Norway?" he asked. "Well," I replied, "I haven't been sitting around thinking about it." I had thought I was one of several names being considered. He invited me to come to Washington to talk with him. I did, and found out I was the Administration's choice for the appointment.

So rather suddenly we were to decide if we were willing. I say "we" because from the start it was evident that Lois would play a major role in the work, should I be appointed. We had to keep everything quiet for the time being while the government checked me out. One exception was that I was permitted to talk to Oscar Husby, chairman of the St. Olaf board. If I were to be appointed, I would leave St. Olaf even earlier than planned, probably at the end of the first semester instead of the end of the 1979–80 school year. Mr. Husby was very supportive, and assured me that the board would release me at the time required.

It was necessary for me to undergo what was called a clearance check. This was conducted by both the FBI and the intelligence branch of the State Department. We were required to supply the names of persons who knew me well, including all the people who had been our neighbors in the past ten years. The investigators visited with dozens of people, asking questions about me as a person, my habits, my work record and my temperament, without saying why I was being investigated. Many of my friends later reported to me that they had been visited, and of course some of them suggested that they had given quite damaging information about me. One St. Olaf faculty member, Miles Johnson, reported that he had asked the person who had come to him, "What's he running for, Ambassador to Norway or something?" Sam Haugen, a near neighbor, reported that he had asked, "Aren't you going to ask anything about his wife?" "No," replied the investigator, "we aren't allowed to." Then Sam offered the advice, "You ought to. She's the best part of the team." Al Anderson, a St. Olaf board member and personal friend, told us later that he had been asked about my drinking habits. His reply had been, "On the drinking scale, Sid Rand rates somewhere between Jimmy Carter and zilch."

The investigations must have turned out favorably, because even before I had been confirmed by the Senate, Vice President Mondale made a public announcement stating that I was to be the ambassador. Naturally, we grew more excited as the days went by, and we were encouraged to see how genuinely pleased everyone on campus seemed to be.

Some time before the public announcement, we were able to share this good news with the members of our family. They were as excited as we were. When Sarah shared the news with ten–year–old David, he asked, "Are you sure that's the same Sidney Rand?" It was just about that amazing to all of us.

In December I appeared before the Senate Foreign Relations Committee, and that proved to be a new and educational experience. Minnesota's two senators, Rudy Boschwitz and David Durenberger, attended. I was introduced by Arlen Erdahl, the representative from Minnesota's First District where St. Olaf College is located, and an alumnus of the college. The committee had fallen behind in its agenda, and I was given only a brief time. That was quite all right with me. Senator Frank Church of Idaho, the committee chairman, asked Senator Jacob Javits of New York, the vice chairman, to question me first. "Mr. Rand," said Javits, "what makes you think you are qualified for this appointment?" I had to think fast. I believe what I said in reply was, "Senator, I have great confidence in the judgment of those who have appointed me, and I have been a college president for more than twenty years. I think that is a kind of diplomatic work." "That's all," Senator Javits said, and then turning to Senator Church he commented, "That's about as good an answer as we get around here." Next, Senator Jesse Helms asked, "Do you speak the language?" I understood him to mean Norwegian, so I replied, "Not as well as I should, and not as well as I intend to." That ended the questioning, and the committee recommended my confirmation. I was later confirmed by the Senate, and over the final hurdle to the ambassadorship.

In January, Lois and I were back in Washington for two weeks of briefings. It was necessary for me to meet with several government departments, including military and intelligence. During that time we stayed in an apartment near the State Department and included some St. Olaf contacts with our other business.

One special series of events took place prior to my confirmation hearing in December. I went to the North European Desk as I had been told to do when I arrived in Washington. Here I met a young man whose primary responsibility was contact with the Embassies in the Scandinavian countries. He was Dennis Goodman, an easterner and a graduate of Princeton, who was to guide me through my orientation. He had never heard of St. Olaf.

When I arrived at his office, there was a cable for me from Bruce Laingen, a St. Olaf graduate who was being held hostage in Teheran. He was a veteran foreign service officer who had been the Chief of Mission when the U.S. Embassy in Teheran was taken over by Iranians. He had heard of my appointment, and sent me congratulations by way of the Norwegian Ambassador to Iran. Of course Bruce was something of a hero in the State Department at the time. "Do you know him?" Dennis asked in surprise. "Yes," I said, "he's a St. Olaf graduate."

In a short time, we were due at the office which coaches prospective ambassadors regarding their appearance before the Foreign Relations Committee. So off we went, Lois, Dennis Goodman and I. As we entered that office, we were greeted by the man in charge, Robert Flaten, a St. Olaf graduate and veteran of the foreign service. "Do you know each other, too?" Dennis Goodman asked in amazement. We acknowledged that we did.

As we returned to Goodman's office, we found a telephone message from Oslo waiting for me. Brenne (Fred) Bachmann, a St. Olaf graduate stationed in the Oslo Embassy had called to welcome me. I returned the call and we had a brief visit. Brenne had graduated the first year I was at St. Olaf, and I also knew his parents. His father, Dr. Theodore Bachmann, was a veteran theological professor.

That call was followed shortly by another. Carol Hamrin, a China specialist, was working a couple of floors above us in the State Department. She was a recent St. Olaf alumna, had her Ph.D. in Chinese studies, and was on special assignment. She had heard I was in the building and called to invite us for dinner. Dennis Goodman could hardly believe all this.

Then we went down to the cafeteria for lunch, and in the line we met John Reinertson, a St. Olaf alumnus recently home from the Middle East and working in the State Department building on international labor issues. We visited briefly. Finally Dennis Goodman said, "Is St. Olaf trying to take over the State Department?"

It was fun to impress an easterner and a Princeton graduate with this kind of record for a midwest church college. I was proud.

Our briefings in Washington included sessions in which Lois and I were both involved, and some in which we were briefed separately. In one of her briefings, Lois was told that since the passage of the Equal Opportunity Act, spouses of diplomats could not be required to assist in the work of the mission. Then the briefer paused and said, "Now this is what you will be doing." This was an accurate forecast.

We were taken to Norfolk, VA, one day to visit the Navy installation there. This included a briefing from SACLANT, the American admiral who was the supreme allied commander in the Atlantic area for NATO. He was Admiral Harry Train, impressive in his knowledge of military affairs and also a high–class gentleman in every way. He entertained us at lunch in his home, one of several stately mansions on the base, each named for a state of the union. We had later visits with him in Norway and in Minneapolis.

One of the special events during our briefing time in Washington was a luncheon given for us by the Norwegian Ambassador to the United States, Knut Hedemann, and his wife Gro. Vice President Mondale was one of the guests.

Meanwhile, back home, the Board of Regents arranged to have Harlan Foss, then vice president and dean of the college, to be acting president while a search for my successor went on. The change took place on February 1, 1980. As it turned out, Harlan was elected to a regular term as president, and served until 1985.

Vice President Mondale had said he would like to come to Northfield to swear me in. Normally the swearing–in would take place at the State Department in Washington, but we were glad that the Vice President wanted to come to St. Olaf for such an occasion. That made it possible for us to make a celebration out of our leaving St. Olaf. On February 14, 1980, the chapel was filled to overflowing with an enthusiastic crowd of students, college staff and friends. George Vest, Assistant Secretary of State, was there, as was Ambassador Knut Hedemann. The program was brief. The Vice President spoke and swore me in. I took the oath with Lois holding the Bible, and then responded briefly. Ambassador Hedemann brought a greeting, and received the biggest round of applause of any that day! This may have been because he was a Norwegian, or because it was announced that he had spent a year at Carleton as a student.

A reception in the Center followed the ceremony, and later in the day the college hosted a dinner for our family and close friends.

One day in chapel, shortly before we left, the students put on a program in which they remembered some of my idiosyncracies and sent us on our way with shouting and singing. They gave us several gifts, including St. Olaf T–shirts, a scroll signed by hundreds of students, and a certificate entitling me to free dance lessons. Faculty and staff hosted a dinner in our honor at which they also emphasized some of the special Rand characteristics in an inventive and humorous program. The Northfield community said farewell with a lovely dinner at Carleton College, sponsored by the Rotary Club. We were surrounded by good feelings and good wishes.

On February 19, we flew to Copenhagen, stayed there two days, and then went on to Oslo. On this trip we went first class, and that was fun. But after that the State Department flew us business class. I don't know what that means, but we enjoyed the first class trip very much!

Vice President Walter Mondale came to St. Olaf to commission me as Ambassador to Norway. Lois held the Bible at the ceremony in Boe Chapel.

The Embassy Seal and I welcome visitors at the gate of the Embassy Residence in Oslo.

On my way to present my ambassadorial credentials to King Olav V, escorted by Marshal of the Court Smith–Kjelland in the King's 1939 Packard.

The new ambassadorial couple in the Embassy Residence.

Which one is the ambassador? Our faithful driver and guide, Willy Waaler, regularly pointed out places of interest as we traveled around Norway.

When my brother Lyman, his son Robert and his grandson Tony visited us in Oslo, the Rand boys played a Rothsay game of croquet in the Residence garden.

Former St. Olaf student Tarald Rike (second from right) and his brother Jon showed us around their home area at Valle in Setesdal, Norway.

Foreign Minister Knut Frydenlund was my chief contact with the Norwegian government. He and his wife Grethe became our good friends as well as colleagues.They always called me Anders, my Norwegian name.

With relatives (from left) Alvin and Clara Serkland, Alice Serkland, and Charlotte and Francis Heiserman.

My sister Mary and her husband Harold Miller.

My brother Lyman and sister Charlotte with me in Fergus Falls in 1978.

Grandchildren (left) Luke and Leah Williams of California, and (right) Amy and
Dorothy Rand of Minneapolis.

Our daughter Sarah
with her husband Ben
and son David.

Grandson David delights in beating me at a game of Rocks.

At a reception with King Olav V in the Twin Cities in 1982.

At a May 17 parade with former Minnesota Governor Al Quie and his wife Gretchen.

Norway's Consul General Harald Lone presented me with the Commander's Cross, Royal Norwegian Order of Merit, in 1986.

A tennis team out of uniform gathers to celebrate Oscar Husby's eightieth birthday. From my left: Hoover Grimsby, Oscar Husby, David Johnson.

In La Jolla with Leah, Luke and Mary.

On the lake at Kavanaugh's Resort with grandchildren Jessica and Bryce.

The Rothsay brand of croquet must be passed along. Granddaughter Jessica takes a lesson.

Grandchildren of Jorgine Vatnaas Pedersen at the dedication of the house in which she was born, which was moved from Sigdal, Norway to the Scandinavian Heritage Park in Minot, North Dakota, in 1991. Left to right with me are Alice C. Serkland (Mrs. Chester), Chester Serkland and Alice Serkland.

Jo Benkow (second from right), president of the Norwegian Parliament, spoke at the May 17 celebration in Minneapolis in 1990. Robert Paulson (at left) and his son Loren were the photographers for the book, *Norway*, which we presented to Mr. Benkow. Lois and I wrote the text.

Gathered with Lois and me in Chicago when Peter was made a Fellow of the AIA are Nancy, Amy, Peter, Dorothy and Mary.

Ron and Mary Taylor with Dorothy, Peter and Nancy Rand.

Sarah celebrates her 1995 MBA from Iowa State with brother Mark, husband Ben, daughter–in–law Kari, son Dave, niece Jessica and me.

At Kavanaugh's Resort each summer we "dress up" one evening for dinner. Here Peter and I await the rest of the group.

Mark, Bryce and Jessica at home in Northfield.

Granddaughter Amy with some of her students in Monduli, Tanzania, in 1996.

ON TO OTHER PLACES
1980 —

Chapter 21

EMBASSY LIFE

When we arrived in Oslo on February 19, 1980, we were immediately ushered into a busy life, quite new to us in many ways, but not so different in others. What I had suggested to the Senate Foreign Relations Committee regarding a similarity between the life of a college president and that of an ambassador was supported by our experience in the Embassy. Both of us were involved. There was much contact with people, socially and otherwise. We traveled extensively. The Embassy proved to be an organization of human beings not unlike college denizens; they operated best when they knew their roles and were shown appreciation for the performance of their duties.

The Embassy Residence was an impressive experience in itself. Located near Frogner Park on Nobelsgate, it is 24,000 square feet in size, consisting of about 65 rooms and numerous other cubby–holes and storage spaces. It is set in a large city block surrounded by an iron fence. Security was tight; we had a guard stationed in the house day and night. The house was designed in what the Norwegians called "Russian country house" style, and had been built by a family named Nobel–Olsen. Mr. Nobel–Olsen was an industrialist who had spent several years in pre–Revolution Russia and admired that architecture.

The home proved to be an excellent place for entertaining groups large and small. We were assisted in all of that by a staff of loyal helpers. Romy Reynosa, a Filipino, was house steward in general charge of operations. Our maids were Anne–Marie (Rie) Kjær–Nielsen, a Dane, and Elvira (Elvie) Tolentino, a Filipino. The cook was an American young man, Kurt Martuneac. There were also a gardener, a caretaker and two part–time laundresses. Lois supervised these people and directed their work. In addition, seven retired Oslo police officers provided round–the–clock security. One was always stationed in a small room by the front door. He monitored the traffic in and around the yard with the help of electronic surveillance, and controlled access to the property.

The first floor of the house included a large entrance hall, two rooms used as public reception areas, a dining room, two offices and a five–room kitchen complex. Our personal quarters consisted of four rooms on the second floor, where there were also guest rooms and a maid's service room. On the third floor were two more guest rooms, a small apartment occupied by Romy, two exercise rooms and a large storage area. Over the kitchen wing were quarters for Rie and Elvie. The basement accommodated food and wine storage facilities, a small guest bedroom, furnace room, laundry and ironing rooms, a greenhouse, a sauna and several storage rooms. Above a detached garage were two apartments, one occupied by Kurt and the other by our gardener.

The Embassy is located near the center of Oslo, about a mile from the Residence. It is on a main street, Drammensveien, across from the Royal Palace. The Embassy provided office space for about a hundred persons, a cafeteria, an atrium, and a garage for embassy vehicles. My office was on the fourth (top) floor in one corner of the triangular building. This embassy was built in 1959, and was an award–winning design by Eero Saarinen. It is somewhat forbidding and fortress–like from the outside, but inside it is functional and attractive with a beautiful four–story atrium.

I was blessed with a capable staff. The reason an inexperienced person such as I can serve as an ambassador is because the State Department has well–trained and dedicated people in an embassy, who know their business and are able to guide a neophyte ambassador. My Deputy Chief of Mission was Richard Barkley, an eighteen–year veteran of the foreign service. He was expert at counseling me regarding approaches to be made to the Norwegian government, decisions on sticky issues and many miscellaneous matters. He had previously served in West Germany and in Panama (where he had assisted in preparing the treaty by which the United States relinquished control of the Panama Canal), and when we knew him had learned to speak German, Spanish and Norwegian fluently. Following his posting in Norway, he has served a second time in West Germany, a special–request assignment in South Africa, and as ambassador to East Germany, a post he held at the time the Berlin Wall fell. His final post before his retirement in 1994 was as ambassador to Turkey. Dick Barkley is an excellent example of the high caliber of the State Department personnel we met during our period of service. The Embassy housed not only State Department personnel, but representatives of the Department of Defense, the Department of Commerce, the United States Information Agency and the Central Intelligence Agency. My job was to coordinate the work of all of them, and keep them from pursuing tasks at cross–purposes with each other. The mission in Norway is considered a medium–sized operation. There are smaller ones, but there also are the huge ones such as those in London, Paris, Tokyo and Moscow. Also, the Norwegian operation, while including several non–State Department missions as mentioned above, is still basically a diplomatic mission. There are embassies where U.S. Aid is the dominant concern, and others where the military is the over–riding operation. Oslo was, and is, a comparatively quiet place for Americans.

My work was varied. I was expected to supervise and coordinate the work of embassy staff, and this task was facilitated by the capable management style of Dick Barkley, who knew the ropes and kept things running smoothly. He was able to sense trouble spots and do something about them before they became serious. There were some inter–office rivalries, and we did take steps to send two people home because of their lack of cooperation with the purposes of the mission. All in all, however, it was a competent staff, and the day–by–day work went well.

Once a week I presided at a meeting of the heads of the various sections. We exchanged information and decided on any necessary course of action.

The ambassador is the representative of the President to the government of the host country. Therefore, one of my chief responsibilities was to make calls on the Norwegian Foreign Minister or the Defense Minister (or other government ministers if a special need arose), to discuss issues of mutual concern, and to convey requests or messages from President Carter or from the Secretary of State. An example of this developed following the Soviet occupation of Afghanistan in December, 1979. As a result, President Carter decided to impose an embargo on trade with the Soviets, and asked other countries to support us in this. In March of 1980, I was asked to call on the Foreign Minister to secure Norway's cooperation. The Minister explained to me that even though Norway considered the United States its chief ally, it was still necessary to keep the peace with the "big bear to the East," as he called the USSR. So Norway would not go along with the embargo. As it turned out, only Britain supported us in this move, and the embargo did not succeed in changing the Soviet position. The occupation lasted for ten years.

Soon after I arrived in Norway, I made official calls on the King (with my papers of appointment in hand), Prime Minister Oddvar Nordli, Foreign Minister Knut Frydenlund, Defense Minister Thorvald Stoltenberg, President of the Storting Guttorm Hansen and a few of the other cabinet ministers. Foreign Minister Frydenlund was my chief contact. He and I became good friends, as did Grethe Frydenlund and Lois.

An important person in our embassy life was Willy Waaler, the ambassador's driver. He was a tall, good–looking Norseman, an expert driver and a man knowledgeable in all things Norwegian. He was a great help to both Lois and me as we traveled in the city and throughout the country. We could not have found a more congenial, helpful person to be our frequent companion in the work.

Travel was an important part of the work of the Embassy. In my briefings before we went to Norway, I was told, "Remember you are the ambassador to Norway, not to Oslo." It could have been easy to remain in Oslo; there was plenty to do there. But we took seriously our charge to go beyond the city, and that added much of interest for us during our time in Norway.

We traveled by car to many places. We went to Bergen for the International Festival; we traveled to Trondheim more than once; we toured the far north, including the Soviet border, Lappland and the coastal area north of Trondheim. We took shorter trips to Setesdal in south–central Norway, to southeast Norway, to Stavanger and to Sigdal and Hadeland. In each case we tried to visit with government officials as well as representatives of the community, church, education, business and the military.

Until the end of the Cold War, The American Embassy maintained an information office in Tromsø, north of the Arctic Circle, and we included that in our far–north tour. Pro–Soviet sentiment was quite strong in north Norway, due to a long, close connection between the people of the two countries in that area. The American office in Tromsø was the eyes and ears for the United States, and also a way to disseminate information regarding our country to that part of Norway.

Two major trips were planned for us by the Norwegians. Each year, the Foreign Ministry hosts a visit to some part of the country for the diplomatic corps and spouses. In 1980, that trip took us to Svalbard (Spitzbergen), an archipelago about 500 miles north of Norway. This is a group of islands which is under Norwegian jurisdiction as a result of a treaty signed in 1924 by 40 countries, on the basis of which all signers are granted equal rights to carry on economic activity in the area; no military activity is permitted. The resource being developed is coal, and only Norway and the USSR operated mines there in 1980. A few thousand residents live chiefly in two towns, Longyearbyen, which is Norwegian, and Barentsburg, which was then Soviet. We flew to Longyearbyen, were shown the mining operation and were entertained at a bountiful luncheon with Russian guests joining our group. On the return journey we were entertained overnight in Tromsø.

The other special trip was to Jan Mayen, a tiny island 350 miles north of Iceland. General Sverre Hamre, Chief of Defense, arranged that trip. We flew in a C–130 aircraft — a real flying boxcar. General and Mrs. Hamre, a few military aides and we made up a party of eight. Seats had been placed in the middle of the huge plane. There were no windows, and the noise was deafening! We flew to Iceland and stayed overnight at the American base at Keflavik. We were joined there by U.S. Admiral Harry Train, NATO Supreme Allied Commander/Atlantic, who had flown in from Norfolk.

Jan Mayen is a volcanic island about sixteen miles long and one to two miles wide. The air strip is packed black lava sand on the beach. The only inhabitants are 28 Norwegian military personnel who make navigational and weather observations. Admiral Train was interested in seeing if the place had possibilities as a naval base. We stayed a few hours and then flew back to Trondheim and home to Oslo.

Due to budget constraints, we cancelled plans to travel to Sweden and England. However, the Air Force arranged a trip for us to American installations in West Germany. We visited Stuttgart, Heidelberg and Ramstein, and were taken on a helicopter trip to the East–West Germany border near Fulda.

In addition to the official traveling we did while stationed in Norway, we took two significant out–of–country journeys of a more personal kind.

In May we returned to the United States for a two–week visit. Before leaving St. Olaf, I had planned to speak at Commencement in the spring of 1980, because that was to be the time for my retirement. With the concurrence of Harlan Foss, we followed through on that. As things developed, the trip home developed into more than we had planned. We headquartered with Peter and Nancy. One day they entertained at a very nice reception in our honor, and many of our friends came.

We had been notified shortly before leaving Oslo that both St. John's University and Carleton College had decided to award me honorary degrees. These were in addition to the one I was to receive from St. Olaf. Thus, one evening we were in Collegeville where our St. John's friends gathered at a dinner and awarded the degree, Doctor of Theology. I was impressed by the fact they would honor me with a degree at all, and even more surprised by some of the things they put in the citation presented in connection with the degree. It read, in part,

> "...we discern your peculiar gifts to all of us as an understanding of the unity of the churches; as an understanding of a deep common inwardness, an inner reality that makes us one. This understanding is clothed in that cherished Norwegian humor which not only entertains but forwards the dialogue and reform... You have

contributed to ecumenism's theological, educational and diplomatic task, the non–sacred element which is also unitive. You have bridged the cultural gaps which exist between educational, business, international and religious communities... You respect continuity and tradition... With a lightness of touch, with charm and wit, but also with deep seriousness and inner freedom you lead others to love God and their neighbor."

It was a humbling experience to be so recognized.

Similarly, when Carleton College, good neighbor to the east, decided to honor me, I was grateful and not a little surprised. There, at a special convocation, I gave an address and received the degree, Doctor of Laws.

At the St. Olaf Commencement I spoke and was awarded the same degree, Doctor of Laws. I felt St. Olaf had thanked and feted me, and us, quite sufficiently before we left for Norway. This latest honor was a kind of bonus. We returned to Norway with grateful hearts.

Speaking of honorary degrees, I have received more than anyone should. In addition to those I've just listed, there have been honors from Concordia College, Augustana College, Colorado College and the College of St. Scholastica.

The other major trip we took while in Norway was to Israel. We decided it would be good to take a break and take advantage of an opportunity. We were half–way there already! So we arranged to be away for two weeks in November. Dick Barkley assured me that I had better plan my own vacation time because no–one in Washington would do it for me. We flew by way of Copenhagen, where our baggage was given a thorough search before we boarded an El Al plane for Israel. We then flew non–stop to the airport at Lod, the ancient Lydda. We had notified the American ambassador, Sam Lewis, that we were coming, so an Embassy car met us and drove us the twenty miles into Jerusalem and to the American Colony Hotel in the eastern part of the city. That was a convenient location from which to see important places, especially those with biblical connections.

We walked several times the few blocks to the old city, and visited such sites as Calvary, the Temple Mount, the Via Dolorosa, the two possible sites of Christ's burial, the Garden of Gethsemane and the ancient temple area. We also visited museums, the business section and the American Consul's home where we were entertained for dinner. We took guided tours to Jericho, the Dead Sea, Masada, Hebron and Bethlehem.

We rented a car and drove to Tel Aviv, Caesarea, Nazareth, Cana and the Mount of the Beatitudes on the shore of the Sea of Galilee, where we stayed at a convent. There we met an Austrian priest and together traveled to Capernaum, the Golan Heights, the "Good Fence" at the Lebanese Border (it's no longer a good fence), and a kibbutz. We continued alone to the Mount of Transfiguration and back to Tel Aviv.

At Tel Aviv we were entertained at a Sabbath dinner in the home of the son and daughter–in–law of our Minneapolis friends, Leo and Lil Gross. The other father–in–law, Maurice Spertus of Chicago, presented us with a scroll of the Book of Esther, done on kidskin in Tunisia several hundred years ago.

It is impressive for a Christian to visit this holy land. It was sad to be there and to become quite aware of the hostility that existed between Israelis and Arabs. There were places we were counseled against visiting (such as the historic Samaria), and we sensed the tension which was evident when our tour guide on a couple of occasions gave us a real pitch for the Israeli cause.

Israel is a land of contrasts. There is desert and there are thriving cities; there are ancient ruins and modern buildings; there are people in traditional nomadic garb or the dress of the Hasidic Jews and there are business people in western dress such as one sees all over Europe and America. There is a variety of languages, and there are obviously differing ethnic backgrounds represented among the people.

I have now been in Israel twice. I can see in my mind's eye the important places I choose to remember. I grieve with others over the unsettled issues that beset the whole area. I have no good answer to the difficulties the land presents. Minds much better than mine have failed to find a way to settle the age–old differences. I believe the land of the patriarchs, the prophets, Jesus Christ and the early church is destined to be a microcosm of the world's problems for a long time to come. The peace accord arrived at in 1993 between Israel and the PLO gave hope of a new day of harmony in this part of the world, but troubles do continue.

Travel certainly occupied a good part of our time in Norway, but another important dimension of the life of an ambassador is that of entertaining and being entertained. There were diplomatic representatives from forty–two countries in Norway in 1980, and the group is known as the diplomatic corps. The one who has been at his station the longest is the dean or "doyen." When we were in Oslo, the dean of the corps was Yuri Kirichenko, the Soviet ambassador. He and I had many a conversation, and became friends of a certain kind.

Much of the entertaining side of diplomatic work involves the other ambassadors. When we arrived in Oslo, we were expected to make courtesy visits on each of them and they, in return, on us. There were other occasions when we were together such as the national day of each country when the ambassador would host a reception. One of the great bonuses of the Embassy experience was the pleasure of learning to know, and in some cases become good friends with, ambassadors and their spouses from other countries.

Numerous invitations of all kinds came from persons and groups in the world of education, business or some other segment of Norwegian society. In December, for example, we were invited by the Phillips Petroleum people to their annual Julebord (Christmas table) at the Hotel Bristol. The Julebord was a popular yearly event for many organizations, but this one topped even the customary festive spread. It was the most sumptuous feast Lois and I have attended. Tables groaning with food of all kinds tempted the guests to eat to their hearts', and stomachs' content — or discontent. Drinks, sweets and smokes were also abundant. It was worthwhile to experience that — once!

Our entertaining included frequent dinners, receptions and teas. When special American individuals or groups came, we would entertain them together with Norwegians with similar interests. These included visits by military personnel, members of Congress, trade delegations and cultural groups. Pianist Andre Watts, author William Styron, Senator Henry Jackson and many other interesting individuals came to Oslo, and we entertained each of them together with Norwegian counterparts. And of course numerous personal friends and relatives visited us, too.

In all of this Lois played a major role. She accompanied me on most of our travels and in most of the official visits we made in Oslo, but it was in the entertaining we did in the Residence that she was all–important. She managed the house, supervised the work of our house staff, helped to plan all functions in the house and managed the finances involved. The ambassador is expected to keep the house supplied with groceries, wines, spirits and other necessary items. When official entertaining was done, we could charge the government for each person, provided more than half the guests were Norwegians. For a dinner we were expected to serve drinks before the meal, a three–or four–course dinner with two wines, and, following dinner, liqueurs and coffee. We were paid $12.50 per person, hardly enough to cover the cost. Reimbursement for receptions and teas was less. We filed a voucher and were paid six to eight weeks later by the disbursing office for northern Europe, which was in Paris.

We estimate that it cost about $3,000 to stock the house when we arrived. In addition, we were required to keep two sets of accounts at all times. We were to have on hand $200 and the same amount in Norwegian crowns in each of two separate accounts, one for food and the other for household supplies. Romy and Kurt did the purchasing, and once a week Lois replenished each of the accounts on the basis of what had been spent during the previous week.

Much of Lois's time was spent on these household matters. She was very good at it, and was appreciated by the house staff as well as by the Embassy administrative office. As a result of this involvement, Lois got to be very close to the house staff. They came to her with personal problems and just to visit. We were told that this was special, that few ambassador's spouses had entered into embassy life as fully as Lois did. We both looked upon our experience as an opportunity to broaden and deepen both personal friendships and our life in general, and to serve our country in a concrete way.

Lois also participated in other activities. She was the organist in the American Lutheran Church. She was the honorary chairperson of the Embassy Wives Club and the American Women's Club. She was also involved in a fund–raising event for the Norwegian Red Cross, arranging for a display of an American Thanksgiving Day dining table. She was active in the International Forum, an organization for diplomats' spouses, both Norwegian and foreign, and in a museum group. She participated in a reading group composed of six Norwegian women and six ambassador's wives. She also had some opportunity to accompany American singers in concert appearances.

Our life in Oslo was not entirely official. We had some time for personal affairs. We were active in the American Lutheran Church, where we learned to appreciate the work of Pastor Harry Cleven and became good friends with him and his wife, Turi. We enjoyed fellowship with many others in the congregation as well.

And of course we visited relatives. Lois's father's people had come from Hadeland, a short distance north of Oslo. We visited there more than once and got acquainted with several Skiaker and Gamme families. We have stayed in contact with them and have returned for visits.

Some distant cousins of Lois's operated Molstad, the nicest women's wear store in Oslo, and we got to know them well. They were Terje and Mary Braathen and Ellen Corneliussen. Mary and Ellen were sisters and were of the Molstad family, related to Rossums and Rognstads of Lois's family in Hadeland. Ellen Corneliussen and her son, Anders, lived across the street from the Embassy Residence. Lois shopped at the Molstad store from time to time, and they also made a gown for her for the King's diplomatic dinner.

Lois's mother's family, the Brendsels, had come from Byneset, a community near Trondheim. We visited there also, renewing our acquaintance with some relatives on that side of the family, and meeting many new ones. Lois's mother came to visit us in August, and we drove to Trondheim for a few days. That trip took us through the beautiful valley of Gudbrandsdal, surely one of Norway's most spectacular. We were royally entertained on that trip and also on another when we were present for the confirmation service for Stein Olav Braa, son of Kåre Braa, one of Lois's cousins in the Trondheim area.

I have fewer relatives in Norway than Lois has. I have told people I found six cousins there and Lois found six hundred. That's close to the truth. My relatives were from the area about seventy miles west of Oslo. My maternal grandparents were born in Sigdal, a quiet, wooded valley in the county of Buskerud. I have six second cousins in that area, all of them descendants of my grandmother Pedersen's family. There are no relatives on my grandfather's side as far as I know. All of his siblings came to America except one sister who remained in Norway but did not marry.

The people who live on the Braatelien farm where my grandfather was born welcomed us warmly and we were there more than once. Their name is Svarstad. We took my brother Lyman, together with his son Robert and grandson Tony there when they visited us, and we were also there with Newell Braatelien and his wife. Newell is my second cousin and the grandson of my grandfather's oldest brother. Bearing the farm name as he did, Newell was a special person when we visited "Braatelia gaard," the Braatelien farm.

It was a warm summer Sunday in July when we were in Sigdal with Lyman, Robert and Tony. Because there would be five of us, I had told Willy that he would not need to drive us — I would drive that day. We attended a worship service in the little Vatnaas church, the place where my grandmother had been baptized, and afterward a "kirke kaffe," or church coffee, at a nearby home. There Lyman and the others experienced real Norwegian hospitality. As one plate after the other of cakes and cookies was passed, they could hardly believe it — and their appetites could hardly do it justice. Then we did a little sight–seeing and soon were at a community hall where the mayor of Sigdal entertained us. Again we ate, a full meal with all sorts of goodies.

As we were to leave for home, I threw my suit jacket in the trunk of the car and closed it. In a pocket were the car keys! So there we were, unable to use the car. It was an Olds 98 with armor plate in the sides and rear. There was no way to get into the trunk. After valiant efforts by the local men proved futile, we had to look for another way home. We hired a bus and driver and returned to Oslo, if not in splendor, at least with a good story to tell about a forgetful ambassador. The next day Willy and another driver from the Embassy went to Sigdal to get the car. Ever afterwards, whenever we were to take the car without Willy along, he would give a second set of keys to Lois!

There are many special memories connected with our Embassy experience. Once a year the King entertains the diplomatic corps at a gala dinner at the

Palace. That was an occasion for white tie and decorations. Some of the ambassadors came with sashes covered with medals. I wore my Knight First Class, Order of St. Olaf decoration. I have said I also should have worn my Sunday School pin with its several bars for perfect attendance. Americans don't wear decorations much! A beautiful dinner was served, followed by a splendid piano recital by Kjell Bekkelund. Afterwards each guest had an opportunity to visit with His Majesty.

Christmas was a special time. Lois's brother, Sheldon, and family came to celebrate with us. One evening we prepared and served a meal, Embassy style, with our house staff as guests. We had meatballs, mashed potatoes and everything to go with it. (Lois says it is the only meal she cooked in Norway.) We went to church on Christmas Eve, and as we left at five o'clock, all the church bells in Norway were ringing. On our way home, we visited a cemetery near the Residence. We had heard of the Norwegian custom of placing candles on the graves, and we went to see them. I must say that both the ringing of the bells and the expanse of lighted candles created an unforgettable impression.

Midsummer Eve, June 23, is another special time in Norway. We were guests of the Braathens at their summer place on the Oslo Fjord for dinner. Late in the evening, when it is only dusk because of the long Norwegian summer day, bonfires are lighted in celebration. We could see not only our own but many others along the shore of the fjord. Sailing on the fjord were many boats decorated with birch branches, another symbol of midsummer.

Visits of friends and relatives were special. The St. Olaf Choir came, and with it a tour group including Harlan and Bea Foss and Oscar and Pearl Husby, who stayed with us at the start of the tour. When they returned to Oslo, Elaine Tracy, Evelyn Jerdee, Solveig Steendal and Ned and Elizabeth Brown stayed one night. Later the Kenneth Jennings family stayed with us. Elmer and Gertrude Holm came for a few days before leaving for a boat tour of the west coast. When they left us, they forgot a garment bag, so Elmer wore the same pair of trousers for several days.

Travel groups came through regularly, and with them usually some folks we knew. In one of them were Pastor Hoover and Shirley Grimsby of Central Lutheran Church in Minneapolis. They were walking by the Residence one day after visiting Frogner Park, and decided to drop in on us. They were turned away by our guards — they had no appointment. We saw them later, of course, but have not tired of kidding them about how we refused to let them call on us.

Other family members came to see us, too. Mary, Gary, Luke and Leah came in the fall and stayed several days. One special memory has to do with our going to the award–winning *Grand Prix*, a muppet–like movie in the

Norwegian language. Luke and Leah enjoyed it very much, and Luke even learned the key phrase used by one of the characters. In a deep, sinister voice he would say, "Det er farlig, det," that is, "That's dangerous." Leah became a special friend of Willy, our driver, and all these years later still thinks of him with affection. To show Mary and Gary a little about our work, we entertained at two dinners, one of them black tie. The guests at the latter included several ambassadors, and featured special impromptu entertainment. The Spanish ambassador, Aurelio Valls, a recognized Spanish poet, recited several of his poems accompanied by his wife, Carmen, on the guitar. Nagwa Hosny, the wife of Ambassador Ahmed Hosny of Egypt, performed a genuine belly dance. Lois played the piano, and accompanied solo and group singing. The evening stretched on far longer than the three–hour standard for ambassadorial dinners. A Norwegian guest, thinking it was time to leave, but knowing that it was customary for ambassadors, the ranking guests, to leave first, said to me after midnight, "When are those ambassadors going to leave? I'm getting tired."

Lois's nephew, Bob Ekeren, called one day from Thief River Falls, Minnesota, to ask if we would care to have a wedding in the Embassy. We assured him we would. He was a bachelor who had finally decided to be married. He and his fiancee, Karen Mundell, flew to Oslo and we had a delightful time. Pastor Cleven officiated, Lois played the piano, and we invited several friends to share the event.

Peter came the last week we were in Oslo, wanting to be sure he didn't miss out on a visit to the Embassy. He came at the right time to enjoy a special weekend with us. We were invited, together with others, to be the house guests of Kjell and Tone Steinsvik, owners of the Blåfarveverket museum and park at Åmot, not far from Sigdal. It was a weekend of good music, good conversation, and cultural enrichment in general. We were sorry Nancy and the girls could not come with Peter, but their schedules prevented a last–minute trip. Sarah and Ben, and Mark and Kathy, had been planning to come in the summer, and unfortunately didn't make it because of our rather sudden departure from Norway.

Bill and Connie Cameron (Lois's niece) also came during that last week, and they made a video tape of much of the activity of the final days, including the farewell reception.

We entertained a group of Norwegian people, officials and others, on American election day evening in November. Results weren't conclusive yet, but radio reports indicated to us that Ronald Reagan was probably going to defeat President Carter. That's the way it turned out, and we knew our days were numbered.

During my briefings before going to Norway, I had been told that it was government policy that when a presidential election was held every ambassador submitted his resignation so that the newly elected, or re–elected, president could make appointments as he chose.

Shortly before President Reagan took office in January, I received word from Washington that my letter of resignation should be on his desk by inauguration day. I complied. Almost immediately I received instructions that I was to vacate my post within two weeks. This was nearly an impossibility; we managed to accomplish it in seventeen days, leaving for home on February 14. After we returned to Minneapolis, I received a letter from President Reagan, forwarded from Oslo and dated February 16, in which he thanked me for my service and said I would hear from his staff about a time to leave my post! Evidently the right hand did not know what the left hand was doing.

When I received the notice to leave Oslo, I had proceeded with plans to settle accounts with Uncle Sam. The Embassy paid us for inventory remaining in the house. Before I had left for Norway I had been told that five percent of my salary would be deducted each pay day and deposited in the Civil Service Retirement Account. When I suggested that I be exempt from that inasmuch as I was in other retirement programs, I was told that the law required this be done. So I inquired regarding the benefits. Then I was told that because I was not a career foreign service officer I was not eligible for the retirement program. Upon inquiring what would happen to my money, and what interest I would be paid, I was told there would be no interest paid but that my money would be refunded when I left my post. It was a kind of no–interest forced savings plan. Perhaps Big Brother knew I would need some money when I returned to normal life.

Before leaving Oslo, I filed with the State Department a request for the refund of my accumulated savings. The Administrative Officer of the Embassy told me it would probably take a couple of months to get my money. In June, 1981, four months after leaving the Embassy, Lois and I were in Norway with a trade relations group headed by Governor Al Quie. Inasmuch as we had not received our refund, I went to the Embassy and put through a call to Washington. I was told that my application was being processed and that I would receive my money in about two months. I was angry! So after returning home I wrote to my friend, Senator Dave Durenberger, and told him the whole story. In two weeks I had my money.

Perhaps the moral of this is that our government is very thrifty in some ways. They believe in using other people's money for as long as possible, interest free.

Before leaving a post, an ambassador makes farewell calls. I called at the Palace to see His Majesty, on the Foreign Minister and Defense Minister and on some of the other ambassadors. We entertained at a farewell reception at the Residence. A rather special experience was a dinner at the Soviet Embassy. When I made my farewell call on Ambassador Kirichenko, he suggested that he and his wife would like to entertain us. I said the time was short and that under the circumstances we could forget about such a party. But Yuri insisted. When I returned to the Embassy and told Dick Barkley, he said, "The Russians never do that. Either you must have been doing something awfully wrong or awfully right!" Anyway, we had the dinner, a delightful evening with a six–course meal, featuring, in our honor, roast turkey as the entree in an otherwise Russian menu. Ambassador Kirichenco and I toasted one another and reminded each other of the importance of our nations remaining friendly and maintaining the peace of the world. Perhaps it was a little bit of glasnost.

We left Oslo on February 14, one year to the day after my commissioning. Arriving late at night in the Minneapolis airport, we were met by Peter and Nancy, and John and Kathryn Kvinge carrying a sign reading, "Happy Valentine's Day! We love you even if Reagan doesn't." We stayed with Peter and Nancy for a few days and then went on an automobile trip to the south.

It had been a grand year of unforgettable experiences. How thankful we both were for the opportunity we had enjoyed. A year was not enough, but it was much better than never having had the experience. We have been pleased in the years since that many friends in Norway, official and otherwise, tell us how well we did and how they wish we could have stayed longer. We are glad that we were able to leave Norway knowing that what we had done and who we were evoked appreciation and gratitude among those with whom we worked.

We have stayed in contact with several of our Norwegian friends and with some of the colleagues on the Embassy staff. All of it has enriched our lives.

Chapter 22

ONLY WHAT WE CHOOSE TO DO

There are many definitions of retirement. I see it as a time in life when a person is free to choose what to do and when to do it. This can mean paid employment, volunteer work, travel, loafing or whatever strikes one's fancy.

I am grateful that I have lived long enough to retire. Not that I disliked my work, far from it. I've been offered opportunities to work in areas which I have enjoyed and where I believe I have been able to make a contribution to other people's lives as well as my own. I have enjoyed variety and satisfying activity in each of my careers.

Even before I completed my education and embarked on what was to be my life work, I thoroughly enjoyed the work at Moen's Lumber Yard in Rothsay, at O'Meara's Store in Fergus Falls, at Woodward's in Moorhead and in miscellaneous odd jobs that came my way.

I entered the ministry with every intention of being a parish pastor for my entire working life. The work was a challenge and completely satisfying. Teaching was also a joy to me. Perhaps that was in my bones — both my father and mother were teachers. Later, the work of administration in colleges and with a board of the church proved to be something I liked. And finally, the ambassadorship was not only a happy surprise but a congenial and agreeable assignment in every way.

There may be something wrong with me! Isn't a person supposed to find his niche in life and stay there? Isn't a person supposed to prepare for a career and pursue it? Can it be wise to move from one kind of work to another? All I can say is that, for me, what has happened in my work life has been a thoroughly satisfying and happy half century.

And now I enjoy retirement. That's a still different kind of career. "You aren't retired," my friends say. They would be correct if retirement meant doing nothing but loafing. Since 1981, when we returned from Norway, both Lois and I have been very busy.

For one thing, I have taken on several jobs that pay salaries. During two quarters in 1984 and 1985 I taught homiletics at Luther Northwestern Theological Seminary in St. Paul. That was a new field for me. I needed to prepare lectures having to do with preaching — the history of preaching, various kinds of sermons and meditations, how to prepare and how to preach. It also meant that I listened to and critiqued sermons preached by students. I must say I heard some very poor sermons and some good ones. That work was interesting, and, as a bonus, I got reacquainted with the faculty of the seminary.

During six months of 1988, both Lois and I were employed in another pursuit. We were asked by Robert Paulson, a commercial photographer in the Twin Cities, if we would be interested in writing the text for a picture book about Norway. Bob and his son, Loren, had contracted with Graphic Arts Center Publishing Company in Portland, Oregon, to do a coffee–table book. They needed someone to write ten thousand words of text about Norway plus captions for the pictures to be included. We talked it over and agreed that we would like to do it. We submitted samples of our writing to the publisher and were hired.

It proved to be a very stimulating experience. Both of us contributed to the research and the writing, and Lois put the manuscript in final form. The long body of text was to be a general description of Norway, and that proved to be simpler to do than the captions. The publisher wanted each caption to say something about Norway in addition to identifying the picture. We were told that nine out of ten persons who look at a book such as this do not read the text. So, with that humbling information, we did our best to write copy people would want to read, and captions that would do what the publisher wanted for the 143 photos included.

Norway went into its third printing in mid–1992. The first printing was 10,000 copies, the second and third were each 7,500. The book sells for $35 to $40. We've given quite a few away, and many people have told us they have bought it and that they enjoy it. The Norwegian Embassy in Washington and the Norwegian Information Service in New York have used it as a gift to inform people about Norway. They have told us it's the best book of its type about Norway in the English language, a view that gives us special satisfaction.

During the school year 1986–87, I served as president of Augustana College in Sioux Falls, South Dakota, a senior college of the Lutheran church. Dr. William Nelsen, who had earlier been the dean at St. Olaf, had resigned after being at Augustana for a term of six years. The board of the college decided to take a year to find a replacement and asked me to fill in. I was to be an "interim president."

At a meeting of the board soon after I arrived at Augustana, a member raised a question about my interim status. Joe Foss, a World War II flying ace and former governor of South Dakota, gruffly addressed the chairman, Richard Gunderson. "Mr. Chairman," he said, "we don't want any interim president around here. I move that we either make Rand the president or get rid of him." So I became the president of Augustana College.

Both of us enjoyed returning to a community we knew well. We lived in an apartment the college provided for us, including rented furniture. Dr. Nelsen and his family were to stay in the president's residence for a year while he served as chancellor of the college with certain fund–raising responsibilities. He resigned in October to become president of Citizens Scholarship Corporation, based in St. Peter, Minnesota. His family stayed on in Sioux Falls until the following summer.

I tried to keep things at Augustana on an even keel. I've said I was instrumental in getting two things done for the college. One was to dismiss the provost, a man who was unacceptable to the faculty and many others. The second was to persuade a Sioux Falls business man, Robert Elmen, to finalize an arrangement for a million dollar gift he had said he was going to make to the college. This enabled us to proceed with plans for a physical education/recreation building, which was begun the next year.

Dr. Lloyd Svendsbye, a former student of mine at Concordia and also former dean at St. Olaf, was elected president. He came to Augustana from the presidency of Luther Northwestern Theological Seminary. After five years, Lloyd decided to retire, and I was asked by the Augustana board to return as president for the 1992–93 school year while another presidential search took place. During that year, we had the privilege of living in the president's home. The college furnished it, and the art faculty provided a marvelous exhibit of paintings, sculptures and other art objects, all of them either part of the college collection or produced by members of the art faculty. This provided a beautiful setting for entertaining, and we enjoyed hosting many groups on behalf of the college. When the board elected its next president, Dr. Ralph Wagoner, we returned to Minneapolis.

In 1990, I was asked to serve another interim college presidency, this time at Suomi College in Hancock, Michigan. Suomi is the Finnish word for Finland. The college is so named because it was founded by Finnish immigrants who came to the Upper Peninsula of Michigan to work in the copper mines.

As at Augustana, the president of Suomi had resigned. He was Dr. Ralph Jalkanen, who had been in office for thirty years. He was not in good health and decided to retire.

So we moved to Michigan. I went there on August first, and lived in motels for two months. Then Lois joined me in an apartment the college had rented for our use. It was located near the campus of Michigan Technological University in Houghton, Hancock's twin city. A canal crossing the Keweenaw Peninsula separates the two towns.

Suomi, founded in 1896, is a junior college of the Lutheran church with an enrollment of about four hundred. When we were there it offered programs in nursing, business and law enforcement, as well as a general two–year course. Most of its students were the first in their families to attend college.

We found a warm welcome and had a rewarding year. The Upper Peninsula is noted for snow, and in the winter of 1990–91 there was a total of only 180 inches, well below the annual average of 200–250 inches. The natives apologized to us for the mild winter.

After a lengthy search process, the board elected Dr. Robert Ubbelohde as president. He had been the dean at Suomi for three years. We returned to Minneapolis in late June, 1991.

We had been commuters during the years at Augustana and the year at Suomi, as we maintained our chief contacts and activities in Minneapolis. Lois especially spent quite a bit of time in our Minneapolis home during the three years we were away.

Since 1981, I have been occupied off and on with short–term tasks of various kinds. During 1990, I joined with Dr. Norbert Hruby, a retired college president from Michigan, to conduct a review of a program sponsored by the Minnesota Private College Council. A grant from the Kellogg Foundation had made it possible to provide leaves of absence for the presidents of the Council colleges, together with special seminars and tours. We tried to assess the effect of the program. It took us about three months of part–time work to complete the study.

I have done other short–term college consulting jobs, which have given me the opportunity to renew acquaintances and to catch up on how things have and haven't changed on the college scene. For someone no longer in the work full–time, these have been good ways to keep informed and up on developments in education.

Both Lois and I have been involved in volunteer activities of various kinds. The remuneration is the satisfaction we get from knowing we are involved with worthwhile causes. We hope what we have done has been helpful to the organizations we have tried to serve.

My board memberships have become fewer, partly because that's what I choose and partly because, as one grows older and is no longer in the mainstream of activity, fewer groups consider one's board membership desirable. Younger people properly take over.

Allianz of America, the former North American Life and Casualty Company, has a rule that requires board members to retire at age 73. I concluded my board service there in 1989, after 21 satisfying years. I had learned much about insurance and about business in general.

The same year, I was persuaded by my friend, Jonathan Messerli, president of Muhlenberg College, to join the board of directors of that institution. In 1987, I had done a small consulting job for Muhlenberg. A college for women, Cedar Crest, located a mile or so away from Muhlenberg in Allentown, Pennsylvania, was facing some kind of crisis, and the two colleges had engaged a consulting firm to study the future relationship of the two schools. Its report, though quite costly, had resulted in an ambiguous recommendation with which neither college was pleased.

I did a quick study including two brief visits to Allentown, and, after gathering the available information, recommended that the colleges not merge but continue whatever joint programs they could. I also recommended the dismissal of all consultants, including me. Muhlenberg paid me $5,000 for that fairly simple and straightforward advice, and a little later President Messerli asked me to join their board. "That way I can get your advice without paying for it," he said. I joined the board, and served for one term of three years.

It is interesting and educational to serve on the board of a college other than one you know well. I had to refrain from comparing Muhlenberg with St. Olaf. The two colleges display ovbious differences, but Muhlenberg has many strengths, and I grew to appreciate them.

My volunteer work in the years since retirement began has included quite a few speaking and teaching opportunities. Both Lois and I have taught classes at Central Lutheran Church, where we are members. They have included Sunday Bible studies and Thursday classes for the Fifty–five Plus group, where I have taught both Bible and catechism. Following the retirement of Hoover Grimsby as senior pastor at Central in 1986, I was elected chairman of the call committee. This involved many meetings over a period of several months, and much of it was during the time I was serving as president at Augustana. The call committee was a congenial group, and our work ended with the calling of Stephen Cornils of Palo Alto, California, as our senior pastor. In the fall of 1994, I was chair of the Every Member Visit program carried on at Central.

Separately or together, Lois and I have spoken more than 150 times regarding Norway. Our experience in the Embassy and our writing of the Norway book have stimulated invitations from church groups, Sons of Norway lodges, service clubs and others. We talk on almost any aspect — the church, Norway and the European Community, education, security issues, the country in general, the people, holiday customs, and the Norwegian migration to the United States.

We have been kept up to date by trips we have taken to visit Norway, by contacts with Norwegians and by news reports. The Norwegian Consulate General in Minneapolis has provided us with lots of information. Since our retirement, the three Consuls General, Harald Lone, Bjarne Grindem and Anfin Ullern, have been supportive and helpful. Consul General Grindem once told us we are Norway's ambassadors to the United States. It is true that our talks give a favorable report on almost all aspects of Norwegian life. I'm sure a Consul General would like that.

I have mentioned that I received the honor of Knight First Class, Royal Norwegian Order of St. Olav, from the King of Norway during the St. Olaf College Centennial in 1974. I was surprised, but pleased, in 1985 to receive an additional honor from His Majesty. This new honor was Commander, Royal Norwegian Order of Merit. This order had just been established, in order to recognize non–Norwegians for service significant to Norway, and I was told that I was one of its first recipients. In 1983, Lois was recognized by His Majesty, King Olav V, with the St. Olav Medal, given for distinguished service in Norwegian–American relations.

Following our retirement, King Olav visited the Twin Cities twice, and each time Lois and I were involved in planning the visits. Other noteworthy visitors from Norway have also come, and I have frequently been asked to emcee dinners held in their honor.

Occasionally I am asked to speak to service clubs or other groups who want to hear something about education. I act like an authority, of course, and proceed to inform each group before whom I appear! I still preach occasionally for church anniversaries and other special occasions.

From time to time I do an errand for St. Olaf College. I like to do that and consider it a privilege to work with a committee or call on a prospective donor in the interests of the college.

During the mid–80's I was a member of a tax study commission appointed by Governor Rudy Perpich to do a thorough examination of the Minnesota tax policy and structure. After two years of meetings and discussions, we compiled a report which fills two good–sized volumes. We made recommendations to the governor and the legislature for modifications in the way Minnesota taxes its citizens. Some of them have been enacted into law, but it takes a long time for legislatures to make basic changes in such an important area as taxes.

I also served for a year as a member of a task force set up by the Minnesota Business Coalition to study the way in which health care is delivered in the state. This group, like the tax study commission, made several observations and recommendations, but the real benefits of this piece of work will probably be seen in changes that are gradually brought about, both by government and by private interests, as the years go by.

In the late 80's, a group was formed at the initiative of Dr. David Preus and Mike Roan, executive director of Project Tandem, a conference–planning organization related to the University of Minnesota. The purpose was to conduct annual forums on the subject of peace at colleges with Norwegian–American roots, and to celebrate the fact that the Nobel Peace Prize is awarded in Norway. I was asked to serve as a member of the group, which also included former Vice President Walter Mondale, former Governor and Congressman Albert Quie, former Governor and Ambassador Karl Rolvaag, and representatives of the five midwestern colleges with Norwegian background.

The forums have been held on all five of the college campuses, and are on the second round. They have proved successful in attracting students from the colleges, and the general public, to hear presentations by Nobel laureates and other distinguished speakers on various themes relating to achieving peace. Some of the laureates who have been involved are Oscar Arias, Elie Wiesel, Norman Borlaug, Betty Williams, and Rigoberta Menchu. Others with Peace Prize connections have been Camilla Sadat, daughter of Anwar Sadat; Elena Bonner, widow of Andrei Sakarov; Bernice King, daughter of Martin Luther King, Jr.; Naomi Tutu, daughter of Archbishop Desmond Tutu; representatives of the United Nations and Amnesty International, and assorted diplomats. At one of the forums, former President Jimmy Carter was a speaker.

My volunteer work has included one activity which has taken more time than some others. For six years prior to the fall of 1991, I was a member of the board of our condominium association. For four of those years I was the president. This responsibility involved several meetings a year, presiding at sessions of the association, meeting with the management company responsible for day–to–day operations, and hearing complaints and suggestions from homeowners. Like so many of my other experiences, it was an education.

One Towers resident brought suit against the board, and I found myself as a witness in court. Fortunately, the Towers Association prevailed. That was the

269

case of a person insisting on his right to various kinds of disturbing behavior which we on the board thought was out of order.

In 1990, I was asked to be a member of the National Architectural Accrediting Board, a twelve member group representing the architectural profession, architectural schools and the various state registration boards. It examines and accredits schools of architecture. A requirement of the board's bylaws is that one member be a non–architect "generalist–educator," and I fall in that category. I served for five years.

When I was invited to join NAAB, I thought Peter had something to do with it. He says not. The suggestion of my name came from Jim Cramer, then Executive Vice President of the American Institute of Architects, and former executive of the Minnesota Society of Architects. I had met him through Peter.

The work of NAAB brought me into contact with a different group of professional people than I had formerly known. It was an educational experience. Twice a year the board meets in some attractive place, and encourages spouses to attend. While I was a member, the meetings were in Washington, DC; Jekyll Island, GA; Santa Fe, NM; Rancho Bernardo, CA; Victoria, BC; Woodstock, VT; Coral Gables, FL; Halifax, Nova Scotia and Grand Cayman Island. Twice a year I was a member of a team of four or five persons which visited schools seeking initial or renewed accreditation. I visited schools at the University of Utah, the University of Idaho, the New Jersey Institute of Technology, Roger Williams College in Rhode Island, Princeton University, Woodbury University in California, Washington University in St. Louis, and Virginia Technological University.

In 1996 I was made an honorary member of the American Institute of Architects, a recognition resulting from my activity with NAAB. I never thought I would share Peter's professional affiliation, but it is a privilege to do so.

For several years I have belonged to an investment club composed of a dozen retired pastors. We meet monthly and each invest $25 at every meeting. We have not gotten rich, but the meetings have provided us with opportunity for good fellowship, exchange of stories and many cups of coffee.

Lois has been busy during these retirement years, also. She's more of a volunteer than I am. For ten years she was a member of the board of directors of the Ebenezer Society which operates housing and service programs for aging persons. She was chairman of the board for four of those years.

Later she became a member of the board of Lutheran General HealthSystem in Park Ridge, Illinois, and served for six years. During that time, Ebenezer was affiliated with Lutheran General, so Lois was, in some sense, an Ebenezer voice on the Chicago board.

Lois has served for over ten years as a member of the board of the Norwegian–American Historical Association which has its office at St. Olaf College. That organization engages in the study of Norwegian immigration to the United States and settlements which resulted. It publishes books, monographs and essays having to do with the Norwegian settlement of America, and maintains archives of immigrant materials. The NAHA was founded by such worthies as O.E. Rolvaag and Theodore Blegen, and continues to do significant work.

For eight years, Lois served as a member of the council which sponsors the David W. Preus Leadership Award. That award, named in honor of the former presiding bishop of The American Lutheran Church, recognizes persons who have demonstrated outstanding leadership through service to others in church or community.

A recent major task for her was to chair the call committee seeking a new senior pastor for Central Lutheran Church. This was a ten–month process which led to the selection of Paul Romstad of Woodlake Lutheran Church in the Minneapolis suburb of Richfield. In March, 1995, he began his work with us amid an enthusiastic welcome.

During the latter part of 1994 and through 1995, Lois and I were co–chairs of arrangements for the visit of Their Majesties King Harald V and Queen Sonja to the Twin Cities and the surrounding area. We were asked to serve in this capacity by Consul General Bjarne Grindem. The Consul General was the official host in this area. We were assisted by approximately eighty persons serving on several committees arranging general plans for the visit and details of the reception and banquet held in the Twin Cities. We were also responsible to coordinate with committees organizing the visits to four colleges and several other venues in the region. We accompanied the Royal Party on their visits to St. Olaf College in Northfield, Luther College and Vesterheim Museum in Decorah, the Norwegian Lutheran Memorial Church and Augsburg College in Minneapolis, Lyngblomsten Care Center in St. Paul, and Concordia College in Moorhead. The visit went well and the Royal Couple gave every indication of enjoying their time here.

All in all, we have been kept busy doing things of interest to us, and, we hope, of value to others.

Chapter 23

ON NOT STAYING HOME

Miscellaneous employment and volunteering have not filled the Rand retirement schedule. There has been time for travel also.

Norway seems to have dominated that phase of our lives. In June of 1981, Lois and I accompanied Governor Al and Gretchen Quie and a small group of business leaders to Norway to promote trade on behalf of Minnesota business. That was only four months after we had left the Embassy, so we were happy to return and to see many of our friends.

While we were still in the Embassy, we had written to Arley Bjella of Lutheran Brotherhood about the sad state of the old organ at the American Lutheran Church in Oslo. Upon our return home, we had talked with him further about it. Arley and Beverly were along on this trip with Governor Quie, and one evening we attended a special service at the ALC, at which Arley presented the congregation with a check from Lutheran Brotherhood to pay for a new organ.

In August of 1983, we returned to Norway, and while there visited relatives and friends in Sigdal, Hadeland, Trondheim and Oslo. I went to Copenhagen for a couple of days to make contacts on behalf of the Søren Kierkegaard Library at St. Olaf. A highlight of the trip in Norway was an evening at Skaugum, the farm home of Crown Prince Harald and Crown Princess Sonja. The other guests were His Majesty King Olav, a friend of the Crown Princess from Switzerland, and, of course, Princess Märtha and Prince Haakon, about 12 and 10 at that time. We sat at a round table and enjoyed a family–like meal. The entree was crayfish, and we all wore bibs. Our plates were removed and we were given clean ones regularly throughout the meal, but Princess Märtha refused to have hers changed. She was counting the number of crayfish she had eaten, and wanted the proof before her. Prince Haakon offered to show Lois how to remove the odor of crayfish from her hands by sprinkling them with salt and rinsing them in the fingerbowl. He assisted her and asked her to do the same for him.

After dinner we gathered in a small living room for coffee and visiting. It was a delightful experience and one we will always remember. The King dozed off as the evening wore on, a habit he had cultivated through the years. When we thought we had stayed the proper time, I proposed that we leave. It would have been correct for His Majesty to make that move, but then again ambassadors, and even retired ambassadors, exercise such a prerogative at times. When we suggested that we should leave, the Crown Princess nudged the King, and he awoke and bid us goodnight. Lois says this is one of the most embarrassing moments of her life.

In December of 1984, we made a one week trip to Norway. I had been asked by Arley Bjella to assist in setting up a fund to sponsor visits to Norway by outstanding Norwegian–Americans. This trip was paid for by Lutheran Brotherhood, and I secured the sponsorship of the Nordmanns–Forbundet (Norsemen's Federation) and the Norge–Amerika Foreningen (Norway–America Association) for the new program. It is called the America–Norway Heritage Fund, and was established with a grant of $100,000 from Lutheran Brotherhood. The two Norwegian organizations select Americans of Norwegian descent who have made significant contributions to American life, and bring them to Norway to make presentations appropriate to their area of accomplishment. So far, educators, business persons and musicians have been chosen. The costs are paid by the income of the fund.

In September of 1985, we returned, along with the Bjellas, for chapter two of the America–Norway Heritage Fund story. A festive dinner was held at the Militær Samfund, a favorite banquet hall, to inaugurate the fund. Dr. Lloyd Hustvedt of St. Olaf College had been made the first awardee, and he addressed the dinner guests. The King led the list of invitees, and also in attendance were the American Ambassador, Robert Stuart, his wife, Barbara, several government and military officials, and leading business people and educators.

Lloyd Hustvedt gave a brilliant lecture, in English, describing Norwegian–Americans he had known as he grew up in a rural community near Northfield. It was an insightful, poignant story, beautifully crafted and masterfully delivered. It fulfilled the purposes of the fund perfectly. When Lloyd finished, the King stood and led the applause, a truly remarkable occurrence. The America–Norway Fund was indeed off to an auspicious beginning. I think Arley Bjella was pleased, and he should have been.

I was surprised and pleased to be selected as the recipient of this award in the summer of 1995, the fund's tenth anniversary. I gave two lectures in Oslo, the first at the American Embassy Residence on the subject, "Religion in America," and the second at the Nobel Institute during the Norway–America Society annual meeting, on the subject, "The New Migration," dealing with the international exchange of students. The fund paid our expenses for this trip, including a weekend at Moster on the west coast where we attended the celebration marking the 1,000th anniversary of Christianity in Norway.

In 1986, we enjoyed a completely unexpected trip. A St. Olaf graduate who worked for the Royal Viking Cruise line contacted me and asked if we would be interested in a cruise on the west coast of Norway. Lois and I would receive free passage if I would give lectures aboard ship regarding Norway. We were more than happy to accept such an offer, so in June we flew to Copenhagen where we boarded a beautiful cruise ship, the *Royal Viking Sky*, and spent the next twelve days along the coast of Norway as far north as North Cape. We made stops at Stavanger, Bergen, Trondheim, Honningsvåg, Tromsø, Molde, Geiranger and Oslo. It was delightful. Lois and I gave joint lectures about Norwegian life, economics and security, and I preached at a Sunday service. A highlight of the trip was becoming acquainted with a charming couple from London, Ontario, who shared the dining table with us. They were Albert and Marjorie North, who have remained our friends. We correspond, and twice we have visited them in London.

At the conclusion of that cruise we had two extra days in Copenhagen, so we took a bus and ferry trip to Sweden, visiting Malmo and Lund.

My next Norway visit was with Mel George, the president of St. Olaf, in the fall of 1986. President George asked me to accompany him on a visit to Trondheim and Snåsa. The founder of St. Olaf, Bernt Julius Muus, was born in Snåsa and attended school in Trondheim. He is buried in the Nidaros Cathedral churchyard in Trondheim, having died while on a visit to Norway in 1900.

In September of 1987, Lois and I together enjoyed another trip not only to Norway but to other European countries as well. The board of directors of the North American Life and Casualty Company was invited to meet at the offices of Allianz, a large insurance firm with its headquarters in Munich. Allianz had purchased North American a few years earlier. So off we went with our expenses paid by North American. We left in advance of the meeting so we could do some traveling on our own.

We spent a few days in Norway, then flew to Geneva where we rented a car. We traveled through Switzerland on a beautiful Sunday, stopping first at Bossey, where I lived for five months in 1962–63. Leaving Switzerland, we drove through Lichtenstein and saw the village made famous by Spyri's story of Heidi. We stopped one night in Bludenz, Austria, where we stayed in a cozy mountainside hotel, traveled on through picturesque Innsbruck, and spent a day and night in Salzburg, the city famous for its musical history and festival. From there we went to Vienna where we spent several days. We had a reservation in what we had thought was a good hotel. It should have been, because it was named the Alpha. It was at least a gamma — or an omega. The weather was warm and there was no air conditioning. Our view overlooked an alley. But we were not in the room too much, so we survived.

We took the city bus tour, visited the famous Schonbrunn Palace, art galleries, government buildings, churches and business district. One evening we were taken to the opera by our friends, Knut and Gro Hedemann. Knut had earlier been the Norwegian ambassador to the United States, and now was the ambassador to Austria. The Vienna Opera performed Puccini's *La Boheme*. Afterward we stopped at the Hotel Sacher, where we indulged in dinner followed by Sacher Torte. It was an unforgettable evening in every way. Another evening the Hedemanns took us to a winery on the outskirts of Vienna for dinner and a festival of new wine. It was the season for that, and a special time for the Viennese.

A gustatory highlight of the Vienna stay was dinner one evening at the Drei Hussaren restaurant, one of those that makes all the lists as one of the world's finest. A friend of ours, Richard Niebuhr, from Aberdeen, South Dakota, had told us we must eat there. We had a table in a quiet corner, were waited on with grace and polish, ate excellent food and listened to good music. Our waiter recommended the Norwegian salmon as the outstanding entree, and we didn't argue with that. I think the meal cost us close to $100 each, but it was the grandest eating experience we have ever had.

From Vienna we drove west toward Munich, part of the time along the Danube. We stopped over night at Linz, Austria, in a motel much like those in America. Linz is the home of the Linzer Torte, nearly as famous as the Sacher Torte. Then on to Munich, where we were housed in the Hilton for three days. While there the North American board met with the board of Allianz. We visited shops and stores, and the grounds and buildings of the 1972 Olympics.

We were also the guests of Allianz at a rural retreat house about forty miles south of Munich in the foothills of the Bavarian Alps. It was a grand chalet–like house called Voglsang ("birdsong"). About twenty of us were in the group, and we stayed two nights. On one of the days I went back into Munich with the group (Lois stayed home to rest), and we attended the Oktoberfest which had just begun. There were large buildings similar to those at the Minnesota State Fair, each of which housed one of the major beer companies and their wares. The menu was beer and ribs. We were there for about three hours. I drank more beer than I ever had, and being one who doesn't care for it, that was quite a feat. Oompah bands provided music, and there were shops selling souvenirs. But the main business was beer.

When we returned to Voglsang, I discovered that Lois had been treated like a queen, being waited on and indulged in every way by the staff. That was a much better way to have spent the time than at the Oktoberfest.

Another day the Allianz folks took us to Oberammergau, where we visited shops and restaurants and saw the site of the Passion Play. It was a beautiful trip through villages as quaint as one sees in the story books.

After a nearly three–year interval since the last trip, we felt it was time to return to Norway for a visit in June of 1990. Although this was a personal trip, and we therefore spent much of our time visiting friends and family, we did also enjoy seeing several of our "official" friends. Ambassador Loret Ruppe invited us to stay at the Embassy Residence during the time we spent in Oslo. We were entertained by Jo Benkow in the president's office at the Parliament, by Bishop and Mrs. Andreas Aarflot in their home, and by Juan and Holly Pellicer, who had become our friends when he was the Mexican ambassador to Norway. Johan Heyerdahl of Nordmanns–Forbundet entertained us at an Oslo Philharmonic concert featuring pianist Eva Knardal. We had expected to have an audience with King Olav, but he was hospitalized following a stroke he had suffered a few days earlier. Crown Prince Harald, who was acting as regent, invited us for an audience instead.

We enjoyed a second trip in 1990, this time paid for by someone else. The Norwegian Ministry of Foreign Affairs invited Mr. and Mrs. Bjella, and Lois and me, to be their guests on a trip to Norway. The Bjellas went at the end of summer, and spent a week traveling. We went in mid–September for ten days of briefings.

The Ministry set up a program for us through which we were briefed by various government offices concerning Norway's policies in such areas as economic affairs, politics and foreign relations. It was an informative series of meetings, and helped us to be better representatives of Norway's interests in the various talks we regularly give. We believe it was due to our activity in making presentations to various groups about Norway that we were invited to be guests of the government for this visit. They housed us in style at the Grand Hotel.

There were some special experiences connected with this trip. We visited Lillehammer and were briefed on preparations for the 1994 Winter Olympics. That was especially fascinating, and answered many questions we and others had been asking. The manager in charge of the entire project, Petter Ronningen, entertained us at lunch and gave us a thorough and most impressive account of the organization and the progress of the endeavor.

One evening we were guests of Jo Benkow, the president of the Storting (Parliament), and his wife, Annelise Høegh, at a dinner party at the Hotel Bristol. We had been asked to suggest a dozen names of guests, and we found that Mr. Benkow had added another dozen, all of them friends of ours. Of special interest was the fact that our friends, Oscar and Pat Boldt, of Appleton, Wisconsin, were in Norway and we were able to include them in the company. It was a rather lavish feast, done in formal Norwegian style with "Velkommen til bords," "Takk for maten," and other toasts.

During the dinner we spoke to Magne Hagen, the King's secretary, concerning His Majesty's health. He told us that the King was at his farm in Bygdøy and was receiving therapy following the stroke he had suffered in June. On this September visit, we had not even notified the Palace of our presence in the city, because we knew the King was not receiving any visitors and we had had an audience with Crown Prince Harald in June. However, we now asked Mr. Hagen to bring our greetings and best wishes to His Majesty.

The next day there was a call for us at the Foreign Ministry, requesting that we contact Mr. Hagen. He informed us that the King had said that if we had time in our schedule, he would like to see us! What a privilege, we thought. Of course we were not too busy.

The following day we went to the farm at Bygdøy, where we had a delightful visit with the King and his dog Troll. It proved to be our last visit with him, because he died the next January. He was his usual gracious self. He was in a wheel chair, his left arm was impaired, and his speech was not as clear as it had been, but he was cheerful and outgoing and asked questions as usual about our lives and about St. Olaf. His first question, as usual, was, "How is our college?" This private visit is a wonderful last memory to have of a kind and gracious man, aptly described as an "uncommon common man."

Our next trip to Norway was a sequel to that visit. The King died in January, and we wondered if we should try to go to the funeral. We mentioned it to Consul General Bjarne Grindem, but did not feel it would be proper for us to think seriously of going, particularly in view of the protocol issues involved in such an occasion. Shortly after that, on a Saturday evening, we received word from Mr. Hagen through Mr. Grindem, telling us that the Palace requested our attendance at the funeral. So we made some fast arrangements, and flew to Norway that next Monday. We were in Oslo just two days.

The Grindems were kind to let us use their apartment in Oslo, an easy commute by trolley to the center of the city. The funeral was held in the Cathedral. We had orders to be in our places before 11:00 a.m., as the service was to begin at noon. We were assigned to a particular seating area, but within that we could sit anywhere. We went early and had excellent seats in row two of the west transept, which we later learned was the section designated for "friends of the Royal Family." The service was to begin at noon, after the funeral cortege had walked from the Palace down Karl Johansgate to the Cathedral. Just before noon, the procession entered the church led by Bishop Aarflot, the presiding bishop of the Church of Norway. At the stroke of twelve, the cathedral bells, and all bells in the country, tolled three times, followed by one minute of silence, observed throughout the nation. The sanctuary was filled with dignitaries from countries around the world and from Norway. The service was the simple funeral service used everywhere in Norway, the only exception being special music by the cathedral choir and the Norwegian broadcasting orchestra, and a brief tribute by Prime Minister Gro Harlem Brundtland.

Following the funeral, the cortege, accompanied by the family and military honor guards, proceeded to Akershus Castle, the final resting place of Norway's royalty.

A little later we walked to the Palace where the new King Harald and Queen Sonja, together with Crown Prince Haakon and Princess Märtha, greeted the people from the balcony. In the snow in front of the Palace, there were thousands of flags, flowers and messages to or about King Olav. Their beloved monarch was gone, but a new King was with them. The crowd broke out in two songs, the Norwegian national anthem and "God Bless Our King."

We were invited to a reception in the Palace, where we had an opportunity to greet the family and wish them well in their new responsibilities. There we had an opportunity to visit with several friends in government positions.

We flew home again the next day, weary but grateful we could share in a momentous event for Norway, and an unforgettable experience for us.

In January, 1992, I made another trip to Norway, this time with a Twin Cities group which was promoting the building of a ski slide in Bloomington to duplicate the famous Holmenkollen in Oslo. Lois was not with us on this trip. We were in Norway for five days calling on people we thought might help with financial support for the proposed slide. It is a large project and the total cost is about seven million dollars, but enthusiastic people are working on it.

In 1993, we were again back in Norway. Anton Armstrong, the director of the St. Olaf Choir and someone we had known well since his student days at the college, suggested that it would be nice if we would accompany the choir on a tour of Denmark and Norway in May and June of that year. B.J. Johnson, manager of the choir, also encouraged us to go. The day after commencement at

Augustana College, we flew off to Copenhagen with the choir. We were there two days, and attended a concert by the choir as well as making another visit to Tivoli. Our friend and former maid from Embassy days, Rie Kjær, came in from Aarhus to visit us and attend the concert with us.

We traveled by bus to Fredrikshavn, where we boarded an overnight ferry to Larvik, Norway. There we left the choir as they headed for Stavanger and Bergen, and we went on to Oslo.

We had several days of visiting with friends and relatives in Oslo, Sigdal, Hadeland and Trondheim. We rejoined the choir for a concert in Trondheim, then for a concert in Lillehammer and finally for a grand concert in the Konserthus in Oslo. Before leaving for home, the choir sang in the American Lutheran Church for its regular Sunday worship, and I had the privilege of preaching the sermon.

There were several other highlights on this trip. A special treat was to be taken by Kåre Braa, Lois's cousin and ever-willing travel guide, to Tydalen, a secluded valley about sixty miles east of Trondheim. Lois's grandmother, Bertha Larson Brendsel, had been born there but we had never visited the area. We stopped at the church and spent time identifying ancestors in the graveyard. In Lillehammer, we viewed the elaborate preparations being made for the 1994 Winter Olympics, the beginnings of which we had seen in 1990. The choir had a special host in Lillehammer in the person of Knut Brakstad, a former St. Olaf student, who was in charge of church and education aspects of the 1994 Olympics. Following the Olympics, he became Personal Secretary to King Harald, and was a key member of the planning group for the royal visit to the United States in 1995.

In Oslo, on that same trip, we were the guests of Hans Brattestå, Director General of the Parliament, and his wife, Christine, at an elegant dinner at the Holmenkollen Hotel. Our friend, Jo Benkow, and his wife, Annelise Høegh, invited us to be their guests at an evening dinner cruise on the Oslo Fjord. The group of sixteen was gathered to honor the president of the Parliament of Hungary, who was there on an official visit.

We were again honored to have an audience with His Majesty King Harald V. People ask us what audiences with the King are like. King Olav was always easy to visit with, and showed interest in St. Olaf College and in news about his friends in the midwest. King Harald, a truly modern man, speaks excellent American English, enjoys a good story, and is quite informal in conversation. Both have always made us feel very welcome.

Our retirement travels have included places other than Norway. At the start of 1982, we went on an automobile trip which took us through the southeastern part of the country to Florida (where we stayed a week at Elmer and Gertrude Holm's apartment in Sarasota), then across the southern states to Arizona and California and finally back to Minnesota. For several years we made an annual winter trip to Phoenix and San Diego. In Phoenix we would visit Lois's parents, Art and Emelie Schiager, and in San Diego we had two families to see — our daughter, Mary, and her family, and my sister Mary and her husband Harold Miller.

Following our Norway cruise in 1986, we visited Albert and Marjorie North on two occasions at their home in London, Ontario. Both times we drove one way through Chicago and Detroit, and the other way north through Michigan into the Upper Peninsula and down to Door County, Wisconsin, to see our friends, the Boldts, at their summer home. The Norths took us on sightseeing tours to various places in Ontario, and to the Shakespeare festival at Stratford.

Short trips are common for us. Destinations such as Rothsay, Fergus Falls, Fargo–Moorhead, Sioux Falls and Ames frequently draw us. We have tried to visit Williams, MN, every two or three years to place flowers on my father's grave.

In the fall of 1991, we made a special visit to Minot, ND. A group of persons in that community had begun a Scandinavian Heritage Park as a memorial to the pioneers who had settled the area. One of their projects was to secure a house from Norway as an example of the kind of home the immigrants had left when they came to America. By strange coincidence, the house they acquired was the one in which my grandmother Pedersen had been born. It had been converted for use as a tool house when a newer home had been built on the Vatnaas farm several years ago. The man engaged to take it down and repair it, and to rebuild it in Minot, was Arne Svarstad, who lives on the farm where my grandfather Pedersen was born, not far from the Vatnaas farm. In October, 1991, the job was done and the house was dedicated. I had the privilege of speaking at the dedication. It was a significant day for Vatnaas relatives, and I think for the Minot community. Peter was able to be there, as were Alice, Chester and Alice Caroline Serkland. I met about a dozen second cousins I hadn't known before. They were from the family of Gul Vatnaas, my grandmother's brother who settled at Clitherall, Minnesota, when he came to America.

Speaking of Minot, I am reminded of the fact that in 1989 I had been made a member of the Scandinavian–American Hall of Fame by the Høstfest organization which sponsors an annual fall festival there.

In connection with travel, I should of course mention Northfield. Not only do we go there often to see Mark and his family, but St. Olaf people are kind enough to invite us to many college events. Lois also continues to go to Robert Tuma in Northfield for her haircuts, and my favorite barber, Dave Downhour, is there. So is our long–time dentist, Elvin Heiberg. The road to Northfield is well traveled.

The current president of St. Olaf, Mark U. Edwards, Jr., and his wife Linda make us feel at home on campus and we appreciate that very much. Mark and I have developed a pattern of somewhat regular luncheon meetings at which we discuss not only the college but theological and other subjects of common interest. He is a Martin Luther scholar who can teach me much in that area of study.

Shortly after leaving Augustana on June 30, 1993, we traveled to northern Minnesota. The congregation of Trinity Lutheran Church in Thief River Falls was celebrating its centennial. That was the church where Lois had been parish worker/organist/choir director/parish visitor/director of parish education/etc. We enjoyed the weekend there, and then drove on to Williams to visit my father's grave. While there we usually stop to see Lois's cousin and her husband, Bertha May and Clyde Tyler, in Baudette.

We went on to Fargo to visit Chester and Alice Serkland, and while there I became ill with a fever of 104 degrees, and finally passed out. I spent several days in the hospital being treated for gastro–intestinal infection. My pulse rate at one point was down to 32. As soon as I was dismissed from the hospital we left Fargo, stopped briefly at Kavanaugh's resort, where the family was gathered and where we should have been for the week, and returned to Minneapolis where I entered Fairview Southdale Hospital. My cardiologist, Dr. Robert Ketroser, ordered a pacemaker. After I had passed out in church in 1992, he had told me that some day I might need a pacemaker, and now that day had come. The gadget is a miracle. I am not aware of its presence as it keeps my pulse rate from going below 60. It can be adapted easily by external controls. Such are the marvels that keep us alive.

Chapter 24

OUR LARGER FAMILY

Retirement has permitted Lois and me to spend quite a bit of time with members of our family. We have been fortunate to live near Peter and his family in Minneapolis, and only a one hour drive from Mark and his family in Northfield. Sarah and Ben are a bit farther off but Ames is only a four hour trip so we can get there fairly easily. We see Mary and her family once or twice a year.

I was fortunate in many ways when I married Lois. For one thing, I acquired another son and daughter. Sarah has lived in Ames for several years, having moved there in 1971 with her first husband, Ray Boosinger. They were divorced in 1973, but Sarah stayed in Ames working for several years in the administration office of Mary Greeley Hospital. Sarah is the mother of David, who was born in 1969. He has lived with his father in Springfield, Illinois, most of the time since 1973, except for a year attending college in Ames, and several months in Northfield where he worked for the Culligan water treatment company with which his uncle Mark is affiliated.

Sarah married Ben Buck, an Ames native, in 1975. It was my privilege to officiate at their wedding in the Lutheran chapel at Iowa State. Ben is a dental technologist on the staff of the Buck Dental Clinic where his father and two brothers had their practice. Since 1989, Sarah has been on the development staff at Iowa State, and travels a great deal calling on prospective donors. She also serves on the board of her former employer, the city–owned Mary Greeley Hospital. We try to see Sarah and Ben as often as possible, and always enjoy our visits with them. Even in retirement, we don't get to Ames as often as we would like.

For several years, Sarah and Ben conducted a side–line business they called Safeguard Films. They video–taped weddings, graduations, family reunions and other special occasions, and copied more home movies than they care to remember. One of their early projects was to make a video insurance inventory for us. They finally decided this business dominated their spare time too much, so they have discontinued it. They are active in their church, St. Andrew's Lutheran, and Sarah is also a substitute organist there and at several other Ames churches.

Mark was in the service from 1970–72. He was stationed in Vietnam during some of the worst of that inglorious war, and came home with his spirit almost broken. He was convinced there was little good in the world. For a time he was uncertain what to do, and seemed to have no sense of direction in his life. But then he decided he should go to school, so he entered Inver Hills Community College and completed two years there, doing well in all his courses. One day he made an appointment to see me in my office to tell me that he would like to complete his college work at St. Olaf. I was surprised but highly pleased. He finished the two years at St. Olaf as a student in the Paracollege, graduating in 1981. The Paracollege was just the thing for him. It allowed him freedom to select what he would study, and he was able to concentrate especially on his interest in writing. His mother and I were proud of him and happy for him.

At Inver Hills, Mark had met Katherine Rush, whose home was in Cottage Grove. Their friendship grew, and in 1981 they were married. I officiated at that wedding, too, this time at Boe Chapel. Mark and Kathy have two beautiful and bright children, Bryce, born in 1985, and Jessica, born in 1987. I had the privilege of baptizing both of them at St. Peter's Lutheran Church in Northfield. Having grandchildren in Northfield provides an extra incentive to make the trip there quite frequently.

Besides being an active homemaker, Kathy pursued many interests outside the home. She earned a Master's degree at Hamline University, was active in the Northfield Arts Guild, served on various commissions and boards for the city and at their church. We were saddened in 1995 when Kathy decided she no longer wished to be married, and moved to her own apartment. She sees Bryce and Jessica regularly. Mark and the children continue to carry on in their home in Northfield, and we treasure the time we spend with them. They live in a beautiful home on which Mark has spent many hours doing finishing work and continually making improvements.

While he was in college, Mark worked for Arnie Nelson, a home builder in Northfield. After college, he found a job with a water treatment firm and for a short time he and Kathy lived in Blue Earth, Minnesota. Then he was offered a job with the Culligan people in Northfield, and they returned to that community. He has done very well, being first a salesman, then marketing manager and then vice president of the firm. In his current capacity he is in charge of sales in not only the Northfield store but in ten others located in southern Minnesota, Iowa, Indiana and Texas. So he, like his sister, has a traveling job. He has done very well and we are proud of him.

Mark takes great pleasure in being part of a four–piece band that started as a bluegrass band, and has expanded through the years to play many styles of music. He has occasionally played drums, but usually plays guitar and sings. Somewhat surprising to us, Mark has joined the Veterans of Foreign Wars, and for several years served as quartermaster of the Northfield post. He has marched in the VFW color guard for parades during Defeat of Jesse James days. When he first came home from Vietnam, I would never have guessed that he would be active in a veteran's organization.

Somewhere along the way, Mark began to call me Dad. I was happy he felt he wanted to do that. He is a wonderful son.

Peter and Nancy continue to live in Minneapolis. In 1979, they sold their home on Eleventh Avenue South and bought a larger one on Humboldt Avenue. It was built in 1910, and since they moved in they have rebuilt the front hall, the living room, the bedrooms used by Amy and Dorothy, and the third floor. They are currently working on the kitchen. Peter has done the lion's share of this work himself, but I have helped him from time to time, removing lath and plaster, putting up sheetrock, sweeping and cleaning and being a general handyman. It reminds me of my days at Moen's Lumber Yard. One day when I was removing lath and plaster in Dorothy's bedroom, I discovered a half–pint whiskey bottle on the sill next to a stud. It was empty, of course! I had visions of some workman being surprised by his supervisor in 1910, and hiding the evidence. Peter and Nancy take great pride in their home, and the renovation, including the parts they have done themselves, is of professional quality.

In his regular employment, Peter has been on the staff of the American Institute of Architects Minnesota since 1981. In 1982, he became executive director along with Beverly Hauschild. Their titles were changed to executive vice president in 1987. The arrangement of having a shared CEO has worked well, contrary to what often occurs.

Peter has also found time to serve on several boards connected with their church, Bethlehem Lutheran, as well as on boards and committees of the Minnesota Council of Churches. He has served as president of Project for Pride in Living, an organization that purchases, renovates and resells housing, especially for lower income families. He has been president of Arts Midwest, a nine–state regional arts board, and is active in architecture organizations at the national level. In 1993, he was made a Fellow of the American Institute of Architects.

In January, 1989, Peter was mugged on a street in Washington, DC, while there for a convention. He was seriously injured and required surgery for a fractured skull and a massive hematoma. We wondered if he would survive. A year after the accident, he was apparently back in good health except for a vision problem in his left eye. One such experience would be enough, but in July, 1995, he was involved in a serious automobile accident near Brainerd, Minnesota, while traveling to Kavanaugh's Resort to join the rest of us for our annual get–together there. A head–on collision caused multiple fractures and internal injuries, involving a long period of convalescence. He has returned to work and is continuing to recover.

His spirit has remained good, and his generally excellent physical and emotional health have undoubtedly been leading factors in his recovery. An abundance of prayers by a host of friends have sustained him and the family, while he went through both these experiences.

Nancy has continued in her profession as a physical therapist. She is a devoted and thorough worker, and shows a deep concern for the welfare of her clients. She is also active in church; she has sung in the choir for several years, and was part of a tour to Europe with that group in 1990. In addition, she has been a busy mother, giving lots of time to being driver, seamstress, organizer and number one cheerleader for Amy and Dorothy as they have been involved with music lessons, skating and other activities. Nancy extends her skills and her compassion to many other people, and during the period of convalescence following Peter's second accident her professional capabilities and insights provided a real advantage for Peter in his recovery.

Mary, Gary, Luke and Leah moved to California in 1978 when Gary was appointed a member of the staff of Scripps Clinic in La Jolla. He is a rheumatologist and his appointment was considered a professional plum. He served as chief of the medical staff a few years after he arrived. We thought they were set for a long and happy life in California, but it was not to be. In 1986, Gary told Mary that he no longer wanted to be married to her, and after some struggle and contention they were divorced. Mary has continued to live in La Jolla, and Luke and Leah have made their home with her, but see their father regularly. In 1989, Mary accepted a job with an organization called MEND (Mothers Embracing Nuclear Disarmament), and a few months later she became a development officer at California Western School of Law. In 1991, she became of director of development. She took to that work very well, finding plenty to do and enough challenge to keep her quite busy. When she took that position, we were amused to realize that we had two children who were executive vice presidents, and two who were development officers.

Some years ago Mary was selected to be a member of Las Patronas, a special group of women interested in supporting the arts. She has worked hard in this organization, especially in promoting and organizing the annual Jewel Ball, their chief fundraising event. For several years, she served as manager of the softball teams on which Luke and Leah played, and has served in various capacities in La Jolla Lutheran Church.

Her life changed dramatically at the end of 1993, when she resigned her position at Cal Western in anticipation of her marriage in February, 1994, to Ron Taylor, who is Chairman and CEO of Pyxis, a San Diego company which manufactures computerized hospital equipment which is used for the controlled dispensing of medications and supplies. Shortly after their marriage they came to Minneapolis for a visit, and we gathered fifty of Mary's friends and relatives for a dinner party in their honor. We have visited them in their dramatic new home in the hills of La Jolla, and rejoice to see them enjoying life together. We are happy for Mary and delighted to have Ron as a son–in–law.

Family includes grandchildren, too.

Together Lois and I have watched David grow up. He was a five–year–old when we were married. Since then he has finished high school, had one year at Iowa State, attended a junior college in Springfield and worked at several jobs. He is the manager of a sports bar in Springfield, Illinois. He was married in October of 1994 to Kari Lesselyoung at Atonement Lutheran Church in Springfield, where his grandfather was the founding pastor. I was happy to be invited to officiate at the wedding together with Pastor Jonathan Berg of Atonement. Through the years, we have appreciated every contact with Dave, as well as the second–hand reports we get through his Springfield grandparents, Fred and Jeane Boosinger, and through Sarah and Ben. We enjoyed meeting Kari and look forward to many happy times with them in the future.

Mark's two children, Bryce and Jessica, have been a delight. We see them quite often and watch with great interest each new development in their lives. Whenever we see them we get hugs of greeting, and they are eager to share with us drawings they have made, books which we must see and read, games we can play together and toys they have received. They have more toys than they know what to do with. They have enjoyed many opportunities at home and in other settings such as art school, Sunday School and public school, as well as musical, athletic and dramatic activities. Bryce has become very interested in singing, and sings in groups at school and church, as well as in a community choir. We have them stay with us over night now and then, and they regard that as a special treat.

Amy graduated from St. Olaf College in 1994 and was elected to Phi Beta

Kappa. She took advantage of opportunities presented by the Paracollege, including special projects of her own choosing and off–campus programs. She has been in Europe three times on study–related visits, including twice in Russia. One of her areas of concentration was Russian, which she began studying while in high school. At St. Olaf, she tutored foreign students and others who needed special help in writing, participated in an ethnic dance group, and continued her study of piano. She spent a summer as a counselor at a church camp in Upper Michigan, and taught two summers at the Concordia College Russian Language Village. In January, 1995, she left for East Africa, to teach English in a girls' high school in Monduli, Tanzania. This is volunteer service, so she had to raise funds for her own travel and support before she left. Her work is related to the Board of Global Missions of the Evangelical Lutheran Church in America, and much of her support came from her own congregation, Bethlehem Lutheran in Minneapolis.

Dorothy graduated from South High School with highest honors in 1994, and now attends St. Olaf College. She has become an accomplished ice skater, winning many prizes in competition. She also plays piano and violin, and has been a member of the Greater Twin Cities Youth Symphony program, as well as being active in church, as a baby sitter, and as an employee of a LeeAnn Chin restaurant and Abercrombie and Fitch. She is a great shopper. The second half of her sophomore year at St. Olaf she spent on one of the foreign study semesters, studying art in Florence, Italy, and theater in London.

Peter and Nancy have taken the girls on several trips. One summer they visited Norway, Germany, the Netherlands, France and Denmark. In 1990, they spent twelve days in England because "the air fare was too cheap to pass up." When Amy finished her semester in Russia in December, 1992, they all met in Germany and went to Italy for Christmas.

Luke is a graduate of the University of California at Los Angeles. He had been a star tackle on the high school football team in La Jolla, but when deciding on college, he chose not to play football. He is 6'2" tall and weighs close to 240 pounds, but he decided he was too small to be a lineman in Division I football. He has been interested in sports all his life, and has played baseball, basketball and soccer in addition to football. At the University he played rugby, which didn't make me happy. I think that sport is a little like boxing; it seems to be dedicated to the idea of hurting someone. As Luke learned to say in Norway, "Det er farlig, det!" He majored in history, and following his graduation completed a 16–month course at the San Diego Golf Academy, which prepares persons to be golf pros and managers of golf courses. He is now employed by a company which manufactures and sells golf equipment.

Leah is also interested in sports, mostly volleyball, basketball and softball. She is six feet tall, a beautiful blond, and strong enough to be a good spiker on the volleyball team. She has been a consistently good student and was president of her senior class in high school. She graduated from high school in June, 1992, and accepted a full scholarship to play volleyball at the University of Colorado. That means all her college expenses are paid for up to five years, provided she continues to play volleyball. When I heard this, I said to Leah, "Why does anybody want to take five years to finish college?" She replied, "Oh, Bop, I'm going to finish in four years!" That was a serious intention; her graduation date is in May, 1996. She has been an outstanding member of the University of Colorado women's volleyball team, captain her senior year, and named to the All–Conference first team.

We are thankful for our grandchildren, and consider it a great privilege to be able to watch them grow up to become responsible young men and women.

A family tradition that has developed during the past several years, and which includes at least part of the family, is a week at a lake. During the last week in July we are at Kavanaugh's Resort on Lake Sylvan near Brainerd, Minnesota. Lois and I rent a cabin, as do the Bucks and the Ekerens. Sometimes Peter, Nancy and the girls spend part of the week with us. Twice Leah has come to be with us, but Mary, Ron and Luke haven't been able to make it. Several members of Ben's family also come. Dave and Kari joined us in 1995.

We enjoy being together and find it a relaxing and satisfying family time. One evening of the week, we all eat together at the dining room of the resort. It is one of the finest eating places anywhere. Often the children have taken us out for dinner on another evening to celebrate Lois's birthday, which really comes on August 1. We don't mind celebrating a few days early.

We also observe such times as Thanksgiving, Christmas and birthdays in order to keep family celebration going. With busy schedules all around, it takes planning to get everyone together, but we try to do it as often as we can. Many of these get–togethers are at Peter's or Mark's. Their homes are larger than ours. However, we have managed to host our Christmas Eve celebration with its traditional Norwegian menu and customs.

Another family tradition that we observed for several years was the annual winter trip to Phoenix and San Diego. That has become less common in recent years. During the first few years after Lois and I were married, it was handy to combine that trip with meetings of St. Olaf alumni. That ended when we left the college, but the trips to Phoenix became fewer after the death of Lois's parents.

We have also maintained contact with other family members. My brother

Lyman and his wife Helen have lived in the Minneapolis area for many years. Lyman spent more than thirty years working for Gambles as a furniture buyer, and was very successful in that business. Following his retirement, he and Helen went into partnership with their son Robert and his wife Rae Ann to buy a large house in Minnetonka. The house accommodates two couples very well. Bob and Rae have a son Tony who is grown and away from home. The joint house idea was suggested by Rae, a brave thought for a daughter–in–law, we believed. But it has worked out well.

We have not seen Lyman and Helen often through the years. Their lives have centered in business and personal activities different from ours. But we make it a point to get together at least occasionally, and always enjoy each other's company.

Helen died in February, 1992, after a period of declining health complicated by cancer. I officiated at her funeral, and Lois played the organ. Lyman is indeed fortunate now to live in a home where Bob and Rae take care of the housework, do the cooking and shopping, and generally make things comfortable for him.

Since my sister Charlotte died in 1978, we have not seen members of her family very often. Her husband Francis remarried and lived near Wadena, Minnesota, until recently, when he and his wife moved to a nursing home at Clarissa. He died in April, 1996. There are seven children in the family. We see Cynthia, Curtis, Heidi and Paul, who live in Minneapolis, more often than the others. Owen, the oldest, is in Iowa, Judy is in Nebraska, and Philip is in New York.

My sister Mary and her husband Harold moved to San Diego in the forties. In recent years they have been in failing health, and in early May of 1992, Harold died following a lengthy illness. He suffered from cancer and kidney failure. Our fairly regular trips to San Diego have enabled us to see them quite often through the years. Mary has now disposed of her home in San Diego and is living in a nursing home in La Jolla. Our daughter Mary manages her affairs.

I stay in touch with my Serkland cousins. Alice lived in Rothsay until failing health necessitated a move to a nursing home in Moorhead where she recently died. Through the years we often stopped to see her. She enticed us with her gracious invitations to lunch or dinner, and we also stayed with her over night on frequent occasions.

Chester and Alice live in Fargo and we see them as often as we get to that area, usually combining that visit with a stop at Concordia College. Alvin and Clara Serkland lived in Fergus Falls until their deaths several years ago.

Dorothy's brother Elmer and his wife Gertrude remain our good friends. We have visited them in their home in Evanston several times, and they even persuaded us to make use of their Sarasota, Florida, condominium for a week. Other relatives of Dorothy whom we see off and on are her cousins, Lanny Seal and her husband Joe, and Kent Olson and his wife Pat. Recently we have had the opportunity to spend quality time with Lanny and Joe's son Dean and his wife Kirsten on a fairly regular basis.

Lois's three siblings are scattered. Her brother Keith is a nuclear radiation scientist and has recently retired from the faculty of the University of Utah. He and his wife Jan live in Salt Lake City. Sheldon, the other brother, is a United Airlines captain, who lives with his wife Jean in Vancouver, Washington. Because his work gives him easy access to transportation, they have visited us wherever we have lived. Lois's sister Ruth and her husband Don Egger have a home in Phoenix, but they actually live in different places because his work is the supervision of the construction of Target stores. He goes to a new location every year or so. We try to plan visits with all these couples whenever we can.

Two years after the death of Lois's father in 1986, her mother Emelie moved to Minneapolis, motivated by a desire to be near one of her children. She rented an apartment at Teacher's Residence, a couple of miles from where we live. After a few months, she decided that was not the place for her. She didn't like our winter because she couldn't walk outside when the streets were icy. We tried to do all we could to help her adjust, but she decided to move to Fort Collins, Colorado, where she would find a more agreeable climate and be near some of her grandchildren. After almost a year there, she moved to Vancouver to be near Sheldon, but after ten months she chose to return to the Phoenix area, where she lived in a retirement complex in Glendale, just outside Phoenix. As her health gradually declined, she moved into a care center. Ruth faithfully took care of all her needs until her death in July, 1994. I conducted her funeral and Lois played the organ. Lois and her siblings had several good days together settling their mother's affairs and reminiscing.

In August, 1993, we attended a Schiager family reunion in Rapid City, South Dakota. It was planned by Lois and her brothers, and brought together 25 of the children, grandchildren, and great–grandchildren of Art and Emelie. The reunion was held in Rapid City because the family had lived in the Black Hills for several years before World War II. We all stayed at the Alex Johnson Hotel, which was the first building Art Schiager worked on when they moved to the Black Hills in 1927. We visited the Norwegian stave church, Mount Rushmore, the Sylvan Lake Hotel (construction supervision by Art), and, in Hot Springs, the Mammoth Site and Evans Plunge, an indoor, natural warm–water pool where Lois, Keith and Ruth learned to swim. Everyone enjoyed the reunion, and we decided to meet again in five years, with Mark and Keith's grandson, Joel (age four at the time of the reunion!) in charge. Perhaps his dad Jerome will help.

We stay in touch with some of the Ekerens, also. Connie, the daughter of Walt's brother Olaf, lives in Minneapolis with her husband Bill Cameron and their three sons. Bill is an attorney and a pilot for Northwest Airlines, and Connie is a high school teacher who now works in a mentoring program for gifted students. Connie's brother Bob is a pharmacist in Thief River Falls and owns the family business, the Ekeren Drug. He is carrying on a family tradition there.

Lois has relatives wherever we go — uncles, aunts and a variety of cousins have enriched our lives as we have visited with many of them wherever we have lived and traveled, whether it be Minneapolis, Sioux Falls, Norway, California or elsewhere.

Our larger family also includes a host of friends. We have lived many places and have maintained contact with friends made along the way. Our Christmas card list includes over four hundred names, of whom close to a hundred live in Norway and other places outside the United States. We are grateful to have this abundance of connections with people and places that have played important roles in our lives.

One of the enriching experiences of our marriage has been that each of us has brought to it a group of cherished friends, some of whom had been our mutual friends before. Together we have made many more friends, so the circle is really "yours, mine and ours."

Chapter 25

REFLECTIONS ON
PLEASANT PLACES

Retirement provides time for thought and reflection. I usually start the day about eight o'clock. After I make my own breakfast, I spend some time with the Bible and prayer. I usually read two chapters of the Old Testament and one of the New Testament each day. That way I read through the Bible with some regularity. Lois and I conclude the day with a reading from the Bible and a meditation from a devotional book such as Christ in Our Home. Often we also read together from some book of special interest to us, frequently an old favorite.

The reason my day starts by myself is that Lois likes to sleep later than I do. She is often wakeful during the night, and as a consequence appreciates sleeping until about nine o'clock. Then she's on her own for her breakfast.

My morning also includes reading the daily paper and working the crossword puzzle. Each of us, in addition, has at least one crossword puzzle book going at all times. We buy the fifty–puzzle spiral bound Sunday crossword books and go through them quite rapidly.

When I am not occupied with meetings or other special assignments, I read, take walks and run errands. In fact, I often ask Lois if there is something she needs, so that I will have an excuse to take a walk. Walking is my only regular form of exercise, and I like it. In the cold weather, I walk through the Minneapolis skyway system to which we have access across the street from our building. In nice weather, I often walk in the old warehouse district nearby or on the lovely parkway which has been built along the Mississippi River only a block from our home. A strip along the river provides a walking lane, a bike lane and a lane for auto traffic. It's an inviting place.

The city library is only three blocks away, and I often go there. The periodicals I no longer subscribe to are available, as are daily papers from the major cities in the country. I also seem to have plenty of books waiting at home to be read. My favorite non–fiction subjects are biography and history. Mysteries are my favorite fiction reading, above all, Sherlock Holmes. I have read that entire collection several times. To show how my memory must be failing, I report that I can read Holmes over and over because I don't remember how each story ends.

What kind of person is Sidney Rand? The ancient Greeks advised, "Know thyself." It is a lifelong task, and I suspect no–one ever completely knows himself, but as one grows older, thoughts related to self–understanding easily arise.

I have enjoyed good health throughout my life, even though I have experienced a few illnesses and accidents. As a child I broke an ankle playing baseball, split an eyebrow playing on the school grounds, and had measles and chicken pox. As a college student I was confined for a couple of weeks with mumps. In seminary days, I broke my nose playing touch football. In later life, I have taken medication for high blood pressure, and was once hospitalized for removal of a rectal cyst. As I have mentioned earlier, I contracted Reiter's Syndrome on a round–the–world trip in 1972, and have carried the bug in my system ever since. Several times since then, various symptoms have recurred.

As I have alluded to earlier, on Sunday, May 10, 1992, I passed out in church. I created a flurry of excitement as I was taken away to an ambulance and then to Fairview Southdale Hospital. I was there three days, and had a thorough examination. The doctors diagnosed an irregular heart beat and predicted I might continue to have that trouble. In July of 1993, after passing out again, I received a Telectronic pulse generator, and since that time the irregular pulse has been under control.

While growing up, my height and weight were quite normal. During college and seminary days, I weighed between 135 and 145 pounds, and was 5'10" tall. Starting in 1945, I put on weight, and in 1990 weighed 185 pounds. Since then I have reduced that to 170 pounds. My height has also shrunk — I am about 5'9" now.

For several years in the 60's and 70's I smoked a pipe. I had no trouble quitting when I concluded that Lois didn't care for it. I enjoy a drink of scotch on the rocks or a gin and tonic, and also, on occasion, a glass of wine with dinner. I do not like the taste of beer, and don't care for carbonated beverages. Coffee, currently the decaffienated variety, water, milk and iced tea are my favorite beverages..

I am a strong–willed person; I want to excel at everything I do. Schoolwork was always comparatively easy, and I usually received high grades.

My employers have commended me for my work, and I have always believed that hard work done well is a necessary ingredient in the good life. I do not take orders or correction easily, preferring to choose my own way to accomplish a task. I have a temper. It is not far below the surface, as Dorothy, Lois, Peter and Mary could attest. In my adult years I have controlled it better than I did earlier, but it is still very much a part of me.

There is also a strong streak of silliness in me — together with an honest sense of humor, I trust. I enjoy repartee, the exchange of good–humored banter, even barbs and put–downs. I am in my element when being an emcee or appearing in front of a crowd. I like to take advantage of a situation to make a joke, often on myself, and sometimes even on someone else. I am sure that I appreciate this side of me more than most persons around me do. But I have frequently been told by people who hear me speak in public that they like the way I am able to treat certain events and ideas lightly rather than dwelling only on the sober side of things.

Three of the granddaughters have standard reactions to my attempts at humor. Amy will say, "Courtesy laugh!" Leah keeps count as the day passes, "That's one...that's two..." Dorothy turns to Lois and commiserates with the words, "Grandma, how can you stand it every day?"

I like space. In a restaurant, I prefer a table in an open area. Lois likes to sit in a booth, so we often find an eating place that has a banquette and chair arrangement. I like space on my desk and space in which to move around. I thrived in the 4,200–square–foot president's residence at St. Olaf, and of course in the 24,000–square–foot Embassy Residence in Oslo. But I am also happy now to be in a 1,200–square–foot apartment in which we get along fine.

As to my inner self, my thoughts and hopes and dreams, I believe they have remained fairly constant through my life. A person's point of view is affected by his experiences, and I know mine have been, but I have gone through no sudden or cataclysmic change. I have had abundant opportunity to formulate and express my thoughts because of my work. The St. Olaf Archives are the depository of many of my sermons, talks and reports, most, but not all, of them from the time I was president there.

I have written some things which are available for anyone who is interested, either because they are published or in some kind of limited circulation. I will mention a few of them.

The book, *Centennial Sketches*, written in celebration of the one hundredth anniversary of Forest City, Iowa, is found in the public library there and in the Waldorf College library, as well as in my own.

In 1960, Augsburg Publishing House published *Christian Faith and the*

Liberal Arts. I was the author of the chapter on administration in a church college.

In 1980, I wrote a piece called "Rothsay Reflections" in response to a request from Gary Wigdahl, who was preparing a centennial history of the town. It never was printed in its entirety. It tells much of the story I recount in the first section of this record.

In connection with a history of Lutheran colleges he was writing, Dr. Richard Solberg interviewed me on the subject of higher education in the Lutheran Church. That interview contains my views on higher education and its relation to the church. It is available in the archives of the Lutheran Educational Conference of North America, as well as in my personal library.

In 1984, Dr. Todd Nichol interviewed me as a part ot the Oral History Collection of the Lutheran churches. . That interview was included in *ALC/AELC/LCA Oral History*, published by the churches which united in 1988 to form the Evangelical Lutheran Church in America. In it I recount some of my reflections on the church, and my own theological and faith journey. It is probably the best and most complete summary of my views on church matters. I have a copy of that, and another is in the archives of the former Lutheran Council, USA.

After we returned from the Embassy in 1981, I wrote my recollections of the experience under the title, *For the Time Being.* The certificate of appointment, which is signed by President Carter, names me "ambassador plenipotentiary and extraordinary" and goes on to refer to the various powers and duties embraced in the appointment. I chose the title for my recollections because that paragraph ends by reminding me that my appointment is "for the time being." In that record I report on what we did the year we lived in Oslo, and also some of my thoughts regarding diplomatic service, the place of the United States among other nations, my views of a culture other than my own and general observations about life in a foreign country. A copy is in the St. Olaf Archives, and members of the family, as well as several friends, have copies which I gave to them.

Lois kept a journal of our Embassy experience. It is more detailed than my report, and has provided me with a good source of information concerning much of our life there.

A book which Lois and I have written together, and which I have referred to earlier, is entitled *Norway.* It is a coffee table book with photography by Robert and Loren Paulson, for which we wrote text and captions. Seven years after publication, it is still available in bookstores.

We have taped or typed the record of some of our travels, and these also include observations regarding people and places outside the United States. They describe the trip I took to the Orient in 1968, the around–the–world trip Dorothy and I took in 1972, my trip to the Lutheran World Federation Assembly in Tanzania in 1977, and my trip to Norway with President Mel George in 1986. Lois also has kept journals of many of our travels, both domestic and foreign.

In March of 1989 I was asked to speak on the subject, "What I Have Learned," at the first meeting of a newly formed group called The College of Senior Clergy, of which I had been elected president. I referred to a talk I had once given at St. Olaf as a Blue Key lecture, titled "How My Mind Has Changed." Building on themes in that talk, I listed some ideas which I thought were appropriate, and I record them here.

1. A sound theology has contemporary value. It is the basis for everything even though times change.

2. The Christian faith is open–ended. There is always more to learn and to appreciate. God is free to act as he chooses; we do not limit him.

3. Fads in religion come and go. We shouldn't get too excited by such movements as New Age or communal living groups. There will always be those who will experiment in their religious lives.

4. There is an ever–present tendency among people of God to put secondary things first. Busyness, self–interest and concern for organization and control have a way of taking over as primary concerns.

5. There is a delicate balance in life between the importance of persons and the importance of groups.

6. It is difficult, but not impossible, to establish community. It is worth time and effort to do that.

7. History is important. We are creatures of history, with memory and imagination.We can transcend the present, re–live the past and project the future.

8. The world is important. Robert Frost's "lover's quarrel" with the world is real. The world is God's, not ours. We are here as caretakers, as stewards.

9. Ideas are costly. What we think is what we become. Ideas lead us and form us.

10. Issues are always political. They attach themselves to people. There are few, if any, truly objective issues in life.

11. Leadership is usually a side effect. It happens by the way, as we serve.

Leaders must first be servants.

12. It is a gift to be able to lay aside the day's concerns at the end of the day. God has given me that gift. I sleep well at night no matter what the problems or cares may be.

13. Accountability of a measurable kind is not common in the church. We are not great at setting standards or holding to them. We make subjective judgments about people, beliefs and organizations.

14. Retirement is a great time of life.

On the same occasion I said something about my experience as an ambassador, so I included some things I thought I had learned doing that:

1. It is a privilege to serve one's country abroad.

2. Being an ambassador is a team effort. I cited Lois's work as a full–time member of the Embassy staff.

3. An ambassador works hard in order to be the best possible representative of his country. An ambassador also experiences many enjoyable and exhilarating times.

4. One learns a new appreciation of one's own country while serving as an ambassador. Many people abroad speak with appreciation of the United States and its place in the family of nations.

5. There are well–qualified, able people in the foreign service. With only a few exceptions, this was the rule in the Oslo Embassy.

6. Other ambassadors teach a new ambassador.

7. You can't make money as an ambassador.

I closed my talk by referring to Harold Ditmanson's book, *Grace*, and said the bottom line of all I had learned was summed up in that word. God is good and is the giver, the redeemer and sustainer of life.

Though my life has been spent in a career serving the church and its institutions, I have never considered myself a theologian. The fact that I did not master the biblical languages and chose church history as my major interest indicates that my competence does not lie in the field of theology as such. However, I reflect on life in theological terms, and I view my life and my work within a framework of theological presuppositions. I understand education to be important primarily because human beings are creatures of God, endowed with minds and wills and imaginations. Education is an exercise in the stewardship of God–given talents, abilities and possibilities. As a teacher and administrator in colleges of the church, I have been guided by a basically theological view of my work and its relationship with other people both in the church and in society in general.

An opportunity for me to express my views regarding the church came in 1970, when I was among those nominated for the presidency of the ALC at the time of the retirement of President Schiotz. Prior to the convention, those nominated were asked to answer certain questions posed by the editor of the *Lutheran Standard*, the official periodical of the church. I had already decided I had no great urge to be president of the church, being quite convinced that I was doing what I should be doing as president of St. Olaf. This gave me a certain sense of freedom in making my reply to the questions.

It was an honor to be among the nominees. I did not want to give the impression that I thought otherwise. However, it was not easy for me to understand why I should be considered a worthy candidate for the church presidency.

In the statement I made to the convention of the church in San Antonio, I said:

"The chief issue facing the church today as always is the simple question, What is the gospel? What is the good news from God in a troubled world? And we need to give ourselves to serious study and concern in order that we might faithfully believe that gospel ourselves and then be diligent in making our witness known in patterns of word and action appropriate to our world. This means a willingness to go beyond the stilted mouthings of timeworn truths, and to go on to shape our thought, speech and action in such a way that, by the working of God's Spirit, persons will hear and be drawn to faith in God. I am certain all other issues are secondary to this one. I am certain also that both the basic and secondary issues need our prayerful attention as individuals, congregations, and as a church.

"As important as the issues facing the church, are the strategies or methods for facing them. I have several convictions in this regard.

1. The church, in all its forms, needs to keep structure and organization flexible and minimal.

2. The church is ultimately people. The aim of the church must always be to involve people, first by a continuing program which confronts each person with the gospel, and then by a program which permits and

encourages the believer to grow in his or her exercise of that faith in personal and inter–personal relationships.

3. The church needs to encourage its members to seek extra–church ways to be Christian. This means activity in political, social, economic and other groups which work at specific problems in society.

4. Worship life needs variety. The church should encourage private and corporate worship which will appeal to the wide divergence of human desires, backgrounds and life goals.

5. The church needs always to find ways to balance despair with hope, to see the grace of God amid the problems of life, to keep the ultimate confidence in God alive even when human situations seem hopeless.

6. The church, as the corporate body of believers, needs to practice humility, knowing its only strength is God–given, not man–inspired, and to live with a sense of humor, knowing that God, not man, is still in charge and has the final word."

I went on to say that I thought church reorganization (which was a topic under discussion at the time) was not a high priority goal, and that any planning that was done should, insofar as possible, be in concert with the Lutheran Church in America and the Lutheran Church–Missouri Synod. I did not believe Lutheran church merger to be as important as working together as effectively as possible. I favored cooperation with other churches, but opposed membership in the National Council of Churches, advocating instead efforts to form another council which would include the Roman Catholic Church.

In conclusion I said, "I am honored to be a nominee for the presidency of the church. I am not certain, however, that I possess those characteristics of mind, heart and spirit which should typify the person holding such an office. I find within me no passion driving me to seek the position. Should such an inner desire be required of the president, I am undoubtedly disqualified."

My statement must have been believed by the delegates. As I recall, I received twenty–six votes on the first ballot, the next to the lowest of the candidates. But maybe the result would have been the same without my speech. As the votes were counted, I was sitting next to H.P. Skoglund, chairman of the St. Olaf board. In his usual direct way he said to me, "Well, Sid, that decides it. I'm glad you will still be at St. Olaf." So was I.

I have occasionally put my thoughts in verse. Much of it is in the form of ditties I have done for the children or grandchildren.

MARY (1949)

Once I knew a little girl
Who spoke so strangely that
I sometimes failed to know for sure
What she was getting at.

She didn't like to stay, she said,
At hoppypittels, so
She stayed real well instead, and then
She didn't have to go.

But to the zoo she went one day
And thought that elegant
For what do you suppose was there?
A real live ephelant!

TO LUKE AND LEAH (c. 1975)

There's a robin near the window
And a blackbird on the lawn;
A woodpecker's rat–a–tatting,
Making noise for the whole town.

The rabbits jump and skip and sit
And have a leaf for lunch;
And when the squirrels find nuts about,
They grab and go munch, munch.

Spiders, ants and just plain bugs
Find homes around our place.
I guess we're raising livestock here;
Good thing there's lots of space.

But something's lacking yet, I think,
Some others ought to be here,
Not animals or bugs or birds,
No, it's Luke and Leah.

301

FOR JESSICA (1995)

I met a cow
That said, " Bow–wow."
"How can that be?"
Said I to me.
"A cow should moo
To me and you."

But then I thought,
"What I think ought
To be the way
A cow can say
To me a moo,
May not be true."

For kids like me
Must always be
Good listeners, and
Then understand
"Bow–wow" can be
A cow's "Whoopee!"

A piece on a more ambitious scale was a chapel talk I gave at St. Olaf on
May 13, 1969. It is my reflection on a year of chapel services:

THE END OF THE YEAR

A hundred–fifty chances,
More or less,
To worship God in this place
Now are gone for this year.
And we may pause
And wonder
Whether it has made a difference.

Some have come each day,
Or almost that.

Others,
Never, once or twice, or ten times.
For some it's been a way to meet their God
And truth,
For some, to be alone, or even lonely,
And afraid.
Why Chapel?
A right question wanting answer.
Perhaps it's but a custom born of need in yesterday,
A place for hiding out
From world and others, even learning,
A place made comfortable
By prayer and hymns and talk.

Here there were sermons poorly preached,
Hymns sadly sung,
Wandering minds and hearts grown hard too young.
At times our absence,
Whether body, mind or spirit,
Was matched by God's,
For he seemed absent too.

"For everything there is a season,"
Said the preacher.
And so,
Perhaps it's well to break the scheduled round
Of classes,
Study and debate,
With coffee, P.O. box,
Or even common quiet, song and joy.

Or is there more than change
In dull routine
Involved in this;
For some, if not for all?
Not only symbol, habit,
Bow to mystery;
A truly re–creating time,
Itself necessity?

Each one must answer for himself.
But were there not
Some truly human, Christian things
That happened here?
A greater, deeper consciousness of self
And God
And of the world around,
Its aches and dreams?

They say one needs but little help
These days,
To know the world's undone;
That's patent, real,
And the world's undone–ness
Never seems to haunt as much
As that undone–ness
Which is me.

That Word I heard,
Here in this place,
Until I thought I must believe it
Or quit coming.
I quit or not, depending on the way in which
My God reached in
With still another truth.

For what each one must truly ever hear
And know,
Is not how evil, empty
Is this life,
Though that each must perceive.
Yet ever and anew
To hear that there is grace
And hope,
For me.

We do not capture God,
Or lead him 'round,
Not here or elsewhere.
But one thing we do.

We let Him be the God He is,
Claim promises,
His presence, power, pardon —
And all good.

No cure–all this
For ills of world or college or of self.
There is none such:
That's first, the foremost fact.
But short of that can there be insight, hope,
Or power yet enough
To keep us from despair?

Or what about the urge,
The drive,
To act and do,
To right the wrong, or change the status quo?
Must this arise from earth
And only us,
Or is it deep without
As well as deep within?

"It's well I leave you," once the Savior said.
"Because the Spirit comes,"
His presence better yet.
It took great faith
To trust such strange elusive truth.
But trusting,
Those disciples knew.

A hundred–fifty chances,
More or less,
To claim a promise,
Trust an Absent One.
That's what we've had.
And some have known
A glory —
His,
And yet, their own.

During my career I have served on many boards and committees, and been active in various organizations. Some of them I have mentioned already, but there are others. I belonged to Rotary Clubs in Forest City and in Northfield. I was active in a development corporation in Forest City seeking to bring business and industry to the community. It was after I became president of St. Olaf, however, that I became involved with a large number of activities and organizations other than the college, as the list which follows indicates. Many of these were related to education, but I also had the privilege of being a member of a hospital board and more than one group related to the legal profession and the judicial system. These were educational experiences for me and added to my understanding of the world of which we are a part. I have been a member of the governing board of each of the colleges where I have been president.

The following list, if not complete, is quite comprehensive:

Chairman, Minnesota Higher Education Facilities Commission – 1964–67
Member, Minnesota Higher Education Coordinating
    Commission – 1967–73
Member, Board of Trustees, Fairview Community
    Hospitals – 1965–80
Member, Board of Directors, Northfield National
    Bank – 1964–80
Member, Board of Directors, North American Life and
    Casualty Company – 1967–80, 1981–89
Member, Board of Directors, Lutheran Educational
    Conference of North America – 1968–71 (Chairman – 1971)
Member, Board of Dirctors, Council of Protestant
    Colleges and Universities – 1967–70 (Chairman – 1970)
Member, Board of Directors, National Council of Independent Colleges
    and Universities – 1972–74 (Chairman – 1974)
Member, Board of Directors, Wheat Ridge Foundation –
    1975–84 (Chairman – 1981–84)
Member, Minnesota Board for Continuing Legal Education– 1975–80
Member, Board of Directors, Association of American Colleges – 1975–78
Member, Men's Committee for the Japan International Christian
    University Foundation – 1966–70
Member, Board of Directors, Fund for Theological
    Education – 1982–88 (Chairman – 1985–88)
Member, Minnesota Judicial Planning Committee – 1975–80

Member, Regional Board, National Conference of Christians
and Jews – 1983–90
Member, Governor's Commission on Tax Reform – 1984–86
Member, Minnesota Business Coalition Task Force on Health
Care Costs and Ethics – 1984–85
Member, Board of Editorial Advisors, Second Opinion, Park Ridge
Center – 1985–1995
Member, Board of Directors, Joint Studies Commission,
Minot State University – 1987–present
Member, Sponsoring Committee for the Peace Prize
Forum – 1988–present
Member, Board of Directors, Muhlenberg College –1989–92
Member, National Architectural Accrediting Board – 1990–1995

Living through the eighth decade of one's life is a special privilege. I am thankful to God for that gift. My life has been blessed beyond measure in terms of my professional career and the many opportunities I've been offered. More than that, I've lived in the midst of family and friendship ties which have been supportive and encouraging all along the way.

Memory is flooded with the recollection of a mother who sacrificed, cared and loved in double measure as she played the role of father as well as mother. A brother and two sisters offered spice and fun and tension and genuine support. Relatives and friends have abounded, both in numbers and in what they have contributed to my life. I have benefited by generous and helpful employers, caring teachers, cooperative colleagues and able mentors wherever I have been.

I have enjoyed two marriages in which I have received much more than I have given, and been loved beyond any deserving. I have lived to see children grow to productive and rewarding adulthood, and now, lately, to watch grandchildren reach their youth with grace and maturity.

In all of this I see the hand of God. I'm grateful that nothing in life has robbed me of a basically childlike faith in God. I believe He is; I believe He is my God. I believe He loves and cares for me as He does for the whole world. I believe Jesus Christ is my Savior as He is the Savior of the world, and that in His church he provides for all His friends a place for growth into the kind of maturity a God has the right to expect of His followers.

There is nothing I can ask of life beyond what I have been privileged to know and experience. In my prayers, I no longer ask for anything for myself; I pray instead for those others whose lives stand in need of the grace and goodness of God and of the very essentials of life.

The world seems to be in trouble as I near the end of my life. I guess I didn't save it, or even improve it much. I'm not sure how much of that I was supposed to do. I believe I was expected to be faithful in what I attempted to do; I leave the rest to God.

I believe Christian people live with a kind of paradox. We are to bend every effort to improve this world in which we live, to preserve it for succeeding generations, to be good stewards of its resources, to work for peace and the overcoming of hatred, prejudice and violence. At the same time we are realists. We know that the world is not going to be perfect, that there will always be troubles and cares, and that God alone is able to bring everything to fruition. Faith makes it possible to hold onto both those truths.

Four score years constitute a generous allotment of time in this world for anyone. I love life. I love Lois and the family, and all the friends who enrich my life. I am awed by the beauty of the earth, even as I am appalled by the way human beings treat it. But I am ready to let go whenever the good Lord says the word, and I shall praise Him for it all.

So I conclude my life memories. Pastor Tallakson was correct when he suggested Psalm 16 as an inscription over my life. It was appropriate when I was a teenager, and it still is more than sixty years later:

"The lines are fallen unto me in pleasant places; yea, I have a goodly heritage."

INDEX

NOTE: Cities appearing infrequently are listed under their state or country. Entries with sub–headings are printed in capital letters.

Springfield, 225, 228, 283, 287
Immanuel Lutheran Church (Forest City), 115, 116, 131
Indiana, 285
International Festival (Bergen), 252
International Forum (Oslo), 257
Inver Hills Community College, 228, 284
IOWA, 61, 100, 285, 290; Ames 228,283, 284, 287, (Mary Greeley Hospital, 228, 285); Clear Lake, 131; Coralville, 219; Crystal Lake, 134; Decorah, 143; Dows, 136; Emmetsburg, 116; Forest City (see Forest City); Gilbert, 131; Iowa City, 218–220, 222; Iowa State University, 283, 287; Mason City, 116, 133, 136; North English, 219, Norway, 131; Roland, 131; Waverly, 143
Iran, Teheran, 234
Ireland, 38
Iron Range, 83, 84
ISRAEL/ISRAELIS, 210, 254, 255; Bethany, 210; Bethlehem, 73, 210, 254; Caesarea, 254; Cana, 254; Capernaum, 255; Dead Sea, 210, 254; Golan Heights, 255; Good Fence, 255; Hebron, 210, 254; Jericho, 210, 254; Jerusalem, 186, 210, 254 (American Colony Hotel, 254; Arab Section, 210; Calvary, 254; Garden of Gethsemane, 254; Hasidic Jews, 255; King George Hotel, 210; Old City, 210; Temple Mount, 254; Via Dolorosa, 254); Lod (Lydda), 254; Masada, 254; Mount of the Beatitudes, 254; Mount of Transfiguration, 255; Nazareth, 254; Sabbath dinner, 255; Samaria, 255; Sea of Galilee, 254; Tel Aviv, 254, 255
ITALY/ITALIAN, 205, 213, 288; Florence, 288; La Spezia, 156; Pisa, 156 (California Motel, 156); Rome, 156, 157, (Coliseum, 157; Forum, 157; St. Peter's, 157; Trevi Fountain, 157; Vatican, 124; Vatican Council, 157)
Iverson, Maynard, 140

Jackson, Henry, 256
Jacobson, Delmar, 216
Jacobson, E.C., 144
Jacobson, Erling, 101
Jalkanen, Ralph, 266
JAPAN, 206; Kyoto, 207, 208; Tokyo, 207, 208, 251
Jaunlinens, Valija, 141
Javits, Jacob, 233
Jennings, Kenneth, family, 185, 259
Jensen, Kenneth, 9, 44
Jensen, Melford, 201
Jenson, Robert, 147
Jerdee, Evelyn, 259
Jewel Ball, 287
Joesting, Herb, 25

Johnshoy, J. Walter, 94, 103
Johnnie & Tinkie Squirrel, 114, 228
Johnson, Amon O., 16, 23
Johnson, Arndt, 9
Johnson, Arthur, 77
Johnson, B.J., 279
Johnson, Carol, 174, 186
Johnson, David, 120, 158, 168. 169, 172, 178, 201–203, 231, 242
Johnson, Henry & Julia, 23, 42
Johnson, Lala, 4
Johnson, Leo, Furniture Store, 60
Johnson, Lyle, 31
Johnson, Lyndon, 194, 205
Johnson, Miles & Myrna, 114, 186, 233
Johnson, O.J., 128
Johnson, U.D., 43
Johnson, Walter, 44
Johnsrud, P.L., 25
Jorgenson, Dan, v
Jothen, Arthur, 75
Judicial Planning Committee, 204, 215
Julebord, 256
Juvrud, Tom, 43

Kansas, Topeka, 62
Kavanaugh's Resort, 243, 245, 282, 286, 289
Kellogg Foundation, 266
KENNEDY, John F., 155, 194, 203; Center, 196
Kent, Eunice, 85
Kentucky, 110
KENYA, 210; Nairobi, 209, 210; New Stanley Hotel, 210; Treetops Hotel, 210
Ketroser, Robert, 282
Kibira, Josiah & Martha, 123
Kildahl, Karl, 69
Kilian, Tom, 131
King, Martin Luther, Jr., 205, 269
Kirichenko, Yuri, 255, 262
Kjær–Nielsen, Anne Marie "Rie," 249, 250, 280
Kleven, Nils, 75
Knardal, Eva, 277
Knutson, Joseph, 112, 146–148
Knutson, Maurice, 169, 172
Koren, Petter, 15
Kunkel, Cecelia, 30, 119
Kvinge, John & Kathryn, 70, 225, 262

La Boheme, 276
Lacey, Chet, 203
Lafitte, Dr., 25
Laingen, Bruce, 234
Lake Lida, 26, 41, 42, 44
Lake Sylvan, 289
LANGELAND, Anna (see Serkland, Anna); Langeland, Magne, 11, 33, 39
Langer, William, 55

Powderhorn Park, 220

MINNESOTA, 51, 61, 62, 100, 101, 107, 116, 129, 133, 134, 198, 269, 281; Albert Lea, 207; Barnesville, 26, 29, 35, 42, 115; Baudette, 282; Beltrami, 11; Bemidji, 16, 72; Blue Earth, 284; Brainerd, 286, 289; Breckenridge, 3; Burnsville, 188; Business Coalition, 269; Clarissa, 290; Clear Lake, 135; Clitherall, 59; Comstock, 62; Cook, 89; Cottage Grove, 228; Council of Churches, 285; Cromwell, 89; Crookston, 116; Detroit Lakes, 26, 59, 135; Dilworth, 57, 59, 62, 79; Duluth, 14, 88; Eldred, 11; Emmons, 116; Fairmont, 131; Faribault, 217, 221; Fergus Falls (see Fergus Falls); Floodwood, 89; Grand Rapids, 82; Hastings, 59, 72, 73; Henning, 58; Hibbing, 82, 89, 90, 221, (General Hospital, 90, 91); Hovland Lake, 42; Keewatin, 81; Kerkhoven, 219; Lakeville, 188; Lawndale, 24; Melby Lake, 42; Milaca, 30; Minneapolis (see Minneapolis); Minnetonka, 290; Nashwauk (see Nashwauk); Northfield (see Northfield); Paynesville, 59; Pelican Rapids, 26, 29; Pengilly, 87; Private College Council, 266; Reading, 15; Richfield, 271; Robbinsdale, 26; Roseau, 16, (Budd Hospital, 16); Rothsay (see Rothsay); Staples, 59; State Board for Continuing Legal Education, 215; State Capitol, 25; State Fair, 276; State Legislature, 59; St. Cloud, 26; St. Paul (see St. Paul); St. Peter, 265; Supreme Court, 215; Thief River Falls, 52, 223, 260, 292; Twin Cities, 25, 26, 95, 188, 191, 242, 264, 268, 271, 279; Ulen, 15, 16, 23, 42, 58; Underwood, 27; Vkings, 199, 214; Virginia, 89; Wadena, 290; Wells, 225; Williams, 16, 17, 19, 281, 282; Wolverton, 62

Minikahda Club, 177

MISSISSIPPI, 12; Gulfport, 12, 205; Pascagoula, 205; River, 293

MISSOURI, Kansas City, 13; Kansas City Chiefs, 214; Springfield, 71; St. Louis, 13

Model T Ford, 37

Moe, Richard, family, 133

MOEN, Bernice, 42; Ed, 17, 36–38, 42; Florence, 45; Luke, 36; Marvin, 36; Ray, 36; Moen's Lumber Yard, 23, 25, 27, 29, 36, 47, 160, 263, 285

Mollard, Sylvia, 207

Molstad, 257

Mondale, Walter F., 204, 232, 233, 235, 237, 269

Mongolian, 208

Monson, Allwin & Dorothy, 54, 56, 112, 114

MONTANA, 61, 100, 185; Absarokee, 75; Billings, 60, 101, 102; Circle, 35; Glacier Park, 36, 227; Glasgow, 101, 102; Glendive, 102; Miles City, 101;

MOORHEAD, MN, 51–53, 60–62, 79, 88, 93, 94, 99, 100, 110, 111, 115, 116, 160, 263, 281; Bluebird Cafe, 27; *Moorhead Daily News*, 36; State Teacher's College, 19, 30, 33, 56–58, 114, 225

Mor Hansen, 14, 15

Mother, 4–10, 13, 15–27, 30–32, 34, 37–40, 42, 47, 52–55, 79, 91, 92, 104, 115, 118, 119, 133–135, 140, 141, 160, 168, 307

Mothers Embracing Nuclear Disarmament (MEND), 286

Muhlenberg College, 267

Mundell, Karen, 260

Muus, Bernt Julius, 205, 206, 275

Myhrum, Walton, 52

Nagurski, Bronko, 25

Narum, William, 186

NASHWAUK, MN, 17, 75–77, 79, 80, 82–86, 88, 89, 92, 93, 95, 99, 100, 116, 120, 160; Butler Brothers Mine, 79; Cleveland Cliffs Mine, 79; Community Building, 84–87; Community Church, 75, 83; Nashwauk Lutheran Church, 81, 87, 88, 96; *Pastor's Aide*, 82

Nason, John & Elizabeth, 215

NATIONAL Architectural Accrediting Board, 181, 270; Nat'l Association of Independent Colleges, 204; Nat'l Association of Schools of Music, 181; Nat'l Association of Schools of Nursing, 181; Nat'l Council for the Accreditation of Teacher Education, 181; Nat'l Council of Churches, 300; Nat'l Institutes of Health, 220; Nat'l Lutheran Council, 136, 145, (Division of College and University Work, 145); Nat'l Lutheran Educational Conference, 204; Nat'l Youth Administration, 59

Native Americans, 165

NATO, 235, Supreme Allied Commander/Atlantic (SACLANT), 233, 253

Nazareth Lutheran Church (Chicago), 109

NEBRASKA, 290; Blair, 152; Omaha, 135; Wahoo, 131

Nelsen, Henry, 133

Nelsen, William, family, 172, 206, 264, 265

Nelson, Arnie, 284

Nelson, E. Clifford, 186

Ness, Stan, 169, 172

Nestande, Constantine, 80

NETHERLANDS, 288; Rotterdam, 157

Neubarth's Jewelry, 59

New Age, 297

New Guinea, 207

New Hampshire, 107

New Jersey Institute of Technology, 270

321

322